Disaster Planning for Libraries

CHANDOS
INFORMATION PROFESSIONAL SERIES

Series Editor: Ruth Rikowski
(email: Rikowskigr@aol.com)

Chandos' new series of books is aimed at the busy information professional. They have been specially commissioned to provide the reader with an authoritative view of current thinking. They are designed to provide easy-to-read and (most importantly) practical coverage of topics that are of interest to librarians and other information professionals. If you would like a full listing of current and forthcoming titles, please visit www.chandospublishing.com.

New authors: we are always pleased to receive ideas for new titles; if you would like to write a book for Chandos, please contact Dr Glyn Jones on g.jones.2@elsevier.com or telephone +44 (0) 1865 843000.

Disaster Planning for Libraries

Process and Guidelines

Guy Robertson

AMSTERDAM • BOSTON • HEIDELBERG • LONDON
NEW YORK • OXFORD • PARIS • SAN DIEGO • SAN FRANCISCO
SINGAPORE • SYDNEY • TOKYO

Chandos Publishing is an Imprint of Elsevier

Chandos Publishing is an imprint of Elsevier
225 Wyman Street, Waltham, MA 02451, USA
Langford Lane, Kidlington, OX5 1GB, UK

Notices
Knowledge and best practice in this field are constantly changing. As new research and experience broaden
our understanding, changes in research methods, professional practices, or medical treatment may become
necessary.

Practitioners and researchers must always rely on their own experience and knowledge in evaluating and
using any information, methods, compounds, or experiments described herein. In using such information
or methods they should be mindful of their own safety and the safety of others, including parties for whom
they have a professional responsibility.

To the fullest extent of the law, neither the Publisher nor the authors, contributors, or editors, assume any
liability for any injury and/or damage to persons or property as a matter of products liability, negligence
or otherwise, or from any use or operation of any methods, products, instructions, or ideas contained in the
material herein.

British Library Cataloguing-in-Publication Data
A catalogue record for this book is available from the British Library

Library of Congress Control Number: 2014955040

ISBN: 978-1-84334-730-9

For information on all Chandos Publication
visit our website at http://store.elsevier.com/

Typeset by Thomson Digital

Dedication

To Deborah

Contents

List of figures   xi
Acknowledgments   xiii
Preface   xv
A note on terminology   xvii
How to use this book   xix
About the author   xxi

1   Libraries and risk   **1**
    1.1   The prevalence of risk   1
    1.2   Natural risks   2
    1.3   Technological risks   3
    1.4   Human-caused risks   5
    1.5   Proximity risks   6
    1.6   Security risks   7
    1.7   Enterprise risks   9
    1.8   References   9

2   Preparedness   **11**
    2.1   Authorization   11
    2.2   Committees: pros and cons   12
    2.3   RAA, step one: history-taking   13
    2.4   RAA, step two: inspection   13
    2.5   RAA, step three: interviews   14
    2.6   RAA, step four: discussions with external experts   15
    2.7   RAA, step five: documentation   16
    2.8   Mitigation: preventative maintenance programmes   17
    2.9   Mitigation: gradual replacement of older facilities   18
   2.10   Mitigation: insurance   19
   2.11   Mitigation: data back-up   19
   2.12   Mitigation: the key   20
   2.13   References   20

3   Disaster response   **21**
    3.1   Staff and patron safety   21
    3.2   Producing a disaster response plan   22
    3.3   Production mistakes   24
    3.4   The issue of library assets   24
    3.5   Emotional reactions to emergencies and disasters   25

	3.6	Leadership in response planning	26
	3.7	Response teams	27
	3.8	References	28

4 **Operational resumption, continuity and recovery** — **29**

	4.1	After the fact	29
	4.2	Resumption	29
	4.3	Continuity	31
	4.4	Recovery	32
	4.5	Management roles	33
	4.6	Operational resumption teams	34
	4.7	Perfection not possible	35
	4.8	References	36

5 **Damage assessment** — **37**

	5.1	The effects	37
	5.2	Internal and external inspectors	37
	5.3	Beginning at the perimeter	38
	5.4	Building exteriors	38
	5.5	Safe entrance and exit	39
	5.6	Building interiors	39
	5.7	Inspecting damaged collections	40
	5.8	Evaluation	41
	5.9	Prioritization	42
	5.10	Recordkeeping	43
	5.11	References	49

6 **Disaster recognition, declaration procedures and crisis management** — **51**

	6.1	How it feels	51
	6.2	Recognizing a disaster	52
	6.3	Information gathering	53
	6.4	When and when not to declare a disaster	58
	6.5	Disasters and crises	58
	6.6	The library crisis manager	59
	6.7	References	60

7 **Strategic alliances** — **61**

	7.1	Determining the need for a strategic alliance	61
	7.2	Key post-disaster vendors for resumption and continuity	64
	7.3	Strategic alliance documentation	65
	7.4	Updating strategic alliances	66
	7.5	Adaptation of central library strategic alliances for branches	67
	7.6	Going it alone?	68
	7.7	References	68

8   Post-disaster management of patrons   69
    8.1   Convergence   69
    8.2   Closure of facilities: process and implications   70
    8.3   Reassuring patrons   72
    8.4   Updating patrons on operational resumption and recovery   74
    8.5   Dealing with volunteers   75
    8.6   Post-disaster programmes   76
    8.7   Message centres and missing children   76
    8.8   References   77

9   Normalization of operations   79
    9.1   Reassuring employees   79
    9.2   Normalization defined   80
    9.3   Problems arising from incomplete normalization   81
    9.4   Normalization checklists   82
    9.5   Testing normalization programmes   85
    9.6   References   86

10 Orientation and training programmes   87
    10.1   Binder dependence   87
    10.2   Definitions: orientation and training   87
    10.3   Purposes of orientation and training   88
    10.4   Assumptions   89
    10.5   Methods of delivery   90
    10.6   Home circulars   90
    10.7   Newsletter/Intranet materials   93
    10.8   Staff orientation sessions   93
    10.9   Management orientation sessions   95
    10.10 Operational resumption and continuity orientation and training   96
    10.11 Management security seminars   96
    10.12 Training the trainers   97
    10.13 Session reporting   97
    10.14 References   98

11 Basic tabletop exercises   99
    11.1   No plan without practice   99
    11.2   Risk assessment and analysis example   100
    11.3   Generic tabletop exercises   101
    11.4   Tabletops for managers   109
    11.5   Pandemic influenza exercise   110
    11.6   Tabletop exercise management tips   112
    11.7   Conclusion   112
    11.8   References   112

12   Process and results   **113**
      12.1   The overwhelming question   113
      12.2   A case history: in the beginning   114
      12.3   The process: preparedness   115
      12.4   The process: response   116
      12.5   The process: resumption   117
      12.6   The process: backtracking   118
      12.7   The process: orientation, training and testing   119
      12.8   A real scenario   120
      12.9   Use of the disaster plan   121
      12.10   Post-resumption   122
      12.11   References   123

Further reading   **125**

Appendix one   **127**

Appendix two   **139**

Appendix three   **151**

Appendix four   **157**

Appendix five   **181**

Appendix six   **187**

Index   **199**

List of figures

Fig. 3.1   Sample Emergency Response Plan brochure   **23**

Fig. 5.1   Damage Assessment Form   **44**

Fig. 6.1   Disaster Recognition and Declaration Procedures form   **54**

Fig. 8.1   Temporary closure signage   **71**

Fig. 10.1   Example of home circular memo: employees' pets   **91**

Fig. 10.2   Example of home circular memo: employees'
personal records stored at home   **92**

Fig. 10.3   Example of a newsletter item on holiday safety   **94**

Acknowledgments

I am indebted to Chandos and Elsevier for their patience, assistance and support. In particular, I should like to thank Harriet Clayton, Fenton Coulthurst, Jonathan Davis, Glyn Jones, George Knott and Geraldine Lyons.

I am pleased to acknowledge the contributions of my interviewees, who gave me their time and numerous useful insights.

I am grateful to colleagues and friends including Ted Baker, Heather Forbes, Elaine Goh, David Goldie, Hilary Hannigan, Drew Lane, David Leggett, Melany Lund, Maureen Phillips, Nancy Richardson and Diane Thompson. David Barker and Chris Galloway gave me different perspectives on risk management. I received technical advice and fresh viewpoints from Bob Gignac, David Miller, the late Bud Mills, and Michael and Barbara Weston.

The late Roy Stokes served as a teacher and mentor. His influence on my work has been inestimable.

I appreciate the assistance that I received as I conducted the research for this book, and thank the following institutions:

- The British Library
- The British Museum
- The Justice Institute of British Columbia
- Langara College Library
- Library and Archives Canada
- The Library of Congress
- New York Public Library
- Thurber Engineering Ltd.
- University of British Columbia Library
- Vancouver Public Library
- Winnipeg Public Library

Lastly, I thank my wife Deborah and daughter Amanda for their encouragement, diplomacy and proofreading.

I am grateful to all who have contributed to my book. Any errors are my own.

Preface

You are a librarian.

You are the Director of the New York Public Library, or a cataloguer at a small college outside San Francisco. Perhaps you hold a high administrative position at the Bodleian or the National Library of Scotland. Or perhaps you run a school library in northern British Columbia.

In fact you might work in any library in the world. And one day your superiors tell you that your library needs a disaster plan. They might use a different term, such as 'contingency plan', or 'business resumption plan' or 'continuity plan'. There are numerous terms for what is essentially the same thing: a plan that will protect your library's staff, collections, facilities and other assets before, during and after a dangerous and damaging event.

A comprehensive plan will take into account the prevailing risks to your library. It will be clear, concise and easy to understand. It will also be developed in a way that will interest readers - that is, everyone who works at your library - and encourage them to become involved in the testing of the plan and any training that it calls for.

Your plan should also be flexible and open to revision and updating. No disaster plan is complete and perfect; all plans could be better in some way. That is why you will hear disaster planners refer to plans as 'living documents', a term that implies that those documents could be revised at any time to meet changing needs. Planners will also tell you - repeatedly - that plans are not products, but processes. A three-ring binder crammed with emergency telephone lists and first-aid advice is almost useless during a real disaster. In threatening circumstances, what will safeguard your library are the protective measures that you and your colleagues have rehearsed and are prepared to take: often simple and commonsensical actions that long and complicated documents might not mention.

This book is a response to requests from colleagues, clients and students over the past 30 years for information on various aspects of disaster planning. I have outlined a general process that a reasonably well-experienced and competent librarian can follow to develop a plan for almost any kind of library. Much of this process could be adapted for the purposes of archives, records centres, bookshops, museums and galleries. All of these institutions face certain risks, including fire, flooding and severe weather, and all must be vigilant regarding security risks.

I offer this process with several caveats. Firstly, I do not cover every risk that threatens libraries and other information organizations. To do so would result in a much larger (and probably multi-volume) work. Secondly, I describe one process only, and there are a number of others. That which constitutes the content of this book has been effective and field-tested numerous times all over the world; I recommend it in part because it has saved many institutions from serious losses. Thirdly, what I emphasize in the following pages exemplifies my personal and professional biases. I was trained as a bibliographer and rare materials specialist, and shortly after I graduated from library school, I became a consultant. A writer with different training and experience might have concentrated on different risks and alternative ways to mitigate those risks. He or she might have focused more attention on IT or climate change or the conservation of digital resources. These are worthy topics, but like any other writer, I can cover only so much, and the wisest course is to describe and discuss what I know best.

To broaden the perspective of this book, I have quoted librarians and other information professionals who have dealt with different sorts of circumstances, sometimes in trying and potentially dangerous conditions. I have reproduced their remarks and observations as faithfully as possible. I have also respected their anonymity, since what they say might be misinterpreted and held against them. Unfortunately the truth can be uncomfortable and potentially controversial when witnesses describe what they saw during a disaster. While it is helpful to quote reliable witnesses, in my opinion it is best to let them remain anonymous.

Finally, I cannot know the future. As much as I have delved into reports from risk managers and insurance companies, and as much as I have reviewed the history of disasters to a variety of information organizations, I cannot predict what will happen in any library or other organization next year, or next week, or even a few minutes from now. I can only consider the past and what it teaches us, and trust that it will hint at what impends. I hope that this book will provide you with the process and guidelines that you need for whatever is in store.

Guy Robertson
Vancouver, BC

A note on terminology

In this book, I have used 'risk' in the singular as an all-encompassing term for risk in general. Depending on the context, the term can also indicate a single and specific threat such as fire, flooding or theft. Synonymous with risk in the latter usage are 'danger', 'peril' and 'threat'.

For purposes of simplicity and clarity, I have used the term 'disaster planning' throughout. In the general field, this activity is also referred to as 'business continuity [or resumption, or recovery] planning', 'contingency planning' and 'emergency [response, or management] planning'. While I have misgivings about the sound and sense of 'disaster planning', I defer to common usage since most readers will be familiar with it.

Disaster planning comprises a series of procedures, plans and programmes that enable organizations to prepare for, respond to and recover from negative events of all kinds. For libraries and other information organizations, the author's recommended classification of such events is as follows:

- An *incident*, for example a minor breach of security, a small loss of data or a minor injury at a site.
- An *emergency*, for example a number of minor casualties, a small toxic spill or the loss of valuable equipment.
- A *major emergency*, for example a serious casualty or casualties, extensive damage to a building or equipment that will involve serious inconvenience, or a power outage that disrupts operations for 24 hours.
- A *disaster*, for example any damage to the building(s) or equipment that will disrupt operations for more than 48 hours, any natural event (for example, high winds, winter storm, earthquake) that disrupts transportation or communications for more than 48 hours, or any serious loss of vital data (for example, borrower data that have been lost).
- A *catastrophe*, for example a large regional disaster that disrupts conditions across an entire region for an extended period of time, and that involves multiple casualties and the loss of facilities.
- A *crisis*, for example an event involving negative media coverage and adverse public relations during or following any of the above circumstances.

All of the above-mentioned terms have been used in different ways by other authors, organizations, professions and industries. I trust that readers will find my usage helpful, even though they may prefer different terms.

How to use this book

If an emergency or disaster has occurred at your library and you do not have a plan, remember that your top priority is human safety. Your initial task might be to contact first responders – police, firefighters and paramedics.

If you have time, consult Figure 3.1, 'Sample Emergency Response Plan brochure' (see p. 23). You might also find the 'Disaster Manager's Kit' in Appendix 4 useful. Do not attempt to study these items in depth while there is any immediate danger to you, your co-workers or anyone else in your library. Follow the directions of the first responders.

In normal circumstances, you can use the different chapters and appendices of this book to update your plan and to develop new material that is appropriate for your operations. Since much of the material herein is generic, you should adapt it so that it addresses your organization's risk profile and site-specific requirements. Do not hesitate to set aside material that is irrelevant.

If you are responsible for compiling a new plan from scratch, you can study this book from beginning to end and extract the information that you need to complete a draft. Your disaster plan will be a living document in that it will never be finished or perfect. The need for revisions and enhancement will be constant, and there will always be reasons to work on your plan. As your organization changes, so must your plan. Thus, it is best to consider your plan a draft, and to be prepared to add, delete or rewrite material regularly.

You can keep this book – along with any others concerning related topics – on your planning shelf for future reference.

About the author

Guy Robertson lives in Vancouver. A graduate of the University of British Columbia's School of Librarianship, he teaches library history and records management at Langara College, and information management at the Justice Institute of BC. He is also an adjunct professor at the University of British Columbia's School of Library, Archival and Information Studies. He has lectured across North America on disaster planning, emergency management, corporate security, forgery, money laundering and fraud prevention.

As a consultant, he has developed disaster plans and training programmes for libraries, archives, records centres, financial institutions, manufacturers, retail chains, hospitals, laboratories, seniors' residences and architectural firms.

Libraries and risk

1

1.1 The prevalence of risk

Risk pervades life.

Everywhere, and at all times, you live under threat from numerous perils. Fortunately you have the time and opportunity to prepare for whatever might happen, and you possess the intelligence with which to mitigate risk. Working against you, however, is human nature, which includes apathy, stubbornness, irrationality and narrowness of perception: traits that hinder effective disaster planning in any organization.

Librarians are no more inclined than people in other professions to plan for and respond to disasters. Librarians are seldom trained in risk assessment and management, and in many cases have relied on others – police, firefighters, municipal planners, insurers, public health authorities and consultants – to prepare them for and occasionally save them from fire, flooding, severe weather, criminal activities and other negative events. But even when external bodies offer assistance and good advice, many librarians have not availed themselves of these things. There are numerous other tasks to complete. The adult services coordinator and her staff are busy weeding the fiction collection; the children's librarians are struggling with the summer reading programme; the technical services department has what appears to be an insurmountable cataloguing backlog; the branch clerical staff is having difficulty handling an increase in borrowing and returns; and the head librarian is engaged full time in persuading the city council and library board not to cut the budget. There are few library employees who have time to devote to disaster planning. Moreover, many employees admit that they find planning and any training associated with it to be onerous and dull.

Thus it is no surprise that so many libraries lack effective disaster plans. In fact, library employees at all levels are often oblivious to the most conspicuous threats to their personal safety and operations. The reason is simple. Whereas daily routines involve the frequent repetition of activities, and ordinary problems and their solutions present themselves with dependable regularity, disasters are infrequent. Decades might pass between fires and floods; such disasters might never occur at most sites.

Because risk so infrequently turns into actual threats, you might take your safety and security for granted. The infrequency of emergencies and disasters can lull you into apathy. If deadly pandemics and fires and terrorist attacks are so unlikely and rare, why should you bother to take precautions against them? Are not the chances of such things happening slim? Why waste time, money and other resources to protect yourself from something that will probably never happen?

These are good questions. The answer is twofold. First, if risk never turns into actual threats, and you are never faced with an emergency or disaster, you may celebrate your good luck. At least you have demonstrated good sense and responsible custodianship by preparing for the worst, which is constantly possible. After all, you

are unable to predict the future with absolute certainty, so you were prudent to acknowledge the possibility of nasty surprises.

But, second, if the risk of a fire turns into a real conflagration that engulfs your main
branch, then you were equally sensible to have a plan to deal with the loss – temporary
or permanent – of that branch building, the loss of the offices, collections, and other
assets that it contained, and the displacement of the employees who occupied it. There
might be those who criticize you for developing disaster plans, and who suggest that
you are 'alarmist' or 'Chicken Little'. You need patience and determination to deal
with such criticism as a matter of course, and to proceed with the development of your
plan. The first step in the planning process is to identify your library's *risk profile*, that
is, the spectrum of risks that prevail at your site or sites.

The following sections describe different kinds of risks that all planners must take
into account.

1.2   Natural risks

'California means earthquakes', says a public librarian from Los Angeles. 'Florida
means hurricanes. Anywhere near the Mississippi River means floods. In America,
nature is brutal.'

In fact, nature is no gentler anywhere else on earth. A large landmass such as the
continental US has a long list of prevailing natural risks, but every square inch of
the planet is exposed to a list similar in length, and always has been. There is no point
in attempting to find a site that is unaffected by the forces of nature. Rather, it is best
to identify whatever natural risks prevail, and to prepare for them accordingly. Among
the most common are:

- *Flooding and water ingress*. Any library site near a river, lake, harbour or other natural
  body of water is at risk from flooding. Even a small local pond can break its banks and
  flood neighbouring sites. Water ingress – defined as seepage of water into a building – can
  also occur through an open window, a leaky roof, a clogged drain or a sewer back-up. Some
  regions have dealt with high levels of precipitation for millennia; others have only recently
  begun to see it owing to changing weather patterns. There is much anecdotal evidence to
  indicate that flooding and water ingress cause more damage to libraries than any other risk.
  'Water in the wrong place' could also be the consequence of technological, proximity and
  security risks.
- *Fire, smoke and fumes*. Naturally occurring fires threaten any library situated near forests and
  other wooded areas. Any vegetation – including farmers' crops, gardens in urban parks and
  tumbleweed – can burn and lead to damage. Smoke and fumes can pose a serious risk not
  only to employees but also to fragile IT equipment. Fire, smoke, fumes and explosions could
  also be consequences of technological, proximity and security risks.
- *Severe weather*. Any weather event that becomes extreme can be defined as severe. Winter
  storms, thunderstorms, high winds and heatwaves are common examples. Note that natural
  risks often overlap. Thunderstorms can involve lightning, which can cause fires. Winter
  storms can cause flooding and water ingress. High winds can damage roofs, and lead to
  water ingress. Heatwaves can result in fires. You must guard against *secondary risks*, which
  can cause more damage than the risks that give rise to them. All natural risks have secondary
  risks.

- *Earthquakes.* Among the most frightening natural phenomena, earthquakes can occur anywhere on earth, but are far more likely to strike regions identified as seismic zones. These include countries around the Pacific Rim, and particularly China, Japan, Indonesia, Canada, the US, Mexico and Chile. Mediterranean countries such as Italy, Greece and Turkey have a long history of devastating earthquakes. Seismologists cannot predict the occurrence of earthquakes with any accuracy. Library buildings and heavy furniture – including shelving systems – are particularly at risk from earthquakes.
- *Tsunamis.* These earthquake-generated sea waves move at high speed and can destroy coastal cities and their outlying communities. They can cause large numbers of fatalities and enormous property damage. Like earthquakes, tsunamis can wipe out not only a region's libraries, but its entire information infrastructure, including archives and records centres, schools and post-secondary institutions, and information technology in public and private locations.
- *Landslides and avalanches.* Such natural phenomena occur most often in mountainous regions, although any natural slope – for example, a hillside in an urban park or along a suburban road – can be the site of a landslide or avalanche. Geotechnical engineers note the possibility of different kinds of landslides, including rockslides, landslips, mudslides and debris torrents. These could cut off libraries and their communities from neighbouring areas, and disrupt schedules and routines.
- *Pests.* Some insects and various other kinds of wildlife can become a pest in or around a library. The most common are silverfish, cockroaches and bedbugs; rodents such as rats and mice; and pigeons. These pests can infest and damage library materials. They are also signs of poor sanitation. Bedbugs can bite human beings, and rats can spread disease, but pests are rarely life-threatening unless they take the form of the poisonous snakes that congregated near the entrance of a school library in Kenya, or in the corners of a library parking lot in Arizona. Bears and mountain lions have been sighted near Western Canadian libraries. Cobras and scorpions have 'made nuisances of themselves near libraries', according to a rural school librarian in southern India.

Less common but still necessary to note for planning purposes in many libraries are:

- *Pandemics.* The last serious pandemic that caused high levels of fatalities was the Spanish Flu of 1918. Recently, in light of the threat of Avian Influenza and Severe Acute Respiratory Syndrome (SARS), governments worldwide have urged citizens to prepare for an outbreak of influenza that could be equally devastating. High-traffic libraries could face lengthy closures in the event of a pandemic.
- *Drought.* Absence of precipitation and the resulting lack of water for human use can occur not only in countries such as Australia, Ethiopia and Somalia, but also in the Southwestern US and in parts of China. Drought can result in crop failure, famine and the displacement of entire populations.
- *Volcanoes.* Most often, volcanoes are located in seismic zones. Notable examples include Italy's Mounts Etna and Vesuvius, Washington State's Mount St Helen and Iceland's Grimsvötn and Eyjafjallajökul. Volcanic explosions are often accompanied by earthquakes. Aside from damaging any community in their immediate area, volcanoes can also disrupt transportation and communications.

1.3 Technological risks

'Anything that can break down will do so eventually, and with gusto', says a British university librarian during a risk management seminar in London before the 2012 Summer Olympic Games. 'You focus on information technology, and worry about computer crashes, but a power outage could shut us down and cause just as much data loss. A fire in the toaster in our cafeteria forced us to evacuate for three hours. You need to consider risks from all of our technology, high and low.'

Among the most common technological risks to libraries are:

- *Power outages and brownouts.* A sudden loss of power can result in darkened stack areas and much confusion among employees and patrons. Outages can affect a single building or an entire city, and have lasted from a few seconds to several days. They can lead to library closures and data loss. A related risk is a power spike or surge, during which electrical equipment could be overloaded and burned out or 'fried'. In such cases, IT failure is common. Disruptions in the power supply might also be due to natural, proximity and security risks.

- *IT failure.* This risk includes the malfunction of computer hardware and software, often resulting in unintended shutdown and data loss. Note that in many instances the mechanical cause of IT failure can be difficult to detect. IT failure could be the result of other problems including water ingress, fire and severe weather.

- *Data loss.* While data loss can be the result of accidental deletion, power outages and spikes, and theft, it can also be due to a deterioration of the media: an aging hard drive or CD, or a back-up tape that has been stored in an inappropriate environment.

- *Gas leaks.* Civil authorities will not hesitate to shut down entire neighbourhoods if a gas leak occurs, owing to the risk of fire and possible explosions. The length of a shutdown will depend on how long civil authorities will need to discover the source of the leak, and to repair any damage to gas lines. Gas leaks might be the consequence of earthquakes, serious fires or sabotage.

- *Toxic spills.* A spill can involve toxic chemicals such as ammonia and chlorine, petroleum products, hospital and laboratory waste, and foodstuffs that will deteriorate quickly if exposed to the elements. Examples of the last include dairy products, meat and fish. Libraries situated near lifelines such as major roads and railway lines are particularly at risk from toxic spills. Those who assess risks to library sites may refer to toxic spills as proximity and security risks.

- *Train derailments.* Derailments can occur on subway and monorail lines that connect urban locations as well as on standard gauge railways for long-distance transportation. Occasionally derailments cause toxic spills, damage to nearby property and the closure of facilities – including libraries – in the vicinity. Hence, derailments are often considered to be a form of proximity risk.

- *Transportation disruptions.* Motor vehicle accidents, overturned heavy trucks and trailers, and damaged roadways can lead to transportation disruptions. More serious disruptions of this kind, however, can be the result of natural disasters such as floods, fires, earthquakes and severe weather. Accidents that cause road closures can also be considered as a form of proximity risk.

- *Telecommunications disruptions.* For communications purposes, modern organizations rely on a variety of technologies, a foundation of which is the telephone system. Most disruptions in telephone service are due to either overloading or line breakage.

Overloading occurs in the following circumstances:

- A regional disaster such as an earthquake, large fire, flood or windstorm.
- The commencement of severe weather, for example snowfall or high winds, in the general area.

- A major disaster with national or international implications, for example 9/11.
- A major political event, for example an election or the resignation of an important government figure.
- A major sporting event held locally.
- Major statutory holidays, for example Christmas and New Year.

Line breakage occurs in the following circumstances:

- A regional disaster, especially involving high winds, winter storms, heavy snowfalls or the ground motion of an earthquake.
- A systems malfunction at the telephone company.
- Shutdowns for emergency repairs or upgrades.
- Sabotage or tampering.

Mobile or cellular networks have been used during landline disruptions, but it is worth noting that in various circumstances these networks could also break down. While telephone companies worldwide are building more redundancy into their networks, there will always be the risk of disruption. Further, an Internet shutdown could affect worldwide communications for extended periods.

Less likely technological risks, but worth noting for the planning purposes of potentially affected libraries, are:

- *Dam failure*. While dam failures pose a flooding risk to communities in their vicinity they could also lead to long-term environmental damage and power supply problems. Dam failure might be due to structural weakness, an earthquake or sabotage.
- *Nuclear power plant failure*. Meltdowns and the unintentional release of radioactive materials are a source of great concern for any organization near a nuclear power plant. Three Mile Island, Chernobyl and Fukushima are examples of plants where events became out of control and had serious long-term effects. Risk from radiation also exists on academic campuses with laboratories that use and store radioactive materials. Librarians on these campuses should take note of any proximity risk from these laboratories.
- *Aircraft accidents*. Fortunately this risk is small. Libraries located near airports would be wise to consider the effects of a crash in their vicinity, but the chances of an aircraft crashing into a library are infinitesimal. Planners might want to include a nearby airport as a proximity risk, not only because of the possibility of a crash but also because of the risk of fire and explosions from airport fuel tanks.

1.4 Human-caused risks

Potentially, the most destructive human-caused risk to libraries is *war*. Library history contains numerous accounts of libraries damaged or destroyed by aerial or artillery bombardment, and of fires set by combatants. Invading armies have threatened library staffs and looted collections. *Civil unrest* and *rioting* can be dangerous for libraries, but these are not often as destructive as war. Sadly, libraries can make an easy target for belligerent forces and people on the rampage.

The most common human-caused threats are less dramatic, but in some cases they can cause extensive damage in libraries.

'One of the more challenging aspects of dealing with customers', says a retired salesperson from a large American computer manufacturer, 'is to convince people that one of the biggest risks to any IT system is human carelessness. People delete enormous amounts of data accidentally. They trip over cables and disable entire departments. They leave their laptops and other portable equipment on buses, trains and planes. They leave the server room unlocked. And librarians have made all of these mistakes.'

Such mistakes are so common that it is safe to assume that librarians make them every day. The foundations of such risks would include:

- *Apathy*: 'I really don't feel like reviewing this data back-up procedure. Boring! I'll do it next week, maybe, if I find the time.'
- *Carelessness and clumsiness*: 'Whoops! I dropped that big old atlas that everyone makes a fuss about, and the binding broke. But I gathered up all of the loose pages, that is except for a few in the middle. I don't know where they went. Sorry.'
- *Forgetfulness:* 'I forgot to lock the server room, and now we're missing the server with all of the borrower data. Sorry.'
- *False assumptions*: 'I thought that the clericals would bring in those boxes from the loading bay, and they didn't. Those old books that we acquired at the auction in New York got wet last night when it rained. There were some packages from children's publishers, too. They got really wet, but they should be fine when you dry them out. Shouldn't they?'
- *Inattention to detail*: 'Did I back up all of today's cataloguing data? Perhaps not. Well, if you lose any, that's a pity.'
- *Ignorance of internal policies*: 'Is it okay to show patrons around the rare book vault? Some fellow asked to see our early edition of Joyce's *Ulysses*, so I showed him where it was in the vault, and he seemed very grateful. He was in there for quite a while. Are you missing that copy of *Ulysses?* No, I haven't had a chance to read the security manual, but I will, maybe next week.'
- *Inattention to laws and external regulations*: 'One of our older patrons had a heart attack in the reference area last week, and none of us knew what to do. Somebody should have administered first aid, but nobody on staff had the training. So that unfortunate patron had to wait until an ambulance arrived, and that took quite a while. Our county's occupational health and safety code demands that we have at least one fully trained first aid attendant on site during business hours, so I guess one of us should take the training. When? Oh, sometime soon.'

Such statements may seem outrageous, but they are reproduced here verbatim from library sources in Canada, the US and the UK. You must never underestimate the likelihood of human-caused risks, which most commonly result in lost data and other valuable assets, damage to collections and facilities, breaches of employee and patron privacy, and loss of the library's reputation as a responsible custodian.

1.5   Proximity risks

Recalling smoke damage to a Midwestern American library branch after fire destroyed a neighbouring building, the local Fire Chief was blunt. 'I don't care how well you prepare yourself on your own site', he said, 'You have to take a look at what's next door, and down the block, and even several miles away – anything that could burn or flood you, choke you with smoke or fumes, knock you down with an explosion, run into you at high speed, fall on you, or rip you off. For your own safety and your library's, have a look around.'

Library disaster planners should take note of the following:

- *Neighbouring buildings.* Risks at sites and in buildings near a library might include:
    - inadequate fire controls
    - inattention to the requirements of the Fire Code
    - older plumbing and electrical circuitry
    - substandard maintenance
    - older structures unable to withstand earthquake loading
    - inadequate security procedures
    - inadequate sanitation
    - inadequate pest control
    - Criminal activities, for example narcotics distribution.
- *Roadways.* A library might be located near major arteries. Risks arising from its proximity to roadways in the vicinity include:
    - road closures following a motor vehicle accident, or a local emergency such as a fire or gas leak
    - difficulties in entering and leaving the area owing to debris, precipitation and abandoned vehicles in roadways after a storm, fire or earthquake.
- *Retail shopping areas.* Proximity to shopping areas is often related to incidents of robbery, arson and vandalism.
- *Parking lots.* Parking lots can be scenes of muggings, vandalism and assault.
- *Air traffic.* See the above subsection on *Aircraft accidents* (p. 5).
- *Gas (or petrol) stations and fuel tanks.* Fuel spills, fires and explosions can occur on any site that contains fuel tanks. In many cases the cause of these problems is human error.
- *Bodies of water.* See the above subsection on *Flooding and water ingress* (p. 2).
- *Crime hotspots.* In urban areas noted for crime, the most common criminal acts might be vehicle theft and break-ins, mugging and assault, vandalism, shoplifting, and distribution of illicit drugs and stolen goods. See the subsection below on *Security risks*.

1.6 Security risks

'Libraries are truly soft targets', says a thief who succeeded in stealing hundreds of rare books and manuscripts from North American academic libraries. 'Librarians are too trusting, and some of them take offence if you tell them that they have security problems. They don't like to hear it, and often they ignore security risks until a rare book goes missing and all hell breaks loose. But if somebody gets caught stealing in a library, they usually don't get more than probation or a warning from the cops.'

The following risks are due to a human agent acting intentionally for criminal purposes:

- *Theft.* In most libraries there is a constant risk of theft. Library assets most often stolen are:
    - printed materials of any sort, but particularly rare and valuable materials such as incunabula, early maps and atlases, and noteworthy editions of famous works; also rare ephemera such as concert posters
    - valuable reports, white papers and other grey literature.

- manuscripts, including valuable correspondence, diaries, journals and hand-drawn maps.
- sound recordings of any sort, but most often recordings by popular musicians, orchestras and bands.
- IT equipment, particularly that which is set up in public areas.

Patrons' items most attractive to thieves include:

- mobile (or cellular) telephones and other handheld technology
- laptop computers
- data sticks
- iPods
- purses and wallets
- keys (especially to cars and homes)
- cameras
- coats, especially leather jackets and woollen topcoats
- jewellery
- expensive pens and other accessories

- *Fraud and information theft*. Like most organizations, libraries could be defrauded by means of bogus documents, false ID, hacking and computer scams. The confidential information in academic and public libraries – particularly borrowers' records – could also be stolen and resold to illicit marketing organizations.

Special and corporate libraries hold information that could be considered confidential, and potentially valuable to outside persons and organizations, particularly those in the media. Special librarians often have access to extremely sensitive files. Unfortunately there is a low level of awareness regarding the risk of 'social engineering' in most libraries. Social engineering is defined as the use of devious and occasionally criminal methods to obtain sensitive information from unwitting sources.

- *Sabotage*. A disgruntled employee could sabotage library operations by erasing valuable data, causing a plumbing malfunction or planting a computer virus.
- *Arson*. Usually the work of a lone miscreant, arson is possible on any site. Parking areas could be the most likely spot for an arson attempt. Arson is a proximity risk for many libraries in urban neighbourhoods. In recent years, arson has become more common during riots and violent protests.
- *Bomb threats*. Organizations with a moderate to high public profile are targets for bomb threats. These threats are made by pranksters, disgruntled employees, and occasionally by hostile political activists.
- *Workplace violence*. This is defined as violence or the threat of violence by any one person in a workplace toward any other person. Incidents of workplace violence in libraries can increase during periods of high stress, low morale and economic uncertainty. Most often, cases involve violence by patrons to other patrons or to library employees. Many reports of violence in public and academic libraries note a suspected emotional problem in the offender.
- *Hostile intruder*. A hostile intrusion is a possible risk. The intruder might have a complaint about library services or operations. There is also the possibility of an intrusion by a 'street person', perhaps one under the influence of drugs, or a disgruntled former spouse or partner. The intrusion might occur in employee work areas, or in public areas.
- *Malware*. Computer viruses, time bombs, Trojan horses, and worms are increasingly sophisticated and common. While many libraries use advanced electronic protection, there is always a risk of a malware attack.

- *Vandalism.* Vandalism at library sites usually has a minimal effect on operations, unless vandals succeed in damaging power lines or computer equipment. At present this risk appears to be minimal. The most common form of vandalism in many neighbourhoods is 'tagging', that is spray-painting graffiti on building exteriors.

1.7 Enterprise risks

In times of economic uncertainty, enterprise risk management (ERM) can be essential to the continuing operations of libraries. Whereas risk managers and disaster planners usually concentrate on physical risks such as those described above, they are increasingly called upon to consider:

- political risk and hostile legislation
- sudden and deep cuts to operating budgets
- sudden postponements of important projects owing to a lack of funds
- the sudden cancellation of library programmes owing to a lack of funds
- demands from boards and other authorities to cut staff and close branches
- the loss of essential expertise and leadership
- lengthy strike action, and other job actions
- serious morale problems
- crises, for example negative media coverage.

'You can ward off a lot of enterprise risk if you know how to respond quickly with maximum impact', says a Canadian academic library director. 'Budget cuts are never welcome, but there are ways of managing them and their fallout. You have to be a good negotiator to manage enterprise risk. Some librarians are better at negotiating than others.'

Library disaster planners should consider all of the above risks and the likelihood of them leading to actual events. The likelihood of any event is in many cases difficult to determine exactly, but all potential events should be carefully considered in a library's risk assessment.

1.8 References

1.8.1 Interviews

In this chapter I have quoted a public librarian in Los Angeles, a retired salesperson who worked for a large American computer manufacturer, a Midwestern American Fire Chief, a British university librarian, a Canadian academic library director and a school librarian in a rural district of southern India.

I have also quoted a notorious library thief, who, while he has been caught on several occasions in possession of stolen books and manuscripts, has never been charged with an offence.

Preparedness

2.1 Authorization

You have a boss.

Hierarchical management structures ensure that most librarians who are responsible for developing their libraries' disaster plans have superiors to whom they are obliged to report. A public library director will report to a board or city council; department heads will report to their director; front-line librarians will report to their department heads and clericals will report to supervisors. Public library boards are frequently required to inform municipal authorities of their library's disaster plan. University library directors will update their respective governing bodies – senates, for example – of their progress in developing plans. If you have been charged with the responsibility of developing a disaster plan, you will probably have a person or group of people authorizing, overseeing and evaluating your work.

If you are a planning consultant, you will have a client contact such as the library director to whom you will submit your drafts and finished documents. The same is true for a planner employed by a city who develops disaster plans for different kinds of city-owned institutions. That planner will submit his or her work to the library director for approval and sign-off. The planner who works alone and without the oversight of a superior is rare.

It is prudent to update your superiors regularly about your planning project. Your first report will be a risk assessment and analysis (RAA), which is essentially a list of the risks that prevail at your site or sites, and an estimation of the likelihood of each risk becoming an actual threat. Many RAAs also include a business impact analysis (BIA). A BIA provides speculative information regarding the effects on your library from any negative event. To prepare your superiors for any bad news and unpleasant surprises, you should let them know at the beginning of your planning project about the possible contents of the RAA. They may be already aware of some of the risks that prevail at your library. For example, Californian library boards and directors are usually well aware that earthquakes could strike their sites; most adult Californians have felt ground motion associated with earthquakes at some point in their lives. If you work in a Californian library, it is unlikely that you will shock your superiors by stating that your library is at risk from an earthquake. But they might be surprised and discouraged to hear that four of your library's larger branches are showing signs of substantial water ingress and mould growth. They might not want to hear that theft of books and periodicals from your central library has increased by 40 per cent over the past three years. And you might hesitate to tell them (but you should) that the central library is situated near older buildings that do not comply with current fire codes, and that if those buildings were to catch fire they could send smoke and fumes in the direction of the central library.

Such information is disturbing, but it is a relief to know that all of these risks can be mitigated: that is, you can manage them in such a way that even if they turn into real threats they will be less likely to harm employees and patrons, and they will not damage your facilities as much as they might have if you had not anticipated them. You cannot eradicate risk, but you can decrease the effects of various threats. Your superiors will be relieved to hear it.

2.2 Committees: pros and cons

Libraries often strike committees to develop disaster plans, or ask established committees such as that responsible for occupational health and safety to do so. The advantages of having a committee in charge of the planning process include:

- contributions from different departments and various levels of management
- different perspectives on risk
- ease in disseminating disaster planning information throughout the library system.

Although it is often left unsaid, there is also the political advantage of sharing responsibility for delivering bad news to superiors. It can be daunting for a single person to tell a board, for example, that a library branch is riddled with mould and bedbugs, and that the cost of removing them will be high. Superiors can make the mistake of 'killing the messenger', and to be that messenger could be uncomfortable. There is perceived protection in numbers; hence, many planners prefer to work with or in a committee. Note that the chances of causing displeasure among superiors are greatest during the compilation and delivery of the RAA, which superiors might consider nothing but bad news.

'I'm glad that we had a committee to handle the disaster plan', says a technical services librarian at a large corporate library in Toronto. 'We were able to cover a broad range of risks, and it's unlikely that a single individual could have identified all of them. And we were able to distribute information throughout the library and our entire organization very quickly. I would not have wanted to work on our plan by myself. Nor would I have wanted to let my boss know all by myself about the risks that our library faces. There was safety in numbers.'

The disadvantages of putting a committee in charge of the process include:

- A longer planning process. Committees can take more time than individuals to make decisions and to draft documents.
- Higher costs. If more library employees are taking time to produce a disaster plan, that plan will cost more to produce.
- Distractions. Committees can lose their concentration and become lost in details and irrelevant matters. Interdepartmental politics can also take up more time than it deserves.

'There's also the possibility that a plan will never get past the risk assessment and analysis phase if a committee is responsible for it', says a university librarian in Texas. 'Our disaster planning committee has been talking about terrorism for a decade, and still hasn't got round to discussing the leaky plumbing in our stack areas and the lack of first-aid attendants throughout our system. They can't get past the risk assessment phase. They've produced memos that say that they're making progress, but nobody believes it any more. The result is that our library has no disaster plan. That leaves us open to the risks that the disaster planning committee has been talking about for all those years.'

2.3   RAA, step one: history-taking

Realize that every site is unique and has a unique risk profile. Sites may share risks but the likelihood of actual threats varies from site to site. Thus, your RAA should be site-specific. If your library system comprises 20 sites, then it is best to cover the risk profiles of each site. There may be the temptation to cover only the larger and more important sites but this approach could lead to serious problems. If an employee is injured at a smaller site during an emergency or disaster, problems of liability could arise. Moreover, employees at smaller sites could feel neglected if you deem only your larger sites as worthy of attention.

The first source of information regarding risks to your library (or any other organization) is its *history*. Sources are as follows:

- Library board records, including reports to a board regarding maintenance and repairs to library sites.
- Centralized administrative records, including a municipality's property management files, warranties, insurance policies and related records.
- On-site records, including building plans and blueprints, maintenance files and accounting files with details of renovations and repairs.
- Media coverage – newspapers, online reporting, audio recordings of interviews – of any emergencies or disasters at a site.
- Published and unpublished histories of the site: these include histories of the entire library system that contain information about a specific site, as well as miscellaneous materials held in local archives, for example photos and ephemera.
- Employees, current and past: employees' memories are often the best source of information regarding events that might have caused considerable damage to a site but which media representatives did not consider newsworthy.

'In fact, I found that employees who had worked at my branch had the best idea of its history', said a public library branch manager in New York City. 'The older employees pointed out where the roof had leaked, and told me about a small fire that had broken out years ago in our cafeteria area. This information had gone missing from our files, but without it our risk assessment would have been incomplete. I'd say that the best place to start when you're compiling a risk assessment is with your fellow library workers.'

2.4   RAA, step two: inspection

Having reviewed the history and other documentation pertaining to a specific library site, the next step is to inspect it. Traditionally, the 'walkabout' inspection is necessary to identify the greatest risks to any site. Much depends, however, on the perceptiveness of the person who carries out the inspection. A stroll through a building is inadequate. A thorough inspection requires:

- Mental preparedness and the willingness to make observations about all risk factors on a site. The inspector's motto: 'Look up, down and all around' to spot risks that prevail on a site.
- A tour of the surrounding neighbourhood, to identify proximity risks. This tour might also take into account proximity risks from farther afield. For example, a chemical plant ten miles from a library branch might involve more serious threats than a mall or block of retail stores on the same block as that branch.
- An inspection of the site perimeter, which might include fencing, sidewalks, paved areas, parking areas, commuter areas and bus stops, commercial and retail properties, private residences, bodies of water, roads and highways, and undeveloped land.
- An inspection of the grounds, which might include: pathways and 'unofficial' trails; parking areas; gardens, bushes and stands of trees; benches and other seating areas; power sources such as generators, poles and cables; fountains and sculptures; and other organizations or buildings with purposes unrelated to library operations. As well as the physical condition of the grounds, you should note any signs of inadequate upkeep such as excess litter and overflowing litter bins. You should also take into account any signs of potential security problems, such as discarded drug paraphernalia, loitering, vagrancy and abandoned vehicles.
- An inspection of the library building's exterior, paying attention to obvious signs of wear and tear: cracking, staining or deformation of walls and roofing; inadequate drainage and the pooling of water in the wrong places; loose or otherwise damaged wiring; damaged doors and windows; clogged or otherwise damaged heating, ventilation and air conditioning (HVAC) vents; uneven walkways and stairs; obsolete or damaged signage; inadequate drainage on rooftops; overgrown vegetation, including trees whose branches could fall and damage building components; evidence of pests such as pigeons; damaged or malfunctioning security cameras; vandalism (for example, 'tagging'); and signs of incomplete or substandard repairs and maintenance.
- A tour of the interior, paying attention to obvious signs of wear and tear: again, cracking, staining and deformation of walls and ceilings; any signs of faulty plumbing or sprinkler malfunction; any signs of damaged wiring or electrical circuitry; substandard lighting systems; damaged (for example, leaky) windows and skylights, or excess pooling of water in doorways and along walkways; loose, shaky or otherwise unstable shelving; damaged or unstable seating and tables; loose or worn-out carpeting; inadequate litter removal; unsanitary washrooms; signs of inappropriate or criminal activity, for example damaged security cameras, discarded drug paraphernalia or damaged assets including books that have been defaced.

2.5   RAA, step three: interviews

Interviews can be formal or informal. You can conduct formal interviews in an office setting with library employees from all levels of the hierarchy. You might rely on a preformulated series of questions for each interviewee, such as:

- How long have you worked at this site? In which departments or areas?
- Do you recall any risks or particular threats (natural, technological, human-caused, and so on) during your time at this site? How did the library deal with those threats?

- Can you point out any current risks that we should address? Do you know of any threat that we should deal with?
- Can you recommend ways to make our library safer and more secure?

You may invite interviewees to provide any other useful information after the formal interview via voicemail or email. Some libraries advise interviewees that all information that they give during or after the interview will be confidential; some libraries guarantee interviewee anonymity. Even so, employees might still be unwilling to divulge information for fear that they could be considered to be troublemakers or whistleblowers.

Be prepared for employees who are nervous about talking about threats to the library. Some employees will consider the risk assessment to be a pursuit of the obvious and thus a waste of time. Others will worry that the points they raise during a formal interview could be trivial or irrelevant. A skilled interviewer will put interviewees at ease, and encourage them to talk openly about anything they believe to be a risk. Remember that what might appear to be an insignificant matter, for example a small stain on a wall, could be a sign of much larger problems such as deteriorating plumbing or a damaged building envelope, advanced mould growth, or faulty drainage. Observing and documenting that small stain could lead to the prevention of a disaster.

Informal interviews may be unstructured and could be held in relaxed settings such as a cafeteria. The interviewer's goal should be to elicit as much pertinent information as possible regarding perceived risks to the library. The interviewer may guarantee anonymity if library policy allows it.

It is appropriate to ask interviewees to provide more information if it comes to mind later. You should invite them to contact you if they think of something that might be a useful addition to the RAA or any other aspect of the disaster planning process.

'I really liked the fact that I could keep in touch with the librarian who was working on our disaster plan', said an academic library administrator in New York City. 'She made me feel like I was making a helpful contribution to library safety. Interestingly, it was my offhand comment about the wet floor in one of our staff washrooms that led to the discovery of a faulty pipe that was on the verge of bursting. That could have caused a great deal of damage. Now our RAA is more than just another document in a binder. It has become an ongoing procedure that allows us to protect all of our operations.'

2.6   RAA, step four: discussions with external experts

Your local fire department can provide invaluable assistance during the RAA phase of your library's disaster planning process. In many areas the fire department will inspect public and academic library sites regularly to ensure that they have no outstanding fire risks. Such inspections, however, might be cursory unless you and the firefighters are willing to perform comprehensive inspections. While firefighters are primarily concerned about the risk of fire, they can also advise you about other risks.

'Our local fire chief was interested in our annual fire drills', said a public library branch manager in Pennsylvania. 'But he also talked about drills to deal with toxic spills. There are highways and railway lines near our branch, and a lot of dangerous chemicals travel within two hundred feet of out front entrance. The chief told us to leave our building as soon as possible after any report of a nearby derailment or overturned truck, and to put as much distance as possible between ourselves and the branch. It's not just fire that we have to think about.'

Firefighters can advise you about sprinkler systems and other fire controls. Almost any firefighter can show you the safest building evacuation routes for employees to take in the event of any sort of disaster. 'They can also tell you when to stay inside your building', offered a public librarian in California. 'In this region, a firefighter will tell you to get out if you spot a fire, and stay in if an earthquake strikes. People who enter or exit a building during a quake are more likely than anyone else to get hurt. It's tempting to run outside when the ground starts shaking, but it's a bad idea. Californian firefighters emphasize that point repeatedly.'

Another source of expert opinion is your local police, who might be willing to inspect your site(s) to determine security risks, and to advise you on the best ways to enhance your security measures. It is worth noting that the police can tell you which measures might not work for you. For example, closed-circuit television cameras (CCTVs) will not necessarily deter malefactors such as vandals, hostile patrons or thieves. In some instances, CCTV systems are warranted and useful, especially when their screens are monitored regularly by security guards. But simply installing a system and asking a guard to glance at a screen occasionally will not provide the highest level of security. The police can tell you if, when and where a CCTV system would be to your library's advantage.

Other external sources of information on your library's risks include paramedics, urban planners, architects, engineers, insurance brokers and adjusters, tradespersons such as plumbers and electricians, and other librarians who have worked on their own library's RAAs and disaster plans. Other local librarians can save you time and effort by sharing the information that they collected for their own RAAs. This does not mean that you should adopt another library's RAA, or any other part of their disaster plan. That library has its unique risk profile, which might differ from your library's profile in important ways. But you can benefit from other librarians' experience, especially if they have identified the risks that prevail in your locality.

2.7   RAA, step five: documentation

Throughout the foregoing steps, you should be taking notes of any risk-related matters that come to your attention. You can scribble observations on paper, or make voice memos on your mobile phone or other portable device. But you must make notes, and when you have completed steps one to four, you should compile those notes in a clear and simple fashion for further consideration. Such notes constitute your risk assessment. You do not need to create enormous amounts of material; in fact a few pages of concise observations might be adequate for your purposes.

Now you may analyse your assessment to discover which risks might turn into actual threats. Risk analyses can take different forms. There is no standard format that is guaranteed to cover all contingencies; in many cases, the risk analysis is nothing more than well-informed and intelligent guesswork. It is nonetheless useful since it will give you an idea of what threatens your operations, and what measures you should take to protect them.

The basic elements of a risk analysis are as follows:

- *Listing of potential threats*: natural, technological, human-caused, and so on.
- *Scope of disasters*: how they could affect your operations in general, including damage to buildings, displacement of employees and loss of collections.
- *Frequency*: how often any kind of event can occur at a particular site. For example, thefts might occur several times a week; a power outage or brownout might occur once a year; and serious winter storms and high winds might disrupt your operations every four or five years.
- *Timing of onset*: how quickly an event will occur, and whether there is any warning. For example, a riverine flood may take days to occur, and in many cases local weather forecasters and municipal emergency workers can provide ample warning. But other disasters can occur suddenly and without warning, for example earthquakes, IT system failures and fires.
- *Impact*: the effects of any event in the short, medium and long term. A fire that destroys a library building will usually have a long-term effect on the operations of the entire library system, whereas a brief power outage might cause no more than temporary inconvenience. If, however, the library has not backed up its data effectively, and the outage causes important data to be lost, then the impact of the outage will be serious.
- *Sustainability*: how serious any event will be in light of the library's vulnerability. For example, if you back up all of your data regularly on reliable media and in secure off-site locations, and if you have tested your back-ups to ensure that your data is recoverable, then your library should be able to sustain the loss of data. If you have not backed up your data, their loss might be unsustainable to your library.
- *Likelihood*: how likely the occurrence of any event is at your site(s). In the south of England earthquakes are rare, but high winds have occurred frequently in the past, and will probably occur in future. Coastal communities in that region face a higher likelihood of gales. Note that while likelihood is related to frequency and scope it is wise to consider it on its own in reference to specific library sites.

2.8 Mitigation: preventative maintenance programmes

Mitigation is the reduction of risks through specific measures. Whatever risk you have identified in your RAA, there are ways to decrease the effects that risk will have if it becomes an actual threat to your library. Generally, the most effective form of mitigation is a well-executed preventative maintenance program (PMP) for each one of your library's sites. A comprehensive PMP includes:

- Regular maintenance of all exterior areas: comprehensive inspections, repairs to buildings and cleaning of vents as required, removal of debris from gutters and drains, repairs to fencing and gates, repairs to exterior lighting, repairs to and updating of signage, care of gardens and pruning of trees, removal of graffiti and 'tagging', removal of rubbish and litter, and clearance of walkways and parking areas.
- A regular janitorial service with the inspection and cleaning of all library interiors, especially in and around high-traffic areas such as lobbies, washrooms, stairwells and public seating areas.

- Regular (i.e., semi-annual) and comprehensive inspections of all fire and smoke alarms and controls, including sensors, extinguishers, hoses and sprinkler systems.
- Regular (i.e., semi-annual) and comprehensive inspections of security systems, including keycard access systems, CCTV systems, Tattle-Tape systems, security mirrors, controlled gates and turnstiles, panic buttons and intercoms.
- An annual inspection of all heating, ventilation and air conditioning equipment, with repairs and updating as required.
- An annual inspection of all electrical systems, including back-up generators, with repairs and updating as required.
- An annual review of security reports and any other documentation that covers breaches of library security such as hostile and intoxicated patrons, thefts, acts of vandalism and faulty security equipment (for example, malfunctioning alarms).
- An annual review of internal signage for legibility, accuracy and proper location.
- An annual inspection of off-site storage facilities, including those for the storage of back-up data and other media.

All inspections and reviews should be documented, and PMP documentation should be retained permanently. Documentation can be made more efficient and convenient through the use of digital photography. The improving quality of mobile telephones with email, voice-memo and camera functions will lead to the increased use of these telephones for documentation purposes.

Ideally, your library's PMP will include training for employees as 'problem spotters'. Librarians and clerical workers cannot be expected to repair leaky plumbing or malfunctioning sprinkler systems, but they should be able to spot these threats and report them promptly to managers who will ensure that they are dealt with before they cause even worse problems. A well-organized system of employee vigilance is the foundation of a first-class PMP.

'People who work at our library treat the preventative maintenance program as a team-building exercise', reported a public library director in Texas.

> *Each of us assumes responsibility for a specific area of the library, and we report any problems to our facilities manager right away. We meet every two months to compare notes and determine whether there are any problems that are occurring in more than one area of the library. Over the past two years, we have spotted an insect infestation, a potentially serious plumbing issue, and a variation in indoor air quality that led to the rebuilding of a couple of air conditioning units. These problems could easily have gotten much worse if we hadn't been vigilant. And I notice that our employees enjoy participating in the process. I think that it has contributed to better morale.*

2.9   Mitigation: gradual replacement of older facilities

As buildings age, they become more vulnerable to various risks. Wear and tear can lead to water ingress and flooding, an increased risk of fire and instability of both structural and non-structural components. In a seismic zone, older buildings can sustain serious damage from even moderate earthquakes. Moreover, surrounding communities and

proximity risks change over time. For example, a Carnegie library building constructed in 1905 might once have been located in a secure, non-industrial neighbourhood.
Over the past century, however, a high-crime area has developed around the library.
Next door to the library is an abandoned department store that has become a haven
for squatters. Local police are concerned about the risk of arson in the area, and are
also concerned about the safety of library employees who park their cars in an ill-lit
and unpatrolled parking lot in which there have been several muggings and assaults.
Adding to the library's risk profile is the fact that the library is in California, which
is a notorious seismic zone. The library's exterior walls have cracked owing to earthquakes, and municipal engineers are worried that the foundations are weak.

Such a building should be replaced as soon as possible, but in an age of budgetary
cutbacks, a new building could be out of the question, at least in the short term. But
this state of affairs should not stop the library's board and management from recognizing the need for a new building and taking the initial steps toward its funding, planning
and design, construction and eventual opening.

2.10   Mitigation: insurance

There is no standard insurance policy or satisfactory general template for a library's
insurance coverage. Since there are so many different kinds of libraries with myriad
different risk profiles each policy will probably have unique elements. Complicating
matters is the cost of coverage. Owing to recent budgetary restraints, many libraries
cannot afford comprehensive coverage, and must rely on policies that insure only the
most outstanding risks, and that contain substantial exclusions and deductibles.

Many corporate libraries are covered by their sponsoring organizations, which purchase policies that address losses of library assets including contents (e.g., furnish-
ings), collections and especially valuable books, documents and artworks. But public
and academic libraries might not have such policies, or may discover that they are
covered only for liability and very limited losses of assets.

As far as insurance is concerned, a little knowledge is certainly a dangerous thing.
The purchase of household insurance policies is not enough to educate anyone on coverage for a complex institution such as a library. The wisest course of action for most
librarians – who probably know little about the technicalities of insurance – is to seek
the advice of insurance professionals who specialize in developing and implementing
coverage for libraries, museums and galleries. Your local insurance brokers can direct
you to these specialists.

2.11   Mitigation: data back-up

It is astonishing how often libraries fail to back up their vital data. Even with clear
back-up policies in place, many libraries do not carry out what should be simple
and essential back-up procedures. Hence, one result of a disaster is often the loss of

substantial amounts of data. Remember that for all of its advantages, electronic data are the most vulnerable assets libraries own. Without a back-up policy and procedures, and the willingness to follow them, librarians leave their institutions exposed to almost every risk in their risk profile.

The basic elements of an effective back-up system for a library are as follows:

- A librarian or senior clerical worker charged with the responsibility of managing the back-up of the library's data.
- A vital data inventory, with a record of where the data are stored.
- Reliable storage media.
- A secure off-site storage facility (for example a branch at a distance of no less than 15 miles from the building housing the library's IT department, or a storage vendor offering secure data storage).
- A secure system of transportation between the library and the storage facility, either via the Internet or by vehicular transport.
- A back-up data storage schedule (ideally data will be backed up securely off-site every business day).
- A testing schedule to ensure that storage media are fully functional, and that all vital data are recoverable quickly and securely.

2.12   Mitigation: the key

In the end, risk mitigation and general preparedness depend on the willingness of you and your associates to make sure that your library has a comprehensive RAA and effective mitigation measures. Anecdotal evidence suggests that those libraries with the highest levels of preparedness for negative events have staff with the following attributes:

- good morale at all levels of the staff hierarchy;
- an acceptance of an information-gathering interview process, either formal or informal;
- ongoing interest and participation in committees concerned with RAA development;
- ongoing interest and participation in programmes to investigate risks and to report trouble as required; and
- ongoing interest and participation in orientation and training related to the disaster plan in general.

With these attributes, your library staff will also accept the need for the next part of your disaster plan, which concerns disaster response.

2.13   References

2.13.1   Interviews

In this chapter I have quoted a technical services librarian at a corporate library in Toronto. American librarians quoted include a university librarian in Texas, a public library branch manager and an academic library administrator in New York City, a public librarian in California and a public library branch manager in Pennsylvania.

Disaster response

3.1 Staff and patron safety

People are paramount.

The purpose of a disaster (or emergency) response plan is to keep people safe. Despite the monetary value of library buildings and collections the safety of the people who use them is more important during a dangerous event than anything else. The importance of personal safety cannot be overemphasized, since librarians are naturally tempted to concentrate on the security of their collections – particularly those of great historical and monetary value – rather than deal with matters of human safety, which they often take for granted. Further, librarians usually know more about their collections than they do about bomb threats, fire drills and evacuation techniques.

'In our library, we always assumed that the police and firefighters would look after our safety', says a corporate librarian in the State of Washington.

> *Our disaster response plan contained advice on how to treat damp books and computer equipment. We were well prepared for an infestation of bedbugs. But when a fire broke out in the cafeteria, we didn't know what to do. It was minutes before anyone triggered the fire alarm and dialed 911 for the fire department. None of us knew how to use the wall-mounted extinguishers. And we were so slow to evacuate the building that two of our staff members and a patron had to be treated in hospital for smoke inhalation. After that, we discarded the old disaster response plan and developed a new set of guidelines that focuses on protecting people.*

The factors that discourage librarians from planning to protect human safety include:

- a focus on the library's physical assets, especially collections
- lack of familiarity with human safety procedures
- lack of interest
- ignorance of occupational health and safety guidelines and regulations
- an assumption that others are responsible for human safety
- an assumption that emergency assistance will always be available
- an assumption that the library is naturally a safe haven, where dangerous events do not occur
- apathy.

Factors that encourage librarians to develop plans that protect human safety include:

- an awareness of risks to human safety
- an awareness of the limitations of first responders and local emergency services
- demands from local authorities – for example, the fire chief – for human safety planning in the library
- demands from the library board that the library develops life safety plans
- advice from insurers, auditors and other external authorities

- concerns about legal liability
- a commitment to compliance with occupational health and safety guidelines and regulations
- concerns about personal safety
- effective leadership from library managers and other supervisory staff
- an interest in human safety issues and planning, often as a break from one's usual professional duties and routine.

'Much depends on organizational culture', says a government librarian in Washington, DC.

> *In our library, which serves a large federal department, the emergency and disaster response planning has always been top-notch, if only because half of our staff members were formerly in the military. Both of our fire wardens were naval petty officers, and are keenly aware of the risk of fire. They organize and oversee our fire drills at least twice a year, and sometimes more often. They also make sure that we have the right kinds of emergency supplies and equipment in the library – a good first-aid kit, flashlights and battery-operated radios – everything we need. And other ex-military people on staff welcome this sort of thing. It's a part of our culture.*

3.2   Producing a disaster response plan

It is possible to spend much time and money on developing a disaster response plan. Even so, time and money do not guarantee good planning nor the kind of plan that is most appropriate to a particular library. The best plans – including some that have contributed to the saving of lives in actual emergencies and disasters – often have the following features:

- brevity: two pages rather than 200
- clarity
- readability
- ease of handling
- attractiveness of design and layout
- ease of distribution to staff members
- ease of updating and revision
- adaptability to other media: from paper to app, and so on.
- appropriateness for particular staff: recognizing physical capabilities and experience in handling potentially dangerous circumstances
- appropriateness for the particular organization's culture
- site specificity: addressing the organization's risks at a specific site or sites.

Figure 3.1 is an example of a plan that has all of these features. This particular response plan is designed to fit in a wallet or purse and to serve as a textbook for the library's orientation and training sessions. Printed on hardy stock, it can last in this form for years, or until the library needs a revised version.

Lancaster Gate PUBLIC LIBRARY

YOUR EMERGENCY RESPONSE PLAN

- FIRE
- EXPLOSION
- LEAKS / FLOODS
- BOMB THREAT
- INTRUDER / THREATENING BEHAVIOUR
- BIO-CHEMICAL MAIL THREAT
- EARTHQUAKE
- HIGH WINDS / SEVERE WEATHER
- TOXIC SPILL
- POWER OUTAGE / BROWNOUT
- GENERAL PRECAUTIONS

Library Security 8494
Police Fire Ambulance 911

GENERAL PRECAUTIONS
- Take first aid and CPR training. Keep your training up-to-date.
- Record injuries in the Accident Record Book and complete the required WCB report.
- Be sure that you know the locations of the nearest first aid kit and flashlight.
- Familiarize yourself with the emergency exits and your Emergency Assembly Area.
- Participate in all evacuation drills.
- Make sure that everyone in your residence knows safety measures against fire and earthquakes.
- Your personal, out-of-province contact number is: ____.

If you have any questions, please contact Library Management at 7050 or 1850.

( )

Copyright © 2013 by Lancaster Gate Public Library
Printed in Canada

Within six hours:
- Call your pre-arranged, personal out-of-province contact number. Give your name, time of call, location, and status.
- If it is safe to do so, inspect your work areas for damage. Do not move heavy equipment or furniture by yourself.

POWER OUTAGE / BROWNOUT
- Keep flashlights and other emergency supplies stored in a handy place.
- Do not attempt to use computers, photocopiers and other electrical equipment.
- Avoid moving around in dark areas unless you have a flashlight. Do not attempt to examine, repair or open electrical equipment.
- Do not use the elevator. If trapped in the elevator, press the alarm bell button and use the emergency telephone to alert Library Security.
- Await instructions from maintenance crews before restarting electrical equipment.
- If power is out for longer than two hours, check food in fridges for spoilage.

- Travel only when necessary. Drive slowly.
- Make sure that your car has an emergency kit and a full tank of gas.
- Listen to your radio for emergency bulletins and traffic advice.

TOXIC SPILL (petroleum, chemical, etc.)
A toxic spill could occur on a major street or at a neighbouring industrial site.
If so:
- Avoid the spill as much as possible. Do not loiter in the area.
- Do not use matches or other open flames in the vicinity of the spill. Do not smoke.
- If you notice heavy fumes or toxic material seeping into the building, evacuate. Avoid fumes, vapour and smoke. Call Library Security immediately.

EARTHQUAKE
During the shaking:
- Take cover under a table or desk. Protect your head. Avoid heavy furniture and shelving units.
- Avoid glass, loose masonry and utility wires.

- Do not take the elevator.
- If indoors, stay indoors. If outside, stay outside.
- In a moving vehicle, stop in a clear area away from falling debris. Do not leave the vehicle.

After the shaking:
- Apply first aid as required
- Avoid unstable shelving and furniture.
- Do not use candles, matches or other open flames. Keep a flashlight handy.
- Do not smoke.
- Do not make telephone calls unless they are lifesaving.
- Turn on the radio or TV for emergency bulletins and updates.
- Avoid entering damaged buildings and loading bays.
- Expect aftershocks.
- Sprinklers and alarms might be triggered.
- Be prepared to remain in your workplace or residence for up to three days.

FIRE
- Douse small fires if possible. For a spreading blaze, trigger the fire alarm and evacuate the building.
- Walk, don't run. Use the nearest emergency exit.
- Do not use the elevator.
- Avoid flames, smoke and fumes. REMEMBER: the closer to the floor, the lighter the smoke and fumes.
- Once outside, go to your Emergency Assembly Area.

- Make way for firefighters and emergency crews.
- Upon arriving at the Emergency Assembly Area, make sure that everyone in your department or work area has evacuated safely. Report any missing person to your Fire Warden.

EXPLOSION
- Administer first aid as required.
- If you suspect that more explosions might occur, move toward a safe area and wait for instructions from your Fire Warden. In the event of evacuation, report any missing person to your Fire Warden.
- For a spreading blaze, trigger the fire alarm and evacuate immediately.

LEAKS/FLOODS/SPRINKLER MALFUNCTION
Most leaks, floods and sprinkler malfunctions are not life-threatening, but:
- Clear the moisture-damaged area. Call Facilities Management at 6365 immediately.
- Avoid wet wires, electrical equipment and power outlets. Do not attempt to use a moisture-damaged computer, printer, fax machine or photocopier.
- Do not walk through water.
- Let Facilities Management know the source of the water: roof, window, pipe, washroom, sprinkler, etc.
- Do not begin clean-up until after the safety inspection of wiring, outlets and equipment.

BOMB THREAT
By telephone:
- Cooperate with the caller. Listen carefully.
- Refer to your bomb threat telephone checklist. If time permits, ask the caller:
  - When will the bomb explode?
  - Where is the bomb?
  - What does it look like?
  - What kind of bomb is it?
  - Why was it planted?

- Try to remember the exact time of the call.
- Try to remember the caller's voice: male/female, accent, intoxicated, familiar?
- Note any background noise during the call: traffic, construction, music, voices, etc.
- Immediately inform Library Security, then prepare to evacuate the building.
- Person in charge of unit: quickly check your immediate work areas for unusual or out-of-place items. Do not touch any suspicious parcel, envelope, box or container.
- Await instructions and prepare to evacuate.

In writing:
- Handle the document as little as possible after you have read it. Save all threatening e-mail and fax messages for future investigation.
- If the message is attached to a wall or other surface, do not touch it or the surrounding area.
- Inform Library Security immediately, then prepare to evacuate the building.
- If you believe that a bomb is about to explode, evacuate immediately to your Emergency Assembly Area.

INTRUDER / THREATENING BEHAVIOUR
- If an unfamiliar person enters your work area, greet him/her politely and offer assistance. Do not allow an unfamiliar person to wander through staff areas.
- If an intruder appears angry or threatening, keep a safe distance away. Listen to what he/she says. Do not argue or raise your voice. Try to calm him/her down.
- Avoid heroics. Do not make abrupt or unnecessary movements.
- Inform Library Security immediately. Avoid remaining alone with any intruder.
- If an intruder leaves any parcel, envelope, or suspicious item near your work area, do not touch it. Inform Library Security.
- If a person has been assaulted, assign someone to remain with him or her. Call Library Security immediately.

BIO-CHEMICAL MAIL THREAT
- Verify legitimacy of suspicious packages with the sender or intended recipient.

- Carefully examine suspicious packages but handle them as little as possible. Do not shake, bend or smell the articles.
- Note excessive packaging or security material such as adhesive tape or string.
- Note protruding wires, aluminum foil or any unusual odour or stains on the envelope or package.
- Do not attempt to clean up any substance that spills or leaks from the package.
- Isolate the article by covering it with paper or a trash can, close the door to the room where the article is located and immediately contact Library Security and Library Management.
- Remove any contaminated clothing and seal it in a plastic bag or garbage can.
- Wash with soap and water to remove any contaminants.
- Wait for emergency response personnel to arrive.

HIGH WINDS/SEVERE WEATHER
- Expect power outages and telephone line disruptions.
- Avoid overhead hazards: tree branches, power lines.
- Avoid glass and debris on sidewalks and roads.

Figure 3.1 Sample Emergency Response Plan brochure.

3.3 Production mistakes

Too many response plans are packaged in three-ring binders, which swell with new and not necessarily useful contents as time passes. Such plans often contain a mish-mash of articles, booklets, items from the Internet, decision trees, organization charts, equipment inventories, bits and pieces brought back from conferences and safety seminars, and lists of emergency supplies, telephone numbers, vendors, consultants and local first responders. It is not unusual to discover that a library has adopted another library's response plan with no changes: one library's plan is simply added to the contents of another library's binder.

Some libraries rely on websites to distribute response plans. These websites frequently contain the same sorts of material in the same disorder that one finds in many three-ring binders. Electronic distribution is no guarantee of a plan's quality, although its shortcomings might become evident more quickly.

'Any response plan for a library that takes more than one hour to read and digest is in need of severe editing', says a corporate librarian in the City of London.

> *When I see that a response plan has a table of contents of more than two pages, I know that it would be useless in an emergency. A good plan tells you what you need to know in a few seconds. In fact, the best plan tells you what you should know before you need that information, and is designed in such a way that you can easily learn and remember its contents. I have no time for unwieldy binders that are difficult to read and require many hours of study – and that do not facilitate awareness of essential emergency procedures.*

3.4 The issue of library assets

If human safety is more important than anything else during an emergency, how can librarians protect assets such as their collections? Should assets be ignored during emergencies and disasters? The answer is yes, but with the stipulation that assets should be safeguarded *before* dangerous events, through preparedness planning and mitigation measures. As a fire or flood endangers a library, the staff should feel certain that:

- Essential data – including digital collections – have been backed up in at least two locations, and that at least one of those locations is outside the immediate region.
- All back-up data are recoverable, that is, in up-to-date media that can be easily accessed on current hardware.
- Fire resistant cabinets and fire control technology will protect valuable books and manuscripts, which are stored in areas not exposed to water ingress.
- Strategic alliances have been set up with vendors for the timely replacement of popular publications, periodicals, furniture, IT and shelving.
- Strategic alliances have been set up with other organizations who can accommodate library operations at least in the short term: community centres, church basements, neighbouring offices and other libraries or library branches.
- Insurance policies will cover facilities and collections.

3.5   Emotional reactions to emergencies and disasters

A person's emotional reaction to emergencies and disasters will depend on a number of different factors, including:

- sociocultural background
- emergency/disaster response training and orientation
- prevailing state of mind
- personality
- age.

Other factors might include the presence of other people at the time of the event, especially if those people are family members or friends; physical conditioning; military and paramilitary experience; and training in dealing with medical emergencies. While much depends on such factors, it remains difficult to predict how a person will react to a particular event. Many Californian and Japanese librarians have lived through dozens of small earthquakes, and are not overly concerned by the small tremblers that occur frequently in their regions. Many believe that they can survive even the largest earthquake by taking precautions that they learned as schoolchildren. But they might not react as calmly to threats to which they are unaccustomed. For example, a Southern Californian librarian might have little experience in dealing with the tornadoes that occur in that region of the Midwestern United States known informally as 'Tornado Alley'.

The level of surprise is also worth considering with regard to a person's emotional reactions. Residents of San Francisco will not be completely surprised to feel the earth move under their feet, since earthquakes are part of their experience in their home state of California. They might not react the same way if they feel the earth move in Germany, or Ireland, or anywhere else that is not considered a seismic zone. A librarian from Alberta, Canada, sums up the essence of surprise as follows:

> *If you see a grizzly bear at a distance of a mile in the Rocky Mountains, you might be frightened, but you would not be very surprised. Grizzlies are common in that region. If you come face to face with a grizzly on a trail in the Rocky Mountains, you might be very surprised. You need to take evasive action immediately. But if you met a grizzly in a street in the South Kensington neighbourhood of London, not only would you be surprised, but also astonished to the point where you might not have any idea about the best ways to react. There are different levels of surprise, which will depend upon your assumptions about what to expect – and not to expect – in and around your location.*

As a librarian, you develop an awareness of many common risks that might turn into actual threats in your workplace. Usually, you are aware of the possibility that faulty plumbing might cause a flood in your workplace; that dishonest patrons might steal books and other items; and that inevitably your circulating collections will deteriorate owing to frequent handling. You are disappointed but hardly surprised to discover that copies of a popular novel have gone missing or fallen apart. You might be astonished, however, to arrive at your library one morning to find it engulfed in flames and surrounded by firefighters with hoses and ladders. Some risks are more likely than others to turn into threats. The more frequently a risk becomes a threat, the less profound your surprise, and the less likely your complete astonishment.

Emotional reactions to emergencies and disasters range from panic, which is uncommon, to confusion, disorientation, depression, anxiety and numbness, from which people frequently suffer during and after negative events. But people are sometimes surprised at how calm they are while a situation deteriorates around them. A public librarian in New Jersey who saw her branch destroyed by fire makes a noteworthy observation:

> *I spent almost my entire career at that branch, and yet as it burned I didn't feel much. In fact I felt numb. When I went home afterwards I thought that I might break down, but I didn't. I suspect that part of my calm attitude was partly due to my fatalism, and partly to my belief that I wouldn't lose my job, that there would be work for me in another local branch. Now, years after the fact, when I think about the fire I regret the loss of the collections, particularly the children's department, but it's not as if I have felt deep personal loss.*

3.6   Leadership in response planning

Library managers are wise to demonstrate an active interest in response planning from the start. Simply to leave planning to subordinates or ignore it altogether is irresponsible.

'I made it clear to my entire staff that I wanted to be involved in any response planning we had on the go', said an academic librarian in Pennsylvania.

> *At the staff meeting where we kicked off our planning project, I pointed out that I was just as human as everyone else, and just as much at risk. I stated that I wanted to participate in all evacuation drills, and to take the necessary orientation and training. And I said that I wanted every manager and supervisor to follow my lead – no exceptions.*

Other aspects of leadership in response planning include:

- A willingness to keep the library board informed regarding response planning, orientation. and training.
- A willingness to listen to staff members' concerns about risks and appropriate response measures.
- Determination to keep the library's response measures – for example evacuation techniques – up to date.
- A willingness to consider liability issues as they might affect the library.
- The resolve to make response plans sustainable in the long term – as a part of corporate culture.

'Really the best sort of response planning does not involve much written material', says a university librarian in Saskatchewan, Canada.

> *You want library staffers to respond immediately and sensibly to whatever emergency or disaster occurs. You do not want people leafing through a three-ring binder*

while the building burns down. Any plan must lead to action, not further reference to the index. Fortunately our head librarian realized all this, and insisted that we keep our planning documents to a minimum.

3.7 Response teams

In many instances, the most effective response team for a library is that which is already in place: the current library hierarchy, with a director at the top and different levels of managers, supervisors, technicians and clericals in descending order of responsibility and control. Certainly other kinds of organizations should rely on special teams for an effective response to a disaster. For example, a manufacturing plant might organize and train the following teams to deal with disasters:

- Management team
- IT team
- Security team
- Communications/Public Relations team
- Emergency Customer Support/Outreach team
- Emergency Staff Allocation team
- Emergency Transportation team
- Plant Operations and Facilities Clean-Up team.

A library, however, is most often able to respond to disasters by maintaining as much as possible its standard management hierarchy. Reasons why include:

- Limited time for orientation and training of each team.
- Budget limitations.
- Strength of the library hierarchy: everyone is familiar with his or her role, location and responsibilities.
- Speed of response: with no time spent on team assembly and activation, library employees can respond quickly to disaster circumstances.

'After 9/11, our library underwent a lot of disaster response training and drills', reported a public library director in New Hampshire. 'We set up response teams, more than a dozen of them. We drafted manuals for each one. As is often the case, time passed and we lost interest in maintaining those teams. We didn't keep the team manuals up to date, and we didn't have the funding to dedicate to teams.'

Then, a burst pipe flooded the ground floor and basement of one of the library's branches, and the branch staff handled the situation admirably. The branch manager turned off the water and electricity, and asked supervisors to close affected areas. Clerical employees on site at the time moved damp books and periodicals to a dry workspace for conservation and 'biblio-triage', which involves deciding which damaged items are worth repairing and restoring and which are to be discarded. A moisture remediation vendor was summoned, and arrived within one hour to commence clean-up of the facilities. Losses were minimal, and the branch reopened the next day.

'If we had tried to activate the library's response teams, we would have wasted a good deal of time', said the director.

The staff on hand at the time did a fine job of responding appropriately to the situation. I'd say that a well-organized staff [hierarchy], knowledge of basic response procedures and a goodly amount of common sense is worth more to us than a small army of response teams. And these days, we simply do not have the money to keep teams going.

This is not to say that response teams in libraries are necessarily unadvisable. In some larger libraries they might be very useful during disasters, in which case those libraries should consider developing the teams listed above for a manufacturing plant, along with more specialized teams for emergency conservation. But the challenges of maintaining such teams persist, and should be considered before the library decides to develop them.

3.8 References

3.8.1 Interviews

In this chapter I have quoted Canadian librarians from Alberta, and American librarians from the State of Washington, Washington DC, New Jersey, Pennsylvania and New Hampshire. I have also quoted a librarian in the City of London.

3.8.2 Print

Robertson, G. (2003) 'Downsizing the binder: effective security planning for libraries', in *Unofficial Wisdom: Selected Contributions to* Feliciter *1995–2009*, pp. 93–104. Ottawa, ON: Canadian Library Association.

Robertson, G. (2009) 'Investigating risk: assessing and analyzing trouble before it strikes', in *Unofficial Wisdom: Selected Contributions to* Feliciter *1995–2009*, pp. 181–4. Ottawa, ON: Canadian Library Association.

Operational resumption, continuity and recovery

4

4.1 After the fact

Disasters come to an end.

All negative events, from the most minor accident to a major global catastrophe, reach a point where the circumstances become less threatening and more manageable. Floodwaters recede, fires are extinguished, high winds subside and the weather improves. Once a disaster scene is stable, that is, safe enough for personnel to work in and around it, then libraries can activate plans that facilitate a return to normal operations. These plans are subsumed under headings such as 'resumption', 'continuity' and 'recovery'. It is worth noting that disaster planners use these terms loosely, and what might be considered more appropriate as a resumption plan might be referred to as a library's recovery or continuity plan. In any case, these plans are intended to deal with matters that need attention after a disaster. What follows are sections that describe different kinds of 'after-plans' and demonstrate how libraries use them.

4.2 Resumption

Whether their planners know it or not, most library after-plans are developed for the purpose of operational resumption. These plans are often less expensive to develop and implement than continuity and recovery plans, and more capable of providing helpful direction after a multiplicity of events, including some not necessarily mentioned in the risk assessment and analysis.

The key components of a resumption plan can include:

- damage assessment procedures
- disaster declaration procedures
- crisis management plans
- clean-up arrangements
- post-disaster procedures for dealing with employees, volunteers and patrons
- staff allocation plans
- strategic alliances with associates, vendors and suppliers
- post-disaster communications procedures
- post-disaster transportation procedures
- post-disaster data management procedures
- normalization programmes
- testing, auditing and revision schedules
- orientation and training programmes

Depending on the aims of the library and the nature of its operations, these components should be designed for site-specific implementation. This means that a component such as a succession plan covers the replacement – temporary or permanent – of key personnel in a specific library. Some libraries may focus on the replacement of senior managers only; other libraries might cover emergency succession for more junior staff in key departments such as Technical Services and Reference. The components appropriate to one library are not necessarily appropriate to another.

'We borrowed our damage assessment component from another university library', says an academic library administrator in Texas.

> *That short cut did not serve us well after a fire broke out in one of the storage areas. The damage assessment procedures covered an entirely different building; they even included the layout for that building. Why didn't anybody at our library have a look at the borrowed component before the fire? I guess we simply assumed that it was generic enough to get us out of trouble. That was a bad mistake, and parts of our building were closed for weeks. If we had a plan specific to our building, we would have been able to resume operations far more quickly. We would have had the relevant details at hand.*

Resumption plan components from other libraries – even from altogether different kinds of organizations – can provide useful information, but their wholesale adoption by your library is inadvisable. Some planners succeed in adapting components for their libraries, but it is not unusual for planners to determine which components are most valuable to their respective libraries, and then develop plans that are specific to their needs. Numerous resumption plan components are available on the Internet, as is much medical and technical advice. You should be wary of taking such information at face value since it could be irrelevant or inaccurate.

'Cookie-cutter solutions', says the assistant director of a public library in California.

> *You can find lots of software packages that will do your resumption planning for you. All you have to do after you've paid the vendor is fill in the blanks, and bingo! You have a full resumption plan. But look a little closer, and you'll find all sorts of things that aren't covered. Those things could slow you down when you try to resume your operations. That's why we in our library started almost from scratch. We looked at the resumption plans of a couple of neighbouring libraries, but in the end our components were ours alone, with attention to the specific facilities and activities at our library. I believe that we have a higher level of protection than those libraries that take their plans off the 'Net'.*

The documentation of a resumption plan is often voluminous. This is unfortunate, since in many cases more documentation leads to reduced effectiveness of the components. The last thing you want to do during a disaster is to find yourself leafing through a three-ring binder crammed with detailed procedures that distract you from essential activities – such as evacuating your building and dealing with frightened employees and patrons. As with response plans, less is frequently more. A concise resumption plan is easier to use and more helpful after an actual disaster.

Ideally, the best resumption plan is one which you need not consult after a disaster. You may have drafted your plan carefully, and included all of the necessary components. With time, orientation and training, you will make the components of the resumption plan part of your organizational culture. Various post-disaster tasks will become almost second nature. Library employees will know their roles, and will know how to work safely towards full operational resumption in a reasonable period of time. There will be little or no need to review the planning documentation.

'I haven't looked at our resumption plan in years', said a public library branch manager in Florida.

> *There's no need. After Hurricane Katrina, we rewrote all of our plans and tested them extensively. All of our employees received basic orientation, and then training in response and resumption procedures. Every new employee receives the orientation shortly after being hired, and we hold semi-annual retraining sessions. The resumption plan sits on a shelf in my office; all managers have copies. But nobody bothers to review the plan, since the training and retraining is the best way to learn what to do after a disaster.*

This Floridian branch manager notes that the resumption plan has been activated after heavy rains caused flooding in two of the public library's branches. Damage to their collections was serious, and a substantial clean-up was necessary: 'We knew exactly what to do after the rains let up. We closed both branches and assessed the damage. This took us about two hours. We decided not to declare a disaster because the branch building had not sustained serious structural damage, and we assumed that we could resume normal operations within 48 hours.'

A construction firm that offers safety inspections and clean-up services dealt with the water damage. A furniture vendor replaced damp carpeting. A paper recycling company removed books that were beyond repair – most were paperbacks and trade non-fiction. Local booksellers replaced most of these books. Fortunately, few hardcovers were damaged. 'We reopened those branches quickly', said the branch manager. 'We followed our resumption plan to the letter, but I'm sure that none of us consulted the plan in its binder.'

4.3 Continuity

Continuity plans facilitate the continuation of operations in all circumstances. When an organization is too important to its community or country to shut down, it must develop plans that allow it to function in most ways in extreme conditions including war, lengthy pandemics, serious civil unrest and the aftermath of terrorism. Military and paramilitary organizations, airlines, large banks, medical centres and laboratories, shipping firms, and certain manufacturers and product distributors have continuity plans, often highly detailed and confidential. These plans include most or all of the components of resumption plans, although there will be additional and more sophisticated planning with regard to IT maintenance, communications, transportation and post-disaster site management. Other components that appear in continuity plans include:

- Advanced alternative site plans for the accommodation of business operations and employees, in some cases for extended periods; hot sites for data recovery.
- Multi-layered data management and recovery plans for accessing vital data at different sites at all times (or '24x7 long term'); frequent comprehensive testing of these plans.
- Strategic alliances with allied operations on different continents.
- Advanced site security plans, with special provisions for the safety of employees.
- Frequent updating of plans to take advantage of the latest portable communications technology.
- Advanced orientation and training for all employees.
- Development and training of specialized teams that will perform essential tasks following a disaster; regular testing drills for these teams.
- Development of a 'clean' team or teams that will perform tasks in isolated locations in the event of a severe pandemic.
- Strict auditing of plans, and revisions as required.

'Not many libraries need military-style continuity plans', says a government librarian in Ottawa, Ontario.

> *Even most military libraries in North America don't have anything approaching the kind of plans you might find in large airlines, big banks and pharmaceutical distribution firms. But librarians should consider the advantages of a continuity component for vital data. The cost of backing up data for fast recovery is becoming more feasible, especially with the advent of cloud technology.*

If librarians are concerned about the security of the cloud, they can develop agreements with other libraries to hold their back-up data in case of a disaster. For example, a university library in California could exchange data with a university library in Massachusetts. With adequate security at both libraries, the distance between them could decrease the risk of data loss for both. Such agreements are common in special libraries in different regions serving the same organization. And there are a growing number of external vendors who offer secure data storage and collocation services for libraries and other information organizations such as archives and records centres.

4.4 Recovery

While 'recovery' is used more loosely than any other term in the disaster planning lexicon, it has a more specific usage in certain libraries that are more likely to sustain large losses. A true recovery plan addresses questions such as:

- How much damage – and what kinds of damage – to a particular library building will justify the permanent closure, demolition and rebuilding of that building?
- If a library building is written off, should the library rebuild on the same site, or a different site? Should the library write off certain buildings altogether if they are damaged, and not rebuild them anywhere?

- At what point will library IT – including software – no longer be worth replacing after a disaster? When should a library buy a new and possibly different software package?
- How much insurance should a library buy to cover the worst losses? What are the current terms of the library's insurance policy, and are they appropriate to cover losses sustained in a particularly destructive disaster?
- How will the library deploy employees from library sites that are closed for extended periods? Should those employees be redeployed at other library sites? Should they be offered part-time or full-time employment? Or must they be laid off temporarily or permanently?
- What are the long-term effects of a catastrophe on employee morale? How should managers improve morale, and over what time period? How can normalization procedures be enhanced to support better morale?

'Our recovery plan is a series of resumption components with those kinds of questions added on', said a Californian library administrator. 'We are keenly aware of the losses that we might experience in a large earthquake. The Northridge and Loma Prieta quakes proved that libraries could be very vulnerable. So we started asking questions about our recovery measures, and we included a section in our disaster plan that covers those questions.'

The administrator notes that questions arising from recovery issues can make senior administrators uncomfortable:

> *Fact is, when you talk about recovery, you are forced to deal with questions that involve large expenditures and system-wide changes. You could be obliged to rebuild your library and re-establish operations in entirely different forms. And people are unsure about taking the responsibility for big tasks like those. That's why senior administrators in all organizations shy away from recovery questions. There could be concerns about internal politics, and about accusations of alarmism. But we couldn't avoid recovery questions, not in a seismic zone like ours.*

4.5 Management roles

Library managers are responsible for deciding what kind of after-plan is best for their operations. Sometimes a management committee makes the decision. Occasionally the director or head librarian determines what sort of plan his or her library needs. In some jurisdictions, external bodies such as City Hall or a University Senate recommends the scope and contents of the plans for the libraries they control. Special libraries take direction from their organization's senior management; and some corporate libraries – for example, bank libraries – are offered planning guidance by the organization's risk management department.

Inevitably, however, library managers must adapt whatever directions and advice they receive from superiors. City Hall asks the public library to write a plan to deal with the aftermath of a flood that damages three branches in the downtown core; the library's director and senior managers develop a plan to cover all aspects of water ingress and damage to facilities and collections. It is the managers' responsibility to include the 'library element' in any such plan.

Library managers must also champion their libraries' plans, and make sure that employees 'buy in' to the different components. This is achieved through measures such as:

- orientation and training sessions
- tabletop exercises
- drills, especially for evacuation in the event of fire, earthquake or toxic spill
- internal promotion through websites, posters and information sheets
- encouragement from management
- management's willingness to explain planning decisions to all employees, and to listen to employees' comments on various aspects of the plan
- management's good example in attending training sessions and participating in drills.

One tool for the promotion of an after-plan is the emergency response brochure described in the previous chapter (see Figure 3.1 on p. 23). Library managers can tell employees that there will be an after-plan to deal with any effects of a negative event, and that they are welcome to contribute ideas and observations to the planning process. 'All comments are welcome', says a technical services manager in Oregon.

> *I didn't know so much about certain areas of my department, especially regarding the software we use. I made a record of every piece of advice that I received, and I saved every email message. I also made a point of thanking my staff for their input. They got the idea that they were definitely part of the process, and our library had full buy-in from the start. I'd say that our resumption plan is all the more effective for that reason.*

4.6   Operational resumption teams

There is more practical justification for establishing resumption teams in a library than response teams, although many libraries insist on maintaining their standard management hierarchies to deal with the effects of disasters. 'I don't see the wisdom in forming a special team to get our servers and other IT running again when we already have a department that looks after that', said a college librarian in North Carolina. 'In fact, I wouldn't trust people from outside that department to work on our IT. I wouldn't ask the reference and information desk staff to get involved in the resumption of cataloguing and item processing in our technical services department. I think people should work on what they're good at, both before a disaster and after.'

She adds that employees might feel high levels of stress after a disaster, and might not perform as well as they would do in normal circumstances. Disaster-related stress could lead to carelessness and errors, especially during activities with which an employee is unfamiliar. Hence, her library adheres to its standard organization chart in all circumstances, including disasters.

Nevertheless, some libraries can benefit from establishing certain kinds of resumption teams. For example, at an Australian college library with valuable collections of manuscripts and a number of artworks, the following resumption teams are in place:

- manuscript damage assessment team
- artwork damage assessment team
- damage recording team (photographs and written documentation)
- emergency conservation team
- damaged item security team.

Each team comprises a maximum of four library employees, all of whom have taken at least the basic level of specialized training in the tasks performed by their respective teams carry, and who meet annually to review plans and procedures. For this library, these specialized teams could prove to be extremely useful after a disaster. Moreover, team members have increased awareness of the library's response and resumption plans, and have acted indirectly to promote preparedness in all library departments.

Thus, in developing an after-plan library managers should not dismiss altogether the idea of establishing resumption teams. Rather, managers should consider how a team might serve resumption purposes better than the standard hierarchy. Justification for the establishment of resumption teams might be apparent in cases such as the Australian college library.

4.7 Perfection not possible

No plan, and certainly no after-plan, is perfect. No plan can cover all contingencies, nor meet all post-disaster needs. Again, this is why planners say that planning is a process and not a product, and why they refer to plans as living documents.

'You're always trying to do better', said a library technician in charge of her San Francisco special library's disaster plan.

> You want your resumption plan to cover every possibility, but experience proves
> that to be impossible. The most any plan can do is to cover most contingencies.
> There will be weaknesses – gaps and omissions – in every plan, and the only way
> to reduce them is to test it often and revise it when weaknesses become apparent.
> Remember that a plan with weaknesses is better than no plan at all.

Some systems librarians claim that resumption plans for a library's IT department can approach perfection. An IT manager at a university library in Connecticut says:

> If you back up your data properly, and make sure that your back-ups are stable and
> accessible in all possible circumstances, you have reduced the chances of a data
> loss disaster to almost zero. If you form alliances with vendors so that your hardware
> and software can be replaced without delay, you have cut potential downtime
> substantially. If you make sure that you have a succession plan for your IT staff, so
> that all key employees have replacements and can delegate tasks after a disaster,
> you have cut your potential downtime even more. In fact, good resumption planning

in an IT department can deliver something very close to perfection. But the IT world is an exception. You couldn't expect the same resumption capability from a circulation department, or the reference division.

You may not be able to achieve perfection in your after-plan, but you can make regular improvements that will allow your library to return to normal all the sooner.

4.8   References

4.8.1   *Interviews*

In this chapter I have quoted an academic library administrator in Texas, an assistant director at a public library and an administrator in California, a library technician at a San Francisco special library, a technical services manager in Oregon, a college librarian in North Carolina, a public library branch manager in Florida, an IT manager at a university library in Connecticut and a government librarian in Ottawa, Canada.

Damage assessment

5

5.1 The effects

Disasters involve damage.

Damage assessment comprises observation, evaluation, prioritization and record-keeping. No assessment is complete without these elements. Failure to include them in the assessment of damage to a library can result in a waste of time and money, as gaps in the assessment process can impede recovery efforts.

Observation can include the use of not only one's eyes, but also one's ears, nose and sense of touch. An insurance adjuster in London provides practical examples of the different forms of observation at an academic library that had been flooded when a pipe burst:

> I noted that water from the pipe had flowed through the ceiling and into wall cavities, and then into the stacks and work areas. There was substantial moisture staining on three walls, soaked carpets and thousands of wet books. Apparently, at its highest the water level had risen just over a foot above the floor.
>
> While the facility manager had turned off the water to the building, I could still hear water seeping into the wall cavities, and flowing into the floor below. Because the power to the building had been switched off I did not hear any electrical circuits shorting out – a serious safety concern in any kind of water disaster.
>
> The odour from the damp carpets was bad. I could also smell wet bindings and paper. Later I examined a number of the more valuable water-damaged volumes, and determined from their condition that they were salvageable. They felt damp, but I assumed from the texture of their paper that a conservator could repair them. I made notes about all of my observations, and commented on the severity of the damage to all of the library's assets. I also made notes during my discussions with the librarians about their conservation priorities – that is, what they had to have available and in good working order before the library reopened, and which books needed the immediate attention of the conservator. As is typical in such cases, I made notes about the books and other assets that were beyond repair.

5.2 Internal and external inspectors

After a disaster, a site will often require a safety inspection as well as a damage assessment. Safety inspectors can include professional engineers and certified tradespeople – carpenters, plumbers and other contractors – appointed by government authorities or hired by library management. In the event of a regional catastrophe, military personnel might perform site inspections. But often the first inspections of a damaged library site are the responsibility of librarians and their subordinates.

'Libraries are not the first priority after a regional disaster', says a public library administrator in San Francisco. 'Hospitals and schools take precedence, followed by high-traffic landmarks such as shopping malls. It's not that libraries are unimportant, but they can be shut down for longer than other facilities without loss of life or serious disruption of essential activities.'

Thus, external inspectors are more likely to devote their expertise to institutions other than libraries, which during the period immediately after a disaster might have to rely on librarians for the initial safety inspections and damage assessment. These tasks can be performed simultaneously, and there are numerous cases where librarians have been able to complete comprehensive and accurate evaluations of the condition of their libraries.

5.3   Beginning at the perimeter

Any inspection begins at a distance from the site, usually from its perimeter. One should note what is evident from that point, and from different points along the perimeter. Inspectors often use binoculars to look more closely at potential hazards.

Be especially cautious if you observe any of the following:

- broken masonry or roofing
- fire, including flames, smoke and smoulder
- shattered glass
- broken or loose wiring
- toppled power lines, or any that appear to be at risk of toppling
- flooding, either across the entire site or in large pools
- sinkholes or ground subsidence
- damaged roads and parking areas
- uneven pavements and walkways
- clogged drains
- toppled trees, or any that appear to be on the verge of toppling
- seriously injured or dead animals
- uncontained toxic materials such as diesel fuel, chlorine and other chemicals.

'It's a good idea to keep a pair of binoculars in your car', says a public library branch manager in California. 'If your building is older, or near older buildings, you should avoid getting close at the start of a damage assessment. You need a bird's eye view of the entire site, if possible, before you enter the building. You don't want to get trapped.'

5.4   Building exteriors

From the site perimeter you might note damage to the exterior of your library. If the damage appears to be severe, you should not proceed further with your inspection.

Closer to the building, you might note more details about the damage and its extent. This damage might include:

- the collapse or partial collapse of walls or roofing
- extensive cracking of the building exterior
- extensive fire damage
- extensive damage from explosions
- extensive water damage from floods, either from local bodies of water or broken pipes
- large amounts of broken glass, or windows that are loose and could fall from their frames
- doors that have jammed owing to shifting frames, walls and foundations
- alarm systems – for smoke, fire and intrusion – that have been triggered and cannot be turned off.

5.5   Safe entrance and exit

The inspection and damage assessment processes include the safe entrance to and exit from any site on which damage might have occurred. Basic rules for librarians include:

- Do not enter any site, building or space that could be unstable or contain toxic materials. If you suspect certain hazards, it is prudent to maintain a safe distance from them. Allow first responders and hazardous material (HAZMAT) specialists to deal with more serious risks.
- Wait until conditions settle down. Avoid sites if weather remains inclement, that is excessively rainy or windy. Do not enter or exit a building in the aftermath of an earthquake, during which large aftershocks are occurring.
- Use your sight, smell and hearing to detect any hazards such as masonry on the verge of collapse, rotting or burning items, toxic materials and damaged electrical circuitry. Move carefully. Leave if you become aware of a hidden hazard, and warn others about it.
- Wear a hard hat if possible. Some situations might demand the use of goggles, dust masks, heavy-duty gloves and protective footwear. These can be included in the library's emergency kit, which some library managers prefer to store in an off-site location – for example, the trunk of a staff member's vehicle – for use in situations where the site is inaccessible owing to potential hazards.
- Keep a flashlight or other light source at hand if the power fails. Do not move into a dark space; illuminate it to ensure that it does not contain hazards.
- Inform other staff members that you are entering the site. At some libraries, initial inspections and assessments are performed by two or more staff members, who stay close to each other during their time in damaged facilities.
- *Look up, down and all around you* to detect hazards. Listen for sounds of crumbling building fabric and breaking glass, water flowing from burst pipes, and the hissing and crackling of damaged electrical wiring. If you smell natural gas, leave the site without delay.

5.6   Building interiors

Having entered a damaged building, and especially a library in a disaster zone, you might observe:

- any or all of the different forms of damage listed in the previous section
- unstable shelving, including that which has toppled or which has settled at an unstable angle and could topple

- toppled and damaged desks, chairs, filing cabinets
- blocked passageways and stairwells
- damaged decorations, ornaments and artwork that could topple or collapse
- a power outage, full or partial
- damaged washroom facilities
- damaged kitchen equipment and facilities
- damaged IT hardware
- poor indoor air quality
- damaged collections of any items held on site.

'I believe that the worst damage to a library is due to flooding', says a librarian in Manchester, England.

> *Fires can be destructive, and high winds can cause all sorts of trouble, but water can be worse than any other natural or security risk. Water gets in everywhere. Even a small amount – a few gallons – can ruin a work of art or a shelf of rare books, and a little more can cause carpets to smell so bad that you'll have to discard them. And much water damage does not become evident until a considerable time after the original disaster. I'm referring to mould in walls and ceiling cavities, and behind large shelving units. In the long term, building materials that have been exposed to floodwaters or plumbing leaks can rot, and costly repairs will be necessary. In a library, water is more destructive than any other risk.*

5.7   Inspecting damaged collections

The sight of large quantities of damaged books is discouraging, and librarians are often inclined to pay most of their post-disaster attention to printed resources. It is necessary, however, to assess the damage to library collections in all media as soon as it is safe to do so. Although some media are more durable than others, no medium is invulnerable, and over time most library collections will cease to exist, either owing to disasters, security breaches or simply to wear and tear.

Occasionally it is possible to preserve an entire collection despite considerable damage, but often a process of 'biblio-triage' is required to determine which items are beyond repair and which can be saved. Librarians can carry out biblio-triage by noting the specific level of damage to a library item. These levels are as follows:

- *Severe damage*: the item is unrecognizable and beyond repair.
- *Serious damage*: the item can be only partially repaired, and at high cost.
- *Moderate damage*: the item can be repaired, but not restored to its original condition.
- *Light damage*: the item can be repaired and, if desirable, completely restored at a reasonable cost.
- *Full clean-and-mend*: the item is sound, but in need of conservation that includes the removal of dirt and the repair of torn binding, illustrations, pages, and so on.

- *Moderate clean-and-mend*: the item is sound, but in need of conservation that includes cleaning and minor repairs. Library technicians and clericals familiar with basic conservation and mending techniques can attend to items with this level of damage.
- *Light clean-and-mend*: the item requires more attention than it would in normal circumstances: more cleaning, or additional tape on the binding.
- *Normal clean-and mend*: no special attention required; the item is in its acceptable predisaster condition.

Different libraries may adopt these levels and customize them for particular collections. More specific terms will be necessary to indicate the levels of damage sustained by certain kinds of rare items. 'For example, our special collections department contains manuscripts and books in English from the fourteenth century to the present', notes a college librarian in New York State.

> *The way in which we assess the damage to an incunabulum is different from the way in which we look at a damaged first edition of a recent American novel. The binding on the older volume might be a slightly battered, but we can live with that. We might schedule it for restoration at some point, but that's not essential. We are far more concerned about the text of the volume – the text block – than the binding. But our American first editions are another matter. The dust jackets and bindings should be in mint condition. Otherwise the book loses some of its value.*

A conservator familiar with a library's collections is the best person to inspect them for damage and to determine what can be saved and what is beyond repair. The conservator has the advantage of familiarity with different kinds of damage to library items; he or she should also know what the conservation of an item will cost, and how much time it will take.

5.8 Evaluation

After the disaster, librarians and external inspectors should discuss what they have observed at the damaged site. A full evaluation usually involves the observations of more than one person, from a variety of perspectives. It is easy for even a large group of observers to miss important aspects of the damage to a library, and in some cases the evaluation will take a lengthy period of time to complete.

It is not unusual for some forms of damage to take a long time to appear. After a power outage, data analysts might need weeks to determine how much data has been lost, and, after a flood, mould in wall cavities might take months or years to become evident. Thus, evaluations should be considered tentative until all possible damage has been ruled out.

'There could be mould in our library walls', says a corporate librarian and records manager in London.

That's the result of a flood from a pipe that burst a decade ago. We have a lot of other pressing matters to worry about and there's talk of moving the library to another building, so I'm not going to do anything more about what might be in the walls. The possibility of mould was noted in the initial damage assessment, but we had to attend to more important things, like hundreds of damp books. We didn't consider mould to be a health hazard because the walls were sealed, and there was no structural damage.

The initial evaluation, however, should give library managers enough information to decide on priorities regarding repairs and restoration.

5.9 Prioritization

What needs to be done first? Which parts of the building should be repaired, and what fixtures should be replaced? Which damaged books should be conserved before any others? And what level of service, if any, can the library offer patrons during the restoration process? Library managers must answer these questions as soon as possible. This can be challenging since it is natural for people to be slow to react to substantial damage to their workplace. 'I was absolutely stunned when I saw what a fire had done to my library branch', said a public librarian in Los Angeles.

I thought that the damage was irreparable, and all I could do was to stare at the shelves. It took me days to comprehend that the building was still sound, and that the major damage was due to the torrents of water from the firefighters' hoses. A restoration company discovered that a frayed electrical wire had caused the fire. A team of contractors rebuilt the charred walls, and I managed to replace the books and other items that we lost. But I had to deal with my emotional reaction before I could get the priorities straight in my mind.

A generic set of post-disaster priorities is as follows:

- The physical safety of everyone who works at the site: librarians and other library workers, patrons and visitors, external workers, and any others in the vicinity of the site.
- The structural integrity of the library building.
- The soundness of the library building's non-structural components.
- The security of the building and the serviceability of alarm systems, locks, CCTV and other security devices; the availability of security staff.
- The general safety of entrances, exits, stairwells and passageways.
- The serviceability of power sources.
- The serviceability of lighting.
- The serviceability of heating, ventilation and air conditioning (HVAC).
- The serviceability of the plumbing.

- The serviceability of elevators and escalators.
- The stability and serviceability of shelving, cabinets, carousels and other storage devices.
- The safety and serviceability of all furniture in staff and patron areas, including carpeting.
- The condition of collections, beginning with the more valuable items (for example, rare books) and concluding with easily replaceable items (for example, current paperback mysteries).
- The repairs to the above, in descending order.
- The reopening of library facilities.
- The re-establishment of positive public relations.
- The recovery of staff morale.
- The normalization of operations.

Some library managers will be tempted to put the condition of collections at the top of the list, but physical safety must be the first priority, for practical as well as ethical reasons.

5.10   Recordkeeping

Traditionally, a damage assessment resides in the records of the assessor(s). These records include paper documents and forms, but increasingly assessors employ digital resources – cameras and other portable IT – to collect assessment data.

With the improvements in the quality of digital photography – particularly in cellular telephones – conservators and insurers are more inclined to accept digital images transmitted directly from the scene of a disaster. 'You can capture multiple images of damaged assets quickly and efficiently with a cell phone, and send everything back to your office for further assessment', says an American book conservator who has worked on materials damaged during Hurricanes Katrina and Rita in 2005.

> *In fact, these days I prefer to work with digital images, especially of damaged books and manuscripts. With my hands-free cell phone I can add a voice commentary to different images. This is far more convenient than the old paper-based method of post-disaster recordkeeping. As long as I back up all of the data that I collect in the field, I am well prepared to compile my final damage assessment, either on paper or as an electronic document.*

Nevertheless, those who assess damage in libraries continue to use documents and forms for the purpose of recordkeeping. Figure 5.1 provides an example of a sample damage assessment form.

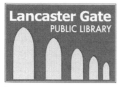

Damage Assessment Form

Note: Record any damage to the Central Library or branch facilities with a digital camera, if possible. Affix digital images to this damage assessment checklist form for insurance purposes.

The delegated librarian will fill out these checklists after completing an inspection of library facilities.

Description of event

At _____ a.m./p.m.	❑ Earthquake	❑ Explosion	❑ Winter storm	❑ High winds
on _____(date), **the library site at**	❑ Fire/smoke damage	❑ Power failure	❑ Toxic spill/vehicle collision at or near the building	
_____ **sustained damage** **from one or more of** **the following:**	❑ Security breach, describe:		❑ Flood/leak/sprinkler, indicate level: top floor, ground floor, basement	

Loss of patron service area(s)	❑ Reception ❑ Stack area	❑ Reference area ❑ Public seating area
Loss of staff work space	❑ Partial ❑ Total	❑ Temporary ❑ Permanent
Loss of parking area(s)	❑ Partial ❑ Total	
Loss of vital records	❑ Partial ❑ Total	❑ Temporary ❑ Permanent
Loss of computer hardware on site	❑ Partial ❑ Total	❑ Temporary Permanent
Damage to server(s)	❑ Partial ❑ Total	❑ Temporary ❑ Permanent
Casualties	Estimated number	
Additional comments		

Figure 5.1 Damage Assessment Form.

Damage to buildings, furnishing and equipment

Damage	Severe	Moderate	Light
Ceilings			
Floors			
Windows			
Internal glass			
Stairwells			
Walls			
Furniture			
Carpets			
IT hardware			
Telephones/fax machines			
Photocopier(s)			
External signage			
Internal signage			
Wiring/cables			
Paper records			
Stationery supplies/forms			
Artworks and decorations			
Staff room furniture/fixtures			
Cafeteria equipment/supplies			
Basement plumbing			
Basement wiring			
Basement shelving			
Basement floor			
Emergency supplies			
N/A			
Additional comments			

Figure 5.1 *(Continued)*

Damage to collections

Bibliotriage level / Items Approximate numbers	Hardcovers	Paperbacks	Periodical hardcopies	DVDs	CDs	Maps and charts	Photos
Severe damage							
Serious damage							
Moderate damage							
Light damage							
Full clean-and-mend							
Moderate clean-and-mend							
Light clean-and-mend							
Normal clean-and mend							

Stakeholders

Stakeholders affected by the event	❑ Library manager(s)	❑ Librarians	❑ Technical staff
	❑ Clerical staff	❑ Patrons	

Additional comments

Figure 5.1 *(Continued)*

General effects of the event on the neighbouring community

❑ Casualties	❑ Missing persons
❑ Communication breakdowns	❑ Transportation problems (e.g. gridlock, lifeline failure)
❑ Power failure: blackout, brownout	❑ Damage to numerous buildings
❑ Resource shutdown (e.g. schools, hospitals)	❑ Neighbourhood shutdown: no street access
❑ Evacuation(s)	❑ Increased absenteeism
❑ Government declaration of emergency or disaster	❑ Supply shortages (e.g. water, food, medical supplies, fuel for vehicles)
Additional comments	

The effects of the event on major lifelines in the area

❑ Gridlock	❑ Detours	❑ Flooding
❑ Power lines down	❑ Roadway damage (e.g. fissures, sinkholes)	❑ Debris blocks (from buildings)

Closures (within ten miles)

❑ Highway(s)	❑ Other arterial route(s)	❑ Side street(s
❑ Bridge(s)	❑ Overpass(es)	❑ Tunnel(s)
❑ Airport		

The effects of the event on telephone lines

Phone lines down	Duration						
	Unknown	2 hours	4 hours	8 hours	24 hours	48 hours	72 hours or more
All lines							
Cellular networks							
Estimated time to phone system recovery							

Some lines functional	❑ Unknown	❑ Local land lines
	❑ Cellular	❑ Long distance

Figure 5.1 *(Continued)*

The effects of the event on power sources

Blackout	Duration						
	Unknown	2 hours	4 hours	8 hours	24 hours	48 hours	72 hours or more
Regional							
Local neighbourhoods							
Central Library/ branches							
Brownout	Duration						
	Unknown	2 hours	4 hours	8 hours	24 hours	48 hours	72 hours or more
Regional							
Local neighbourhoods							
Central Library/ branches							

Additional comments

Figure 5.1 *(Continued)*

5.11 References

5.11.1 Interviews

In this chapter I have quoted a British insurance adjuster in London, librarians in London and Manchester, American librarians from California and New York State, and an American book conservator.

Disaster recognition, declaration procedures and crisis management

6.1 How it feels

All hell breaks loose. Now what?

Initial reactions to the circumstances of a disaster vary, from lethargy and confusion to excitement and recklessness. Widespread panic is rare. 'I watched my old branch burn to the ground', said a librarian in British Columbia. 'I just didn't know what to make of the situation. It seemed so unreal. I stood and watched the firefighters spray the building with their hoses. A wall caved in, and I saw one of the shelves in the reference section collapse.'

Outwardly, she remained calm. But, inwardly: 'I had worked at that branch for almost twenty years, and I was seeing it disappear. It was as if my career were being wiped out. I felt a great deal of anxiety and a tremendous sense of loss. I worried that I had lost my job. But I didn't flip out. Actually I ended up feeling kind of numb.'

Such emotional responses to many emergencies and disasters are common. While the first feelings may dissipate quickly, a person in such circumstances might feel confused and uncertain about what to do next for hours or days. 'Our library had an extensive disaster plan, with all sorts of advice about what to do during and after different emergencies', said a head librarian in a public library in southern Germany. 'Ironically that binder was soaked to illegibility when the local river flooded our town and left the library in a metre of muddy water. None of the library staff knew what to do when the water started to subside and we were able to enter the building.'

So the head librarian gathered his staff in the parking lot:

> I asked if anyone knew what to do. Somebody said that we would need buckets and mops. Somebody else mentioned that the power had been shut off, so we would need flashlights as well. And then one of the reference librarians suggested that we contact our city hall, to let them know what was going on. She recommended that I declare a disaster, but without the disaster plan binder, I was not sure how to proceed.

Eventually a police officer arrived on the scene. He noted the damage to the library, and promised to inform the town's administrators and elected officials. Later that day, local media reported that the library would be closed for a week. 'Unfortunately I made the mistake of telling the media too much', went on the head librarian.

> Some of what I said was inaccurate. We did not manage to save much of our collection, which had been under water for too long. Books were falling apart, and our CDs were unplayable. I had raised false hopes, and later I was forced to retract what I had said. But I am only human, and had to learn how to handle a disaster the hard way – through unhappy experience. In future I will try to gather better information.

6.2   Recognizing a disaster

In the note on terminology at the beginning of this book, a disaster is defined as an
event involving:

> *any damage to the building(s) or equipment that will disrupt operations for*
> *more than 48 hours, any natural event (for example, high winds, winter storm,*
> *earthquake) that disrupts transportation or communications for more than*
> *48 hours, or any serious loss of vital data (for example, borrower data that have*
> *been lost).*

This is a generic definition that will not necessarily suffice for all libraries. Examples of exceptions include:

- An investment brokerage library which contained up-to-the-minute data on currency values
  and fluctuations, as well as online information on commodity prices. A power outage of even
  one hour or less caused serious problems for the library and its patrons. Despite a fast return
  to normal operations, this was a disaster.
- An engineering library which held data on ongoing projects: background information and
  financial records, plans and drawings, and third-party reports. A half-day closure of the
  building owing to a fire in a neighbouring structure interfered with the transmission of mis-
  sion-critical information, and delayed vital decisions. Despite the brevity of the closure and
  negligibility of other losses, this was a disaster.
- A small pipe which burst in the ceiling of a rare-book library at a large university. Several
  shelves of modern first editions were sprayed with water, and dozens of dust jackets were
  dampened. The clean-up of the area around the shelves, the stabilization of the humidity and
  the drying and restoration of the dust jackets required the closure of the library for no more
  than one day, and most of the library's operations were not disrupted. Insurance covered
  the damage to the books. Nevertheless, the librarians in charge were wise to consider water
  damage a disaster.

Since every library has a unique risk profile – that is, the full set of risks that prevail
on its sites – librarians should determine for themselves and their facilities what they
would consider to be a disaster. Some libraries have a higher tolerance for negative
events than others. That is, the losses that they might sustain during a flood or bad
winter storm might not lead to heavy financial losses or extended downtime.

'When a hurricane hit our community some years ago, there was considerable
property damage', says a librarian in a town in southern Texas.

> *A roof leak caused a flood that soaked our carousels of paperbacks. They were*
> *so soggy that you couldn't turn the pages without tearing them. We decided that*
> *it wasn't worth the time and effort to try to save them, so we discarded them. The*
> *cost of replacing them wasn't high, since we purchased used copies of various*
> *popular titles from second-hand bookstores. Our library didn't have to close,*
> *and a team from the town hall arrived quickly to do the clean-up. All things*
> *considered, this event was not really a disaster. It was more of an emergency, or*
> *major nuisance.*

6.3   Information gathering

Before deciding whether to declare a disaster, you should try to gather the information necessary to make the appropriate decision. You can use the damage assessment form in Figure 5.1 to record this information. In some circumstances, however, you might have to determine the extent of the damage and proceed with a disaster declaration without compiling such information. Some disasters will force you to act quickly, and to postpone recordkeeping until people are safe and the situation is stable. This information, either carefully recorded or noted without paperwork, will include your observations regarding:

- casualties – employees or patrons;
- damage to facilities, including structural and non-structural elements, IT hardware, furniture, and shelving;
- damage to collections;
- loss of data;
- effects of the event on the neighbouring community;
- effects of the event on roads, bridges, overpasses and tunnels in the vicinity of the library;
- effects of the event on power and telephone lines, sewerage and water supply; and
- effects of the event on local transportation systems: buses, railways, taxis, airports, postal delivery and courier companies.

There are a number of sources for this information. Immediately after an event, the main source might be word of mouth. News reports can be broadcast within minutes, and it is advisable to treat them with caution. Often the initial reports following an emergency or disaster are inaccurate, and could lead to inappropriate decision making and unnecessary disaster declarations.

In many post-disaster situations you will have opportunities for direct observation of damage to facilities and collections. To observe matters in the areas near your library, you can perform inspections on foot, or use binoculars to spot trouble at a distance. The use of vehicles for the purposes of neighbourhood inspections can be dangerous if there has been damage to roads. Additional risks arise from buildings on the verge of collapse, downed power lines and poles, gas leaks, fires, flooding and miscellaneous debris.

'I swear by my army surplus binoculars', says a Tennessee public librarian whose branch is located near the banks of the Mississippi River.

> I can get up on the roof of my library and have a good look at not only the river, but also the entire surrounding area, including the residential and retail parts. I might have to wait for hours before the media start broadcasting useful information, but with the binoculars on a peg in the staff room, I'm way ahead of them. And if there's an evolving situation that forces me to evacuate the library – like when the river breaks its banks – I need to see where the water is as soon as I can.

A sample Disaster Recognition and Declaration Procedures form appears at the end of this chapter (Figure 6.1, pp. 54–57). This form may be used for future reference,

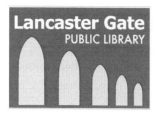

Disaster Recognition and Declaration Procedures

Record of Events

Step One: Recognition of Events
Step Two: Information Gathering
Step Three: Decision to Declare a Disaster
Step Four: Disaster Declaration

Step One: Recognition of Events

When a serious adverse event occurs, the librarian or delegate will investigate the circumstances as quickly as possible and determine whether the event at the library site is:

a. An incident: a minor breach of security, a minor plumbing leak, or a minor injury at the library site.

b. An emergency: several minor casualties, a small fire or flood, or substantial damage to the front entrance.

c. A major emergency: a serious casualty or casualties, damage to the building or loss of physical assets that will involve substantial inconvenience, or a power outage that disrupts library operations for up to 48 hours.

d. A disaster: any damage to the building or physical assets that will disrupt library operations for more than 48 hours, any event (toxic spill, severe weather) that disrupts transportation or communications for more than 48 hours, or any serious loss of vital data (catalogue records that have not been backed up).

e. A catastrophe: a large regional disaster that disrupts conditions across the region for an extended period, and that involves multiple casualties, the loss of facilities, and an unusually high number of insurance claims.

f. A proximity event: an incident, emergency or disaster near the library that could affect operations. For example, a fire in a neighbouring hotel or mall could force firefighters to seal off the area for several hours and cause serious inconvenience. TV news broadcasts that show the library in the background could lead to concerns among patrons. The library may not be directly affected by a proximity event, but indirectly it could face serious consequences.

g. A crisis: an event involving negative media coverage and adverse public relations during or following any of the above circumstances.

Remember:

• Incidents, emergencies and major emergencies can be controlled and rectified by civil authorities and library management. Civil authorities cannot control disasters, catastrophes, and crises.

• Following severe weather or any other disaster that affects the region, communications and transportation systems will slow down and possibly stop altogether for up to several days.

• The local risk profile is unique. What occurs in Californian, Asian, and South American earthquake zones will not necessarily occur in the local region.

• It is not necessary to declare an incident, an emergency, or a major emergency. As serious as these events can be, they need not affect library operations for an extended period, inconvenience patrons, or cause large financial losses.

• In the event of a disaster or a catastrophe, a declaration is essential to begin the library's business resumption activities. In itself, the declaration indicates that the library acknowledges the gravity of the situation and is working to resolve the problems that the disaster has caused.

Figure 6.1 Disaster Recognition and Declaration Procedures form.

Based on the above classification scheme (a-g), the library has experienced:

_____

_____

_____

_____

_____

Step Two: Information Gathering

Having confirmed the occurrence of an event and determined its effects on library employees, the librarian should collect the following data as soon as possible:

a. The effects of the event on the library's facilities, including service areas, office space, computer systems, and communications equipment:

_____

_____

_____

_____

b. The effects of the event on employees and patrons at the library during the event (note number of casualties):

_____

_____

_____

_____

c. The effects of the event on neighbouring areas in general:

_____

_____

_____

_____

d. The effects of the event on major lifelines including the streets or roads outside the library, local bridges and overpasses, and other nearby arteries:

_____

_____

_____

_____

e. The effects of the event on telephone poles and lines in the vicinity:

_____

_____

_____

_____

Figure 6.1 _(Continued)_

f. The effects of the event on power sources in the immediate vicinity, particularly power lines
    and poles:

    _____

    _____

    _____

    _____

g. The effects of the event on local sewerage and water supply:

    _____

    _____

    _____

    _____

h. The effects of the event on transportation systems including local airports, bus routes, postal
    service, and courier companies:

    _____

    _____

    _____

    _____

Indicate the source(s) of the above data:

- ❏ LGPL administration
- ❏ Other library sites
- ❏ BBC Radio and other local stations
- ❏ BBC Television and local cable networks
- ❏ Internet sources
- ❏ Word of mouth
- ❏ Direct observation (from the windows and top floor of the library: Emergency supplies should
  include a pair of binoculars)
- ❏ Local Council
- ❏ Remote sources in other parts of the UK or in other countries

Note: After a disaster, reporting of circumstances can be extremely unreliable. The librarian or delegate
        should try to confirm the informatin before transmitting them to interested parties such as the
        Library Board.

Step Three: Decision to Declare a Disaster

The librarian need not declare an incident, emergency, or major emergency, although these events might
require immediate action from library management. The librarian or delegate's response could include:

- ❏ Immediate notification (through 999) of first responders such as police, firefighters, and
  paramedics
- ❏ Notification of all staff, on- and off-site at the time of the event
- ❏ Activation of strategic alliances (e.g. with moisture control vendor)

To declare a disaster is to recognize that the above measures may not be enough to contain the event
as it unfolds. A disaster will have far-reaching effects, and will require the activation of all disaster plan
components at the libary.

Figure 6.1 *(Continued)*

In declaring a disaster, the librarian or delegate will carry out the following tasks:

❑ Inform available library management that a disaster has occurred at the library

❑ Ensure that all necessary strategic alliances are activated

❑ If necessary, approve the activation of the library's alternative site; or investigate the possibility of using an Emergency Operations Centre

❑ Make oneself available for on-the-spot decisions regarding business resumption and ongoing service to members

Having declared a disaster, the librarian or delegate will record the following information:

a. Date: _____

b. Time (GMT) of event: _____

c. Basic description of event (e.g. fire, flooding, toxic spill, etc.)

_____

_____

d. Available senior managers informed of the declaration:

_____

_____

_____

_____

_____

_____

e. Time at which the senior managers were notified, and by what means (telephone, email, messenger, etc.):

_____

_____

_____

_____

f. Strategic alliances were activated; time of activation:

_____

_____

_____

_____

g. Brief description of damage to neighbouring sites, including retail areas, parking lots and malls:

_____

_____

_____

_____

Figure 6.1 *(Continued)*

and may account for your decision to declare a disaster. Remember that while this and other forms may be helpful, they might be of limited use until after situations have stabilized.

6.4   When and when not to declare a disaster

If the process of information gathering leads you to believe that a disaster has occurred at your library, you must decide whether to declare it, and if so, how. You must also consider the scope of a declaration. Those people and official bodies who will require information on a library's condition after a disaster include:

* all library employees;
* senior departmental/ministerial managers (government libraries);
* library board members (public libraries);
* elected municipal officials, including aldermen and council members (public libraries);
* senior municipal administrators (public libraries);
* senior academic administrators and governing bodies (colleges and universities);
* school boards and superintendents (school libraries);
* senior management, including CEOs, VPs and managing directors (special and corporate libraries); and
* patrons/the general public (public and many academic libraries).

Your disaster declaration can include the following steps:

1. Notification – often by word of mouth – of employees in the immediate area.
2. Notification of all other employees – at other branches and offices – by telephone, email or messenger.
3. Notification of external administrative stakeholders – board members, academic administrators, senior managers, and so on – by telephone, email or messenger.
4. Notification of patrons and the general public by signage posted at library entrances, website announcements, reports via social media, TV and radio broadcasts.

Before activating this declaration process, however, you must make sure that the damage to the library and the disruption of its operations justify the declaration.

6.5   Disasters and crises

A crisis is defined as an event involving negative media coverage and adverse public relations during or following an occurrence as significant as a disaster. It is worth noting that not all disasters lead to crises. In fact, some of the more damaging disasters are best left undeclared. For example, at a Californian public library a toilet overflowed and flooded the computer operations room on the floor directly below it. Servers holding the library's borrower data and catalogue records were badly damaged, a considerable amount of data was lost, and owing to the inadequacy of the library's data back-up procedures, much of the lost data could not be recovered.

The head librarian decided to declare a disaster to the general public. He telephoned local radio and television stations and offered information regarding the damage to the library. But the stations' producers were unconcerned about the library's problems. They told the librarian that the story was not of interest to their listeners and viewers. The library was forced to make due with signage at entrances apologizing for any inconvenience. The final cost of dealing with the water damage and restoring the lost hardware and data was estimated to be more than US$300,000. This was a blow to the library, its employees, stakeholders and patrons, but apparently of little interest to the media.

Nevertheless, it is prudent for librarians to prepare for crises. They might be aware of the need for an appropriate response to a crisis arising from issues of censorship or political correctness; but they might not take into account the importance of crisis management after a disaster.

6.6   The library crisis manager

In many disasters, the person who speaks for the library and who manages the disaster declaration and related information is the head librarian or most senior library manager. He or she should have traits and skills including:

- 'grace under pressure' (Ernest Hemingway's definition of courage);
- the ability to speak publicly and often without notes to a variety of audiences;
- good listening skills;
- effective information-gathering skills;
- the ability to digest a flow of quickly-changing information, and to develop coherent messages from it; and
- a willingness to admit ignorance.

'It is not a crime to tell media people that you don't know what has happened or is happening', says a retired Canadian TV news producer.

It is vitally important for any organizational spokesperson to tell the truth at all times. Try not to sugarcoat the facts, or omit important details, and do not lie. Remember that reporters can be first-class researchers. They can hunt down information that you might be tempted to hide or ignore, and they will not hesitate to mention in their reports that what you have said has differed from the truth. Once a person gets caught [lying], they lose credibility, and so can their organizations.

A sample crisis management plan appears in Appendix 1. This plan covers the activities of a library spokesperson as well as a crisis management team.

6.7   References

6.7.1   Interviews

In this chapter I have quoted and used material supplied by librarians in British Columbia and Western Canada, Germany, Texas, Tennessee and California.

Strategic alliances

7

7.1 Determining the need for a strategic alliance

You need help.

After a disaster, your library's business resumption, continuity and recovery processes might not be successful without the assistance of external vendors. Without prior agreements between your library and its key vendors you could encounter serious post-disaster problems including:

- slow emergency response times
- unprepared, ill-equipped response personnel
- a lack of necessary components and tools
- long waits for a vendor's arrival at library sites
- worsening damage to facilities and systems
- employee displacement
- loss of facilities and assets that could have been saved
- increased risks to employee safety
- difficulty in resuming service to patrons
- higher operational continuity and recovery costs
- prolonged inconvenience for employees and patrons
- the postponement of important projects
- difficulty in finding vendors to provide services, owing to heavy post-disaster demand.

'Lots of plans discuss the use of library employees for clean-up and related tasks', says the Manager of Reference Services at a public library in Florida. 'While library employees can do certain things, there are many post-disaster activities that they should leave to the experts, that is, the people who have the training and experience necessary to deal with disaster damage. Otherwise, various tasks might not be carried out properly, and safety issues could arise.'

He recalls the attempts of his library's staff to deal with flooding from a burst water main in the street outside a single-storey branch: 'The water flowed through the entrance area and into the stacks. At one point, there were five inches of water on the floor. Municipal workers arrived, shut down the main, and pumped out the water from the branch. After that, according to the foreman, the library was responsible for the clean-up. Honestly, we didn't know where to start.'

After consulting sources on the Internet, the Manager discovered that there was conflicting advice about the best ways to dry out and clean carpeting, conserve damp books and prevent the growth of mould. His colleagues removed a section of carpeting and dragged it into the parking lot adjacent to the building. Two clerical workers became ill during this task, and another pulled a muscle in her back. Meanwhile the odour from the carpeting grew especially foul. Finally, the Manager and the Chief Librarian agreed that library employees should not make further attempts to deal with soggy carpeting.

In the end we called in a moisture control outfit. We should have done that in the beginning. The moisture control team arrived with protective gear including goggles, facemasks and heavy-duty gloves. They ripped up all of the carpeting and took it to the dump. It was not worth saving, and neither were several hundred books, mostly paperbacks. But the team freeze-dried several dozen cartons of hardcovers, including a number of my beloved reference volumes. When the hardcovers were returned to the branch, you could hardly tell that they had been soaked. I do not believe that we could have done as good a job of conserving them as the moisture control team.

The Manager regrets that his library did not have a strategic alliance in place before the flood occurred. Such an alliance involves a pre-arranged agreement between an external vendor and a library.

Before you can arrange alliances, you must identify the kinds of alliances that your library requires. Taking into account your library's risk assessment and analysis, you should consider the following as primary categories for strategic alliances:

*   structural damage assessment
*   building and site clean-up
*   post-disaster site security
*   IT systems: hardware
*   IT systems: software
*   telecommunications
*   transportation
*   alternative sites
*   employee counselling
*   emergency moving and storage.

These categories are basic to most organizations, regardless of their risk profiles. For your library, secondary priorities for strategic alliances will include:

*   emergency conservation of damaged books, manuscripts and other items
*   office supplies and furniture
*   communications with patrons
*   communications with sponsoring bodies, for example City Hall, academic governing committees
*   communications with the general public
*   crisis management
*   accounting.

To determine what other kinds of strategic alliances your library needs, it is useful to ask the following questions:

*   If a particular employee was unavailable after a disaster, who on staff could replace him or her temporarily? If no other employee could fill in for him or her, should the library seek an outside replacement?
*   If a specific physical component was unserviceable after a disaster, could the library replace it with another component already available on site? Is the replacement component ready to operate? Or should a replacement be brought in from an external source?
*   Will the library be forced to deal with additional expenses without this employee or component on site after a disaster?

- Will the library suffer negative media coverage if this employee or component is unavailable after a disaster?
- Will library security be compromised in any way without this employee or component?
- Will the absence of this employee or component result in higher recovery costs once the resumption phase is complete?
- Will the absence of this employee or component result in inconvenience to patrons?

In the above questions, 'component' can refer to physical assets including:

- computer hardware and other IT
- software
- electronic data
- hardcopy books and periodicals
- paper records/files
- facilities, including the building(s), or specific parts of the building(s)
- furniture and fixtures.

'Many libraries have disaster plans that contain a lot of information on the best ways to restore damaged books and other library resources', says an administrator at a British university library.

> *There are numerous notes and tables concerning damage from fire and water, and not infrequently details about preserving bindings that have taken a hit. But there is usually little on the actual process, the tasks in their proper order, of rescuing a collection when it has been damaged. In my experience, the compilation of such notes and tables is more a feel-good exercise than anything else.*

This administrator warns that substandard planning for the treatment of damaged books can be 'politically appropriate' nonetheless, in that senior librarians have approved the plans and will reject any attempt to enhance them for the purposes of practicability.

> *Negative library politics will play a role in disaster planning, particularly when we take into account the substandard planning that the higher-ups have given the nod to. Nobody wants to be accused of supporting the wrong thing. And so the bad plans survive, until disaster strikes and the plans fail. What follows is finger-pointing and refusal to accept responsibility. I have seen this sort of thing a number of times in my thirty years as a librarian.*

He admits that higher-ups might have little knowledge of disaster planning, and might not be able to identify weaknesses in their libraries' plans. Also, many senior library administrators worry about the costs of disaster planning, and will settle for inferior plans in the hope that disasters will not occur, at least not while they remain in their jobs. He continues:

> *Thus you become aware of a lot of 'magical thinking' around disaster planning. Senior people believe that things will work out, and that they can get away with third-rate plans. They assume that when all hell breaks loose somebody or some*

*firm will appear out of nowhere and rescue them [en] and so disaster plans are
not really necessary in the first place. I think the root of negative library politics is
based on magical thinking.*

7.2   Key post-disaster vendors for resumption and continuity

To ensure that your library can resume basic operations in no more than 72 hours, you
should arrange strategic alliances with the following kinds of vendors:

- A moisture control vendor that can respond to your library's call for emergency assistance after a fire, flood or any other disaster that involves water damage. This firm must have the necessary equipment (e.g., dehumidifiers, fans) and experience to repair damage quickly and at a reasonable cost, and to work with insurers as required.
- A conservator (or conservators) who can arrive at your library sites quickly, ideally within one day after the disaster has struck. Conservators should be aware of the kinds of materials that they will be expected to work on. In your strategic alliance with a conservator, you should describe those materials in detail, with particular attention to their age(s), pre-disaster condition, provenances and general make-up. If your library has French, Venetian and English incunabula, your description might include photographs of bindings and texts, along with mentions of special features such as bookplates and marginalia by former owners. The more information that conservators have beforehand, the more successful they can be in rescuing and restoring valuable materials.
- A courier service that will handle emergency communications and deliveries in the event of a regional emergency.
- Alternative sites for temporary work processes; for example community centres, schools, vacant storefronts and other library branches are all potential sites for resumption and continuity purposes. Site qualifications include adequate security, power outlets and satisfactory lighting, washrooms, parking, reception area space, kitchen facilities and office furniture. Note that while your library may maintain a good back-up site, management should still develop strategic alliances for alternative sites in case branches are damaged or inaccessible, or in circumstances where employees need additional space for other emergency purposes.
- An IT systems vendor (or vendors) who can resupply hardware and software at short notice. It is essential to provide this vendor with an up-to-date inventory and systems configuration diagrams so that they can stockpile the necessary components in case of an emergency. Ideally this vendor will have an effective disaster plan that covers post-disaster service at client sites.
- A telecommunications vendor that can rebuild the library telephone systems and other networks in the event of a communications breakdown. This vendor should also be able to rectify cellular telephone problems.
- A general contractor or contractors to repair damage to office fixtures. The library's facilities manager might already maintain a list of preferred contractors such as plumbers, electricians, carpeting maintenance vendors and carpenters to work on-site in normal circumstances. The library should arrange strategic alliances with these contractors so that they will arrive at a damaged site as soon as possible after a disaster to make the necessary repairs.
- A security firm that can provide temporary guard service around the site perimeter, or in any damaged library building. CCTV systems can provide only limited security after a disaster,

since not only are they prone to cease functioning when damaged or without power, but also they cannot serve to warn people away from unstable buildings nor prevent illicit entry of sites.

- An employee assistance program (EAP) provider that can offer support services such as psychological counselling after a traumatic event. Some libraries have access to counselling services for employees who have personal problems; in many cases these services are appropriate for employees who have been emotionally traumatized during an earthquake, fire or explosion.
- A removal (or moving) company to remove essential materials from damaged library spaces. It is advisable to let professional movers shift heavy furniture and equipment. Employees run the risk of injury (particularly to lower backs and knees) when they try to move shelving units, large filing cabinets, photocopiers and other furniture that has been shifted or overturned during a disaster. Ideally the moving company will also be able to provide temporary storage space at a reasonable, pre-arranged cost.

'Moving companies are a godsend when you have to move a lot of books and furniture from a site', says a head librarian at a college in California.

> *Every library should have movers to handle the moving and storage of building contents. Movers are much better at their work than library staffers, and they know how to lift heavy items without injuring themselves. I have three moving companies at the top of my list of strategic alliances, in case the situation at my library is too great for one moving company to handle.*

7.3   Strategic alliance documentation

General characteristics of effective strategic alliances include:

- A contract or letter of agreement whereby vendor and customer (e.g., the library) agree on terms such as services to be provided, response times, costs of service, vendor's access to library facilities, data resources and alternative site after an disaster. Contracts or letters of agreement should be renewed regularly. It is appropriate for the vendor to present revised documents for the library's consideration. It is also normal for vendors and their clients to recognize the possibility of a *force majeure* and its effect on the vendor's ability to provide post-disaster services. Note that it is acceptable to build post-disaster strategic alliances into standard service contracts, especially those related to IT systems maintenance.
- An exchange of information regarding resources and abilities. For example, the library organizes a strategic alliance with an online book vendor to resupply hardcover and paperback volumes that have been lost in a branch fire. The vendor indicates that it will need seven business days to deliver the replacement volumes. The library ensures that the vendor has a list of the lost volumes. Note that by means of the strategic alliance, the library guarantees its preferred customer status after a disaster.
- The library does not ask for more goods and services than are necessary after a disaster, or more than the vendor is capable of providing.
- A fair pre-arranged price. Premiums added after disasters are unethical, unless both parties agree on them. The library should not be obliged to pay more than the strategic alliance states.

- A best-efforts clause. The vendor agrees to make the best possible effort to provide post-disaster supplies and service, and the library agrees to make the best possible effort to take delivery of the supplies and services.

The library can also organize internal strategic alliances between different branches, especially those in a particular area or region. Such alliances would let branches know what to expect from senior management after a regional disaster, and would motivate branch managers to determine their site-specific post-disaster needs.

'I run a branch in a neighbourhood 15 miles from the central public library', says a branch head in Pennsylvania.

> *I have solid alliances with the two branches closest to mine. If something happens to my branch, its services will shift over to one of the others automatically. We have in place a system of announcements that will advise patrons of the change to our operations. I'd say that this kind of alliance would work for many public libraries, and would take pressure off their central administrations.*

The library's strategic alliance documentation should be:

- accurately dated and signed off by a senior manager
- contractual if possible
- detailed and explicit regarding the needs of the library
- detailed and explicit regarding the roles and responsibilities of the vendors
- detailed and explicit regarding pricing
- shared with all members of library management teams
- shared with the library's insurers and external auditors as required
- regularly audited and updated
- inclusive of all appropriate plans, drawings, software, and letters of approval and permission
- tested whenever and wherever appropriate.

Senior library managers including the library director, the IT manager, the facilities manager and their delegates should hold strategic alliance documentation. Vendor names and telephone numbers should be included on the library's contact list.

7.4   Updating strategic alliances

The library's facilities manager should audit and update all strategic alliances annually. The basic questions include:

- Do library sites continue to need the services of the vendor in a specific strategic alliance? For example, if the vendor provides repairs to a certain brand of hardware, and the library no longer uses that hardware, then the library no longer needs the strategic alliance.
- Is the vendor in the strategic alliance agreement still in business and capable of providing the service(s) described in the agreement?
- Does the vendor have adequate emergency management measures in place? For example, does the vendor have emergency transportation and communications plans? If the vendor

operates from a distant site, does it have adequate travel and long-distance delivery arrangements in the event of airport and road closures?

- Is the vendor's pricing and promised service level appropriate when there have been material changes of risk at a library's sites? For example, when a particular strategic alliance agreement came into effect, a library used five photocopiers. In the past year, however, it has acquired another three photocopiers to handle increasing workloads. The revised strategic alliance should take into account the additional photocopiers and their emergency repair requirements.
- Have the vendor's contact names, e-mail addresses and telephone numbers changed during the past year?
- Has the manner of taking delivery of various items changed at the library's sites (for example, new loading bays, sign-off procedures)? Has the vendor been informed of these changes?

Strategic alliance documentation should be permanently retained. Superseded contracts and supporting documents should be considered inactive, and may be stored off-site.

7.5 Adaptation of central library strategic alliances for branches

Once the library has established strategic alliances for operational resumption at its central location, branches can establish similar alliances to meet their needs. In many cases, vendors can supply post-disaster services to both the central location and the branches, and system-wide alliances are desirable. To qualify as a system-wide strategic alliance vendor, a company should have the following qualifications:

- the ability to respond quickly to client calls at one site, or at several sites simultaneously
- experience in making comprehensive damage assessments at a variety of sites
- reasonable repair costs and a willingness to offer economies of scale
- well-trained and experienced field staff, with competent project management
- proof of staff members' trade certification available upon request
- high-quality equipment and a fleet of well-maintained vehicles
- the ability to make quality repairs for the short or long term
- a documentation system for recordkeeping at a number of a client's sites
- a willingness to make comprehensive follow-ups for quality control
- a willingness to consider the human factor at disaster sites
- a good reputation in the library's region
- a good reputation among insurers, and references from insurance clients
- the ability to travel to various points around the library's region, and between different client sites
- emergency and disaster management planning in place for project staff and field crews.

While senior managers including the director should retain the master copies of all strategic alliance documents, the library's branches should keep copies of those documents for quick reference.

If different vendors are selected to provide post-disaster service to branches, those vendors must still provide the highest quality of service. It is appropriate for branches to select their own vendors for reasons of:

- a distance greater than twenty miles from the central location, and possible post-disaster communications problems
- proximity of the vendor to the branch
- experience of the vendor in dealing with problems specific to the branch and its neighbour-hood (e.g., damage from winter storms, riparian flooding, high winds)
- direction from insurers
- strong recommendation from the branch staff
- strong recommendation from the facility manager
- a previous alliance that can be adapted for resumption and continuity purposes
- a potential for site isolation owing to road closures, communication problems and severe weather.

Note that a vendor is not necessarily qualified to enter into a strategic alliance with the library simply because it has done business with the library in the past.

7.6   Going it alone?

In their belief that they can mange post-disaster circumstances without external assistance some large libraries may choose not to enter into strategic alliances. Such libraries might have departments that include conservators, facility management personnel and advanced communications systems. Even these libraries, however, might need help after a disaster that causes serious damage.

'Especially with extensive IT operations, and all the new computer equipment that libraries need these days, I'd say that almost every library needs reliable outside arrangements with the right people', says an IT specialist at a university in Colorado.

> *At our library we have alliances with every IT vendor we deal with. We have alliances with a full range of contractors. While we have a conservator on staff, she has alliances with several other conservators in our state. We think that we're reasonably well covered if a disaster occurs. We even invite vendor representatives to our disaster response training sessions. I don't know how we could resume operations without all of that outside help.*

7.7   References

7.7.1   Interviews

In this chapter I have quoted a British library administrator, and librarians in Florida, California, Pennsylvania and Colorado.

Post-disaster management of patrons

8.1 Convergence

What on earth is going on?

After a regional disaster, people want to know what has happened at local sites that they frequent, such as:

- banks and other financial institutions
- clubs and associations
- community and recreation centres
- educational institutions
- galleries and museums
- local grocery stores and markets
- malls and shopping districts
- medical clinics
- parks and recreation centres
- petrol stations
- places of worship
- post offices and government service centres
- railway and bus stations
- restaurants and bars
- sports venues
- theatres and concert halls

Certainly libraries belong on this list as well. Often they are located close to one or more of the above sites. Many public libraries have regular patrons at every branch; and there are patrons who visit their local branch every day. Other kinds of libraries also have their devoted patrons. Academic librarians know of people—erstwhile students—who, long after graduation, continue to browse in their stacks and use their collections. Corporate libraries attract in-house patrons who spend substantial amounts of time conducting research or simply browsing. Some school libraries are visited more often than classrooms by students.

'Fact is, library use can be habit-forming', says a branch manager in Toronto, Canada. 'That's not a bad thing. We encourage people to use our libraries, and spend a good part of our budgets promoting our services. We shouldn't be surprised to see patrons who prefer our facilities to almost anywhere else. Libraries are a second home for some patrons, a refuge for others. Inevitably we become a focal point in people's lives.'

For days after a regional disaster, people might be inclined to stay in their residences, owing to disruptions in transportation and communications systems. There might also be concerns about personal safety in areas where buildings have been damaged and could be on the verge of collapse. Eventually, however, people become curious about their usual haunts, those places that they rely on for entertainment and necessities. The urge to have a look at familiar places can be strong, to the point where people will attempt to bypass hazards to reach a grocery store, bank or library. Hence, patrons might converge at a library, even when it is closed, and linger in the hope that somebody will arrive with information about its reopening and post-disaster circumstances.

Convergence can also occur in cases where only a library has been affected by a disaster – a 'single-site event'. Curiosity will inspire patrons and others to investigate any damage and to try to find out how long any closure will last. Patrons might also make enquiries at other library branches about the safety of employees at the damaged branch.

'When a fire struck one of our suburban branches, patrons who used it regularly travelled to other branches and our central library to ask if the branch staff was okay', said a public librarian in British Columbia. 'We dealt with dozens of enquiries at our reference desks, and some members of the public were very upset. The closure of the library disrupted people's routines, and it was clear that regular patrons missed interacting with their acquaintances who worked at the branch.'

Despite the clearest signage regarding the closure of a library and the inadvisability of remaining on or near its site, some patrons might stay on or close to the site for lengthy periods. They might ignore requests to move along.

'After one of our earthquakes, we cordoned off our entire site and put up big signs telling people to stay away,' reported a branch manager in California. 'There were serious concerns about ruptured water mains, downed power lines and gas leaks in our neighbourhood, and the police and firefighters wanted everybody to keep their distance.' A number of cracks had appeared on exterior walls of the library; most of the windows had broken. Piles of debris blocked entrances and exits. A dog had been killed by falling masonry in the rear parking lot, and its carcass stank. But these circumstances did not deter patrons from arriving at the library, wandering around its exterior, closely examining wall cracks and shattered glass, and taking photographs of the front entrance, with its twisted frame and bulging metal doors. The Californian branch manager went on to say:

> *Despite repeated warnings from the police, patrons kept showing up. So did our employees. When a police officer told people to stand clear of the library, they stood on the sidewalk across the street and discussed the damage to the building. I arrived at some point and tried to reassure everybody that the library would reopen in the near future, although frankly I could not have been sure of that. For several days thereafter, people – our employees and regular patrons – continued to show up and stand around for a time, waiting for updates. I don't know how many times I had to tell people that I didn't know what was going on.*

After many disasters, patrons want to know when the library will reopen. They might ask library employees where they can return items that they have borrowed. They might also ask about the status of their borrower records. If the library is closed, will fines for late returns be cancelled? Will items on hold be available after the library reopens, or should patrons pick up items held for them at other library locations? What about the usual library programmes such as children's story-time and reading group meetings? Will these programmes recommence at some point?

8.2   Closure of facilities: process and implications

The need to close a library arises from concerns for the personal safety and security of employees and patrons. The length of the closure will depend on how soon safety and security can be restored, through the stabilization of building components and the

We're sorry.
The library is closed temporarily.

We look forward to seeing you soon.

Please return books and other items to another branch.

Check our website for more information.

Closed for repairs.
We'll see you soon.

Please return borrowed items to another branch.

Check our website for more information.

Figure 8.1 Temporary closure signage.

reactivation of security systems. Closure involves a process that includes the following steps:

- Damage assessment and the identification of potentially dangerous areas on the library site, or in the library.
- The decision to cordon off the entire site, or areas of the site.
- The acquisition of cordons and signage materials, ideally available in the library's emergency supplies.
- Placement of cordons – for example, yellow warning tape – and posting of signage at appropriate locations on-site (Figure 8.1).
- The assessment of the need for security guards and/or police patrols around the perimeter of the library site.
- Announcements through local media regarding the closure, often 'until further notice', and with information on alternative locations for the return of borrowed items and for the continuation of programmes and events.
- Announcements through websites, apps and recorded telephone messages regarding the closure, with information on alternative library locations for the return of borrowed items and the continuation of programmes and events.

During a library closure, and especially until physical risks have been mitigated, general sanitation and the condition of collections and other assets will suffer. If pipes have ruptured and flooding has ensued, books, periodicals, carpeting, furniture and IT hardware might be drenched. If water damage is not dealt with promptly it may worsen until various items are beyond repair. A fire that triggers sprinklers can result in an unfortunate mixture of charred and soggy items, as well as structural damage. Earthquakes can lead to flooding, structural damage, gas leaks, toxic spills, the outbreak of fire, and the dangerous shifting and collapse of furniture, including shelving units. Those who must contend with such conditions days or weeks after a library building has been approved for re-entry and eventual reopening might find the situation disheartening.

These, however, are worst-case scenarios. Often a library is beset with a mild or moderate problem, such as a minor flood or a power outage. These are emergencies, but they are not often life-threatening as true disasters can be. Reopening can take place after a brief closure. Even so, there can be a layer of dust throughout the library, and a more vigorous janitorial clean-up will be required. And no matter how small the problem, library employees should expect patrons' questions about what happened.

'Ironically we had as many questions at our reference and circulation desks after a four-hour power outage as we did when our library flooded', said an Austrian public librarian.

> *When the light went out, we got back in business very soon. When the floodwaters hit our basement and ground floor, we were closed for almost a month. After both of these events, we listened to patrons' comments for weeks. I believe that patrons need opportunities to express their concerns about their favourite institutions after any sort of emergency or disaster has occurred. For dedicated regular patrons, the library might become an extension of one's self, and damage to the library can be a personal loss. The same applies to long-term employees.*

8.3   Reassuring patrons

Convergence in the vicinity of a damaged library and questions to employees about a disaster's effects are not the only signs of patrons' unease regarding their library's plight. In general order of frequency, other signs include:

- repeated offers of assistance
- unwelcome provision of assistance that involves illicit entry into a closed library
- letters to local newspaper editors regarding damage to the library
- complaints to trustees and other authorities regarding perceived slowness of repairs
- growth of rumours through social media
- unwanted donations, particularly of patrons' cast-off books and magazines
- promises of financial donations that are made spontaneously and are not kept.

Successful reassurance involves attention to these signs as they appear. Employees at all levels in the library hierarchy should be aware of the effects of these signs, and be prepared to counter them as follows:

- *Repeated offers of assistance.* Respond with polite expressions of gratitude and friendly refusal on the grounds of safety and security: 'Of course we look forward to seeing you back in the library when it reopens, or at another location in future. You're always welcome. We're just waiting for things to calm down.'
- *Unwelcome provision of assistance that involves illicit entry.* Respond with firm but friendly direction not to enter the library. Ask members of the public to respect signage regarding the closure. If these measures fail, call in additional security – police patrols and/or private security guards posted around the library. Note that many patrons who make illicit entries into damaged sites and buildings are misguided, but not necessarily ill-intentioned. Arrests

and criminal charges are last resorts unless the intruder's intentions are clearly unlawful, and involve crimes such as theft and looting.

* *Letters to local newspaper editors regarding damage to the library.* These are often expressions of disappointment that a disaster has damaged a library, and should not be considered hostile. Library managers or employees responsible for the library's public relations should respond appropriately, and mention that it is encouraging to see how much patrons care about their library. It is also wise to assert that the library is working hard to resume operations as soon as possible.

* *Complaints to authorities regarding perceived slowness of repairs.* These are also expressions of disappointment. Such complaints are directed less towards library employees and more towards authorities not immediately involved in library operations: local politicians, academic and municipal administrators, and trustees. These authorities might simply pass on the complaints to library managers either directly through meetings or discussions, or indirectly through letters to editors that address the complaint rather than the complainant.

* *Growth of rumours through social media.* These can be difficult to counteract, and can lead to prolonged misunderstandings between a library and its patrons. Sometimes it is best to allow the rumours to subside, which many do over time. In other cases, it is advisable to dispel the rumour directly through the library's website. You will note the absurdity of some rumours after a disaster. Conspiracy theories might appear on blogs – for example about a government's intention to sabotage library operations and public access to information by means of arson, power outages, or intentional flooding. Forbearance is necessary in such cases, and often it is best to ignore the bloggers, since responding to their bizarre postings can give their ideas new life.

* *Unwanted donations, particularly of patrons' cast-off books and magazines.* Such donations are usually as well-intentioned as they are unwelcome. It is not appropriate, however, to scold patrons who donate items after a disaster. Rather, expressions of gratitude are in order, after which unwanted items can be politely refused, or accepted and recycled.

* *Promises of financial donations that are made spontaneously and are not kept.* You should note that such promises are often honoured, and that after a disaster a library's fund-raising efforts can be more successful than they would be under normal circumstances. But sometimes members of the public – and occasionally library employees – promise to donate money during and after a disaster, and do not follow through on their pledges. These people might have spoken in the heat of the moment, before they had time to consider the implications of their words. They might not have the money, or they might simply change their minds. In any case, library fund-raisers are wise not to pursue them more vigorously than before, since to do so might cause embarrassment on both sides, and not result in a donation.

'You should remember that people are just trying to help', says a Canadian university librarian in Winnipeg.

Helping the library can be an effective way of helping yourself emotionally to get past the loss – temporary or permanent – of a cherished institution like the branch near your house. You shouldn't simply shut people down, and you should do your best to reassure patrons. Reassurance comes from librarians who listen to patrons, who let them express their concerns, and who offer the right kind of post-disaster message. Sometimes I think that a soothing conversation with a

small group of concerned patrons is more powerful in the long run than an
extensive PR campaign.

8.4   Updating patrons on operational resumption and recovery

Libraries can also reassure their patrons by releasing regular updates about repairs to library facilities and plans to reopen. Updates can reach the public through different channels, including:

- newsletters, flyers and brochures
- newspaper articles based on interviews with library managers
- radio and TV interviews with library managers
- social media
- website announcements.

While it may sound obvious, updates should be as positive as possible. There is no point in distributing pessimistic announcements unless the consequences of a disaster are dire, and resumption and recovery are not possible. But in some cases where libraries are close to reopening and resuming normal operations, updates are unintentionally and unnecessarily negative. For example, a library branch in a Midwestern American city was damaged by fire and flooding from sprinklers. Within five weeks the building had been repaired to the point that it could reopen. The collections had been either restored or replaced. New fixtures and furniture had been installed. The operational resumption process was successful. However, the pre-opening update released to the media and general public sounded grim. It opened with a three-page description of the damage from the fire, along with photographs of sprinkler-soaked books. There was no mention of the fact that the damage had been repaired and the books replaced. There was a list of programmes that had been cancelled, but no mention of the fact that they would be rescheduled. There was a description of the new furniture, 'which some patrons might find reasonably comfortable'. Finally, there was a paragraph in which the head librarian expressed his regret that the cat which had lived in the branch for years had been euthanized. The cat had not been injured in the fire, but 'it was believed to be old, and the time had come for us all to say goodbye'.

A librarian at a different branch of the library recalls that update clearly.

> *It was so depressing that it was almost funny. There was lots of good news, but the*
> *author of that update wouldn't share it. He seemed determined to cast a pall over*
> *the reopening. And of course that branch's regular patrons mourned for the cat for*
> *weeks. Some patrons stayed away, and started using other branches. It was a PR*
> *nightmare, and it took months for old patrons to return and for the branch's circula-*
> *tion statistics to recover. We've learned our lesson. Next time there's a disaster in*
> *our system, we'll try to accentuate the positive as much as we can.*

She added that despite the extensive damage and its description in the update, there were few donations to the library earmarked for the branch's recovery.

8.5   Dealing with volunteers

The acceptance of assistance from volunteers after a disaster will depend on circumstances including:

- the actual need for volunteer assistance
- concerns about legal liability if a volunteer were to be injured
- concerns about insurance for volunteers in the library workplace
- concerns about the library's ability to give proper workplace orientation to volunteers
- concerns about the kinds of assistance that volunteers can offer
- concerns about volunteers' acceptance of supervision by library employees
- concerns about attracting too many volunteers to a particular site
- labour union contract coverage of volunteers in the library workplace
- overarching administrative policies regarding the use of volunteers
- site safety and security
- questions about how the library will express its gratitude to volunteers.

A natural source of volunteers after a disaster will be the Friends of the Library and similar organizations. Members may be eager to help the library, but sometimes they are not physically fit for work that could include activities such as:

- moving damaged books and other items
- performing damage assessments
- re-shelving items that have fallen on the floor
- moving damaged furniture.

Nor are the Friends necessarily trained to carry out standard library tasks in reference and technical service departments. A public librarian in New England describes the situation with volunteers who showed up at a branch after a ruptured pipe caused a flood:

> We had dozens of volunteers showing up to help us not only from our Friends association, but also from the general public. There were regular patrons, and folks we'd never seen before. Many of these people were elderly and retired, and we had to turn them away for fear that they could hurt themselves if we allowed them to load wet books onto carts. That's hard work. We also worried that these people could slip and fall, and the library would be legally liable for any injuries. We didn't want to take chances in this situation.

But the librarian and her colleagues did not want to discourage volunteers entirely:

> We let them serve coffee and cookies to people who showed up out of curiosity. The coffee urns were set up in a parking lot across the street. There the Friends of the Library put up their banner, and people gathered around them. The Friends actually attracted new members. They also assured people that the library employees were safe, and that the library would reopen soon. And they collected donations of books and other items, which they sold in a rummage sale weeks later. Frankly, everybody had a good time and we in the library managed to call in support from a moisture control outfit, supervise the clean-up, and reopen in a week. That [operational

*resumption] would not have possible if we had been obliged to deal with volunteers
in the library.*

Thus, it is prudent to consider carefully how much volunteer assistance your library is
prepared to accept. In many cases, it is best to limit volunteer activities to the kind of
auxiliary tasks described above.

8.6   Post-disaster programmes

Immediately after a regional disaster, some libraries can offer emergency information
programmes including:

- direction to government emergency services
- meeting spaces for organizations which have been displaced
- provision of pamphlets and other items containing post-disaster safety information
- temporary shelter for people who have been displaced
- message centre services: billboards for posters, announcements and personal messages
- meeting areas for friends and family members to assemble.

It is essential to recognize a library's limitations after any regional disaster. The above
programmes are possible only if library facilities are safe and serviceable, and if the
surrounding neighbourhood has not sustained damage such as downed power lines,
toxic spills and gas leaks. And even in cases where facilities are intact, there are limits
to how much service library employees can render, especially when large crowds of
patrons arrive on-site and demand temporary shelter.

Most libraries can provide only the most basic forms of shelter. They are not hotels.
They do not have large enough kitchens, lavatories or sleeping spaces to accommodate
large groups. Except in the worst circumstances – where leaving the library would involve
life-threatening risks – patrons should not be permitted to treat your library as they would
a hostel or community centre. To do so can lead not only to serious sanitation problems,
but also to damaged furniture and fixtures and the displacement of collections.

'I'm thankful that there's a recreation centre on the same block as my library
branch', says a reference librarian in the southern US. 'When big tropical storms and
hurricanes hit us, people can camp in the gym. The big washrooms have showers and
lockers as well as toilets, and there's a cafeteria. The recreation centre is much better equipped than my branch to handle people who have been evacuated from a local
neighbourhood.' With the recreation centre providing shelter to displaced people, the
branch can offer information services that fit in with the library's usual mandate.

8.7   Message centres and missing children

If local telephone networks and Internet servers are down, libraries can set up message
centres that will allow basic communication between members of the public. Such
centres are temporary, and in urban areas might not be necessary for more than a few

days. As well as standard reference services, centres might comprise a bulletin board for brief messages and enquiries. A librarian should be available to advise patrons about directing enquiries regarding missing persons to the police and other agencies.

Libraries are not ideal places to receive children who have been separated from their parents or caregivers during and after disasters. Nevertheless, it would be unconscionable for library employees to force a young child to leave a library when hazardous circumstances prevail. There have been numerous post-disaster instances in which librarians have kept children in their libraries until parents or the police retrieve them.

'Most parents would be desperate to find their kids after a community gets hit by something bad', said a public branch manager in the Midwestern US.

Library policies might say that we shouldn't hold on to lost kids, but I don't think any of us would simply turn a kid out during a severe snowstorm, or when a hurricane hits. We might even know the kid's family. So we'd tell the little boy or girl to stick around until the parents show up, or the police come by. My library has a collection of books that will keep a kid happy for hours, until the right people show up. I don't think it's a stretch to say that this is appropriate library service.

8.8 References

8.8.1 Interviews

In this chapter I have quoted Canadian librarians from Toronto, Winnipeg and British Columbia, librarians from Austria, and American librarians from California, the Midwestern and Southern US, and New England.

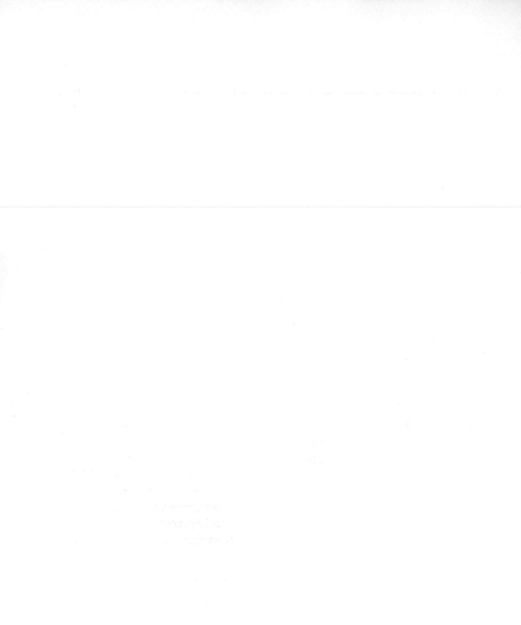

Normalization of operations

9

9.1 Reassuring employees

Good news is always welcome. After a disaster, library employees hope to hear encouraging things.

The questions that employees ask when they see damage to their workplaces revolve around the following:

- the safety and security of the library
- repairs to the library
- the condition of collections
- responsibility for the clean-up
- length of the closure
- the potential permanent closure of the library
- potential loss of jobs
- the reopening of the library and the resumption of normal services
- continuation of salary payments
- the long-term implications for employees at the site.

Since they rely on the library for their livelihoods, employees need reassurance that the library will resume operations after a disaster. Unfortunately, rumours – many of them false – might circulate and cause morale problems. In some cases, the major concern after a disaster is the loss of jobs. What if the library is permanently closed? If so, will employees lose their jobs? Such worries are natural, and senior library managers should address them as soon as possible. Often closures are temporary and employees should expect a quick return to work. Depending on the characteristics of a particular disaster, the message that senior managers circulate might include the following content:

- 'While the library has sustained damage, repairs will be made as soon as possible.'
- 'We will make the best possible effort to repair or replace damaged items, including books and other popular assets.'
- 'Employees unable to work at a library site owing to a closure may find work at other library sites.'
- 'No permanent lay-offs are planned.'
- 'There will be many tasks to complete once the damaged site reopens; it is not as if work will disappear.'
- 'Programmes and events cancelled because of the disaster will be rescheduled.'
- 'Our patrons are supportive, and look forward to seeing us again.'
- 'We will recover from this, and in time our workplace will return to normal.'

'It's necessary to repeat these key points to nervous employees', says a college librarian in New Mexico.

Employees need to hear these things from senior managers repeatedly after a
disaster, so that morale does not deteriorate altogether. Some rumours are really

*strong, and managers must work hard to dispel them. It can be a challenge to
do so, but if managers are to avoid extended morale problems, they must repeat
the message almost* ad nauseum. *People who fear unemployment can be inclined
to spread false rumours in the same way they spread gossip. This can be a real
nuisance.*

Effective management involves counteracting rumours through a variety of media,
including channels such as Twitter, websites and newsletters, but senior librarians often prefer face-to-face meetings with their staff to reassure them directly.

'One of our older branches was badly flooded, and we lost much of the collection',
said a regional library coordinator in the Midwestern US.

*Our staff members were really shaken up, especially the ones who had worked at
the branch for a long time. I didn't think that sending out an email was enough. I
decided to be there with the staff, to offer as much support as I could, and to let them
know that while we had lost a lot, we could rebuild our collections if we worked
together. This approach worked well.*

The coordinator notes that what started as a disaster soon lead to a series of positive
outcomes.

*Once the moisture control people had dealt with the water damage to the building
and fixtures, we started sorting through the soggy books and periodicals. We had to
discard a lot. Instead of asking the janitors to put the soggy items in a dumpster, I
insisted that we recycle as many as possible. During a meeting at the branch, I mentioned to staff that recycling those beloved items was in some sense a way of keeping
them in use, so that they wouldn't be lost completely. It sounds corny, I know, but it
helped several staff members to come to terms with the loss of items that they had
worked with for many years. The fact that I mentioned the recycling in person had
a bigger impact, and we were able to resume operations more quickly, and get back
to normal sooner than most people expected. There's a lot to be said for getting the
message out in person.*

9.2   Normalization defined

Normalization is the general consensus among employees that the library and its operations have returned to normal, and that the changes to the library during and following a disaster are acceptable. It is likely that after a disaster there will be far-reaching
consequences. Changes in facilities, personnel and collections are frequently permanent, and accordingly a library's corporate culture can change. Employees will need
time to adjust to new circumstances. Among those post-disaster circumstances that
require substantial time for acceptance are:

- sudden and substantial changes of front-line personnel
- sudden and substantial changes in senior management
- serious damage to library facilities or their immediate vicinities

- a move to new facilities owing to the loss of library facilities
- loss of or serious damage to collections
- substantial replacement of fixtures at library sites
- an ongoing crisis arising from a disaster
- substantial changes to library work processes, especially when downtime has created backlogs and affected work-flow.

Normalization is a subjective quality that is closely linked to morale levels and productivity. The purpose of your library's normalization programme is to support a return to general normality after any emergency or disaster.

'You shouldn't underestimate people's feelings about even the smallest items', says a librarian in Yorkshire, England.

> *Employees can become emotionally attached to things that most of us would consider rubbish. For example, we had a minor flood that drenched a number of old children's hardcovers – picture books for small children. A couple of staff members in the children's department were very unhappy when they learned that we had tossed out the damp books. Even though they knew that we had no choice – that the books were beyond rescue – those staff members could not accept the loss. One of them retired shortly after that, and she told me seeing the picture books being put in the skip had made her feel ill.*

9.3   Problems arising from incomplete normalization

It is essential to acknowledge the insidious and less obvious effects of an emergency or disaster on employees. The following problems could arise if normalization is incomplete:

- absenteeism
- post-traumatic stress disorder (PTSD)
- prolonged sick leave
- requests for transfer to different sites
- employee resignations
- loss of expertise
- prolonged crisis
- loss of good reputation among patrons
- decreased productivity
- poor quality work, including unfinished and poorly-executed tasks
- a disinclination to contribute to new projects and initiatives
- tension and increased stress
- ongoing rumours
- a general decrease in morale and a poor working environment.

Any or all of these problems is possible following a disaster and a delay in normalization. Additional problems that could add to the above are:

- the disinclination of managers to recognize patterns in absenteeism and resignations
- a disinclination to discuss post-disaster problems, either formally or informally

- failure to acknowledge change officially through the appropriate 'corporate ritual'
- ineffective corporate communications, especially from senior management
- ineffective orientation and training on new systems and equipment
- the disinclination of managers to discuss specific problems with individual staff members.

'You can't take for granted that things will simply return to normal after a disaster of any kind', says a municipal emergency response coordinator in Los Angeles.

It's uncommon for a public or academic library to cease operations permanently, even after a serious regional event such as a flood or an earthquake. With multiple sites and public expectations that they will survive, modern libraries are hardy institutions. They tend to recover in most cases. But, having said that, you must admit that they can experience ongoing problems, usually intangibles that require a lot of analysis and discussion.

He goes on to say that poor morale can persist indefinitely unless library managers make an effort to counteract it:

You see managers in different workplaces struggling with poor morale, and spending money on programs to improve it. But the foundation for any boost in an organization's morale is teamwork. When people understand that they're not alone, and that they're part of a team, they feel better in themselves, and clearer about their roles in the organization. That certainly includes most libraries and other information outfits, particularly after a disaster.

9.4   Normalization checklists

9.4.1   For employees

To ensure that normalization takes place and employee morale is restored in a reasonable time, the following processes and procedures should be carried out:

- Debriefing with employees in each department and branch as soon as possible after the disaster response phase, approximately 72 hours after a disaster.
- Recognition of employees' efforts during the disaster response phase, especially during follow-up meetings.
- Announcement of recovery accomplishments in the library newsletter or intranet.
- Discussions between managers and individual employees regarding specific problems either at sites or in the home.
- Recognition of the need for a recovery period, during which employees might not be as productive as before.
- Approval of time off for all medical appointments, for the individual employee or for a member of that employee's family.
- Availability of ongoing professional counselling for emotional/psychological problems, especially those arising from PTSD.
- Press releases and media packages covering the library's success in getting back in business.

- Availability of senior managers for interviews regarding the wind-up of operational recovery activities.
- 'Rap and wrap' sessions for final debriefing and celebration of effective business recovery.

'I'm a believer in "verbal therapy', says a library manager in Nebraska.

After any kind of trouble, if a library employee becomes very quiet, I get concerned. I want that person to talk about how he or she feels, and release the tension. If people don't do that, you see other emotional problems setting in – anxiety in particular, and sometimes depression. That's why you want to get people talking as much as possible after a disaster, discussing anything that has happened in their homes as well as what has occurred at the library.

After one of his branches was badly damaged in a winter storm, the library manager held a number of discussion sessions during which he encouraged employees to describe what they had been through:

It was a real relief for attendees. They talked about the damage to their homes and to the library. They expressed regrets about the personal property that they had lost, and about their dealings with insurance adjusters. And then they talked about the damage to the library, and how shocked they were to see how vulnerable it was. At that point a supervisor chimed in and said that as long as the library could rely on its employees, it would survive. When the idea of teamwork was emphasized, I think it made it much easier for employees to accept what had happened in the library – lots of flooding, loss of a lot of books and other assets – and to get on with the resumption of service to our patrons.

To deal with any cases of PTSD, professional counselling should be available through the library's employee assistance programme (EAP). While PTSD sufferers can benefit from 'rap and wrap' sessions and related activities at the library, they should consult professionals who have the requisite training to treat what has become a common post-disaster problem. Your library's Human Resources department should make sure that EAP providers have counsellors experienced in dealing with PTSD.

'In the 1980s I was working in California, when an earthquake caused a lot of damage and a number of casualties', says a retired reference librarian.

I saw some ugly things in the aftermath, and I found them very disturbing. I started having a recurring dream about a badly-injured man I saw on the street, and I couldn't get the image out of my head during my waking moments. I'd feel as if the event was happening all over again, and I'd feel very unsettled and anxious. My concentration was bad, and I had difficulties dealing with patrons at the reference desk. I became impatient with kids and some of the older patrons who needed help looking for information. Eventually I went to see a psychotherapist who helped me to overcome what he considered PTSD. It took time for the unpleasant images to stop recurring. I'm glad that my employer sent me to see that psychotherapist, because I'm not sure how I would have dealt with the problem otherwise.

9.4.2   For patrons

Employees should recognize patrons' needs to normalize their relations with the library. Post-disaster patron behaviour might include:

- an inclination to discuss personal disaster circumstances at length with employees at the reference desk, circulation counter and other public areas
- misplacing or losing borrowed items
- forgetting to pick up items on hold
- making unreasonable complaints regarding library services
- demanding that fines be forgiven
- blaming the library or its employees for problems encountered with other institutions, e.g. other government agencies or academic departments.

'After our winter storms, which sometimes involve high winds as well as heavy snowfall, we have patrons lining up to tell us all about what happened to their roofs and trees', says a circulation supervisor on the Canadian Prairies.

> *I've learned to listen to what people say, and that means I have to establish eye contact and acknowledge what people tell me. It can be tempting to break away from a patron's monologue, but this is not a good idea. Patrons rely on the service workers they regularly see to hear them out. Our head librarian was wise to tell us to listen to people, even if it slowed down our work.*

She says that she learned much about handling post-disaster chatter by observing her local bank workers and grocery store clerks:

> *In fact, most retail workers learn methods of listening to their customers, hearing them out, but not being monopolized by them to the detriment of service to other customers. I found that bank tellers are very good at listening to the customers' tales of woe while attending to their financial needs. Some tellers develop listening skills that you could almost describe as therapeutic. I've advised my co-workers to pay attention to the ways in which tellers serve them. I think that library personnel could learn a lot.*

To deal effectively with patrons adversely affected by post-disaster circumstances, managers should ensure that all employees are aware of the need for:

- patience in handling all patron enquiries
- patience and diplomacy in dealing with patrons' complaints
- a refusal to argue with patrons who appear to be angry or agitated
- the expression of the library's commitment to continue service to patrons
- patience in dealing with patrons who take up more time than usual at the reference desk, circulation counter and other service points
- the 'personal touch', i.e. avoidance of unnecessary formalities with long-term patrons
- reassurance that, despite its losses, the library will continue to operate.

'There's no doubt that after a serious event, library employees are going to have their own concerns', says a corporate librarian in the City of London.

They might have had damage to their houses, and they might have had trouble in reaching their places of work. This is particularly true in large cities, where even a minor event can wreak havoc with transportation systems. So you should not be surprised when employees are not in top form, and being patient with library users will be even more challenging than usual. So, gentle reminders about best possible behaviour are in order.

9.5 Testing normalization programmes

Your library's Human Resources department can test your normalization programme through tabletop exercises and can enhance it to meet specific needs. The main issues relate to:

- The ability of your Human Resources department to recognize the need of employees for professional counselling.
- The ability of your library's EAP provider(s) to offer post-disaster counselling, particularly for sufferers of serious anxiety, depression, PTSD and any related conditions.
- The ability of your library's communications vehicles and post-disaster messaging systems to reach all employees and to keep them informed regarding disaster response and operational resumption progress and accomplishments.
- The ability of your Human Resources department to manage the reassignment of employees at all levels to different library sites as required temporarily after a disaster.
- The ability of your Human Resources department to manage temporary and permanent succession planning for all levels of staff, but particularly for key technical employees, e.g. IT specialists.
- The willingness of individual supervisors and managers to make sure that employees accept necessary post-disaster changes to your library's facilities, processes and procedures.
- Your Human Resource department's overall role in your library's business resumption and recovery processes, and its own level of preparedness for disasters.

'HR people may not have to worry about damaged books, but they might have to handle the consequences of losing employees', says a corporate headhunter in New York who provides consulting services to large public, academic and government libraries.

Replacing an IT expert even for a short time can be hard, and post-disaster problems are exacerbated when a library's IT documentation is out of date or simply unavailable, and any incoming replacement has little or nothing to give him or her direction. And if you lose other key people in a technical services department, you can see big backlogs developing – the sort that can take months to reduce.

He goes on to mention his concerns about the potential effects of a global pandemic, which might result in serious absenteeism and staff attrition in many libraries. But he suggests that awareness of pandemic risk will inspire Human Resources departments to enhance their normalization programmes and succession plans; he also believes that a library's determination to protect employees from pandemics will lead to more online library services.

It's not as if I want human contact in libraries to disappear, It's just that pandemic risk is another reason to continue the development of online library services that are already in place. For the purposes of a library's disaster plan, improving online services is a smart idea. Employees who work away from the public are less exposed to the pandemic. The good news about online services as far as your employees are concerned is that it can protect them as well as keeping them busy and working.

And good news is always welcome.

9.6   References

9.6.1   Interviews

In this chapter I have quoted librarians in California and Nebraska, and elsewhere in the Midwestern US and New Mexico, and on the Canadian Prairies. I have quoted British librarians in Yorkshire and the City of London. I have also quoted a corporate head-hunter in New York and a municipal emergency response coordinator in Los Angeles.

Orientation and training programmes

10

10.1 Binder dependence

If your disaster plan lacks an orientation and training programme for employees, you do not have a disaster plan. Rather, you have a three-ring binder stuffed with advice and information that few people will see – let alone learn to use – in an actual disaster.

'I call it "binder dependence syndrome", says an emergency planning consultant in London.

> *Many people believe that once they have taken delivery of a binder of planning material, they are protected against all prevailing risks. This is an example of magical thinking at its worst, and possibly its most dangerous. A paper plan is nothing but paper, an online plan is nothing more than another website that most people skim once and forget. What drives home the essential aspects of any disaster plan is the orientation and training programme. Unfortunately, many clients are not sure what it will involve. They automatically assume that it will be outrageously expensive, or too time-consuming, or not really necessary. Planners have to be clear from the start what effective orientation and training are.*

10.2 Definitions: orientation and training

Employees require orientation and training to ensure that disaster planning components are effective and that the library is prepared to deal with adverse circumstances of all kinds. The following definitions clarify the differences in meaning between these terms:

- *Orientation* is defined as basic introductory instruction in the general areas of your disaster plan. Coverage of topics is concise and 'high-level'. Orientation is intended to encourage employees to think about various aspects of response, resumption and continuity, and to apply them in their workspaces and residences. Orientation should reinforce self-reliance, safe and effective behaviour during emergencies, and problem-solving skills under challenging conditions.
- *Training* is defined as advanced instruction in specific areas of your disaster plan. Coverage of topics will concentrate on certain activities related to emergency preparedness, response, resumption and continuity. Examples include situation management for senior administrators and branch managers, emergency response procedures, damage assessment, post-disaster public relations, basic and advanced emergency conservation techniques, strategic alliance activation, alternative site activation and management, and normalization procedures.

'While orientation is usually basic and intended for all employees, training can be highly specialized and aimed at a specific group of employees', says a rare book librarian in Texas.

> *For example, everyone in my library takes basic orientation – mostly concerned with personal safety – regarding response to fires, floods and hurricanes. But the training for the rare book librarians in charge of a collection of incunabula will focus on the emergency conservation of our oldest printed materials, with attention to different kinds of damage to texts and bindings. Such training will be different from that which a librarian receives if he or she is in charge of a collection of first editions of modern literary works. In many ways the latter are more fragile than the former. The training for each specialist will vary according to the conservational demands that will arise in his or her department during and after a disaster.*

10.3   Purposes of orientation and training

In general, the purposes of orientation and training programmes are as follows:

- To familiarize employees with the components of a disaster plan.
- To encourage employees to evaluate the plan and to indicate any inaccuracies, weaknesses and omissions.
- To allow employees to suggest improvements and refinements to the plan.
- To allow library managers to consider the most effective methods of mitigating risks.
- To give employees opportunities to 'buy into' the plan.
- To make the plan part of a library's corporate culture.
- To reduce barriers to risk mitigation, and operational resumption and continuity, e.g., bystander behaviour, complacency, waning interest, decreasing participation and excess documentation of procedures.
- To make the plan sustainable – that is, able to stand the test of time – and adaptable as a library changes and grows in the long term.

According to a corporate librarian in New York City:

> *We might not want to admit it but a lot of orientation and training is really promoting disaster plans and 'selling' them to employees. We want people to understand how useful plans can be when a disaster occurs. We want to stimulate enthusiasm and interest. The more effectively we can promote plans through orientation and training, the better the chances are that the plans will work when something bad happens. So there's more to training sessions than employee education. There has to be a certain amount of sales management for any disaster plan, to make sure that employees take it seriously.*

A corollary purpose of orientation and training is to present employees with additional perspectives on their facilities and workplace practices. There are often opportunities to streamline practices when one considers ways to resume them after a disaster. For example, when a disaster planning trainer pointed out the risks to the paper files of the administrators at a university library in California, the administrators saw that their records management was inadequate. They updated their retention schedules and finally shredded or recycled several tons of old and redundant files. They also developed a business case for the digitization of current vital records.

'It came to our attention during the business resumption training sessions that we were very behind in dealing with our paper systems', says one of the senior administrators.

In fact, the situation was embarrassing. But the training we received gave us the justification and required path to better and more secure records management. By converting paper to digital records, we have a much greater level of records security and [operational] continuity. Even after a catastrophe, we'll have access to the records necessary for serving our campus patrons. And we're saving money on space, which has always been at a premium in our facilities.

10.4 Assumptions

Most orientation and training programmes are based on the following assumptions:

- The library requires effective disaster planning, and an essential aspect of that process is orientation and training for employees at all levels.
- The library maintains a comprehensive disaster plan that comprises measures for preparedness, response, resumption and continuity.
- The library is willing to comply with the relevant standards of disaster planning, including the local fire code and guidelines provided by various levels of government.
- The library will audit and update its disaster plan(s) regularly, with attention to organizational growth and development: new facilities, employees and workplace practices.
- The library will revise procedures related to response and resumption and so on in light of extraordinary events such as unusually severe weather and other environmental disasters, shortages of commodities such as fuel, severe economic downturns, catastrophic acts of terror and the outbreak of war. Various emergency measures may be *ad hoc* and useful only once, for a brief period. Training to address the library's needs under these circumstances should be available.
- Regular (i.e., annual) updating of disaster plan(s) may include additional orientation and training for management and staff.
- The library will assume in-house responsibility for orientation and training as much as its resources allow.

'Assumptions may seem obvious when you see them in written form', says the Californian senior administrator quoted above.

However, it's good to ask yourself if they're reasonable and realistic. A series of assumptions will give you an idea of how practicable your planning really is. If any of your assumptions is unreasonable, then you should revisit your planning process. There could be a disconnect between the library, its administration and people in positions of power outside the library. It's worthwhile to examine assumptions carefully, even though most of them will be no-brainers.

10.5   Methods of delivery

For your library's purposes, the following methods of delivery can be appropriate:

*   home circulars
*   newsletter/intranet materials
*   staff orientation and training sessions
*   management orientation sessions
*   management security seminars.

These methods should include and rely on:

*   plain language, i.e. jargon-free presentation of material
*   strict time limitations, e.g. ideally no more than 90 minutes for a tabletop exercise
*   realistic scenarios, circumstances and problems
*   a focus on specific problems
*   encouragement of practical problem solving
*   acceptance of best possible (but not perfect) solutions
*   interaction between participants and presenters/facilitators
*   free-flowing exchanges of ideas regarding questions at hand
*   opportunities for follow-up enquiries, recommendations and discussions
*   concise reporting of session results; reports to be permanently retained.

Every library will have different methods of delivering orientation and training, but programmes should contain some or all of the above elements. Your library might already have training procedures in place; these could be adapted for the purposes of your disaster planning. What follows are descriptions of standard methods of delivery.

10.6   Home circulars

Home circulars are an inexpensive and effective way to get employees to focus on specific disaster scenarios and related matters. Advantages include:

*   The opportunity to personalize disaster-related challenges, and literally to bring home information about risks and the best methods to mitigate them.
*   The opportunity to encourage employees to make the appropriate preparations in their residences for themselves and their family members.
*   The opportunity to consider disaster-related challenges not only in their workplaces, but also in transit to and from workplaces, and in their residences. This advantage is crucial for business resumption and continuity.

Ideally home circulars will be brief. They may be distributed in memo form, or they can be laid out like a pamphlet (see Figures 10.1 and 10.2).

'If you can get the families of your employees interested in disaster preparedness and security procedures, you'll reinforce your employees' commitment to these things in the workplace', says a public librarian in Mississippi. 'People like the idea of being safe wherever they live and work. Sending out home circular memos can be a great way to get employees involved in the disaster planning process, and underscore points made during orientation and training sessions.'

Memo to: All library employees
From: Head librarian
Date: July 2015

Re: Disaster preparedness for your pets

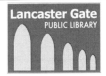

Severe weather, floods and other regional disasters can threaten pets, but there are effective ways to protect them.

Before a disaster:
• Make sure that you have a pet carrier large enough to hold your pet. Ideally you will have one carrier per pet. Carriers must be properly ventilated so that pets aren't overcome by heat and humidity. A dog or cat should be able to turn around in its carrier.
• Make sure that your evacuation strategy includes getting your pet to a safe place. If you can't take a pet with you, make arrangements to leave it with friends or relatives, a veterinary clinic, an animal shelter or a pet daycare. Check to make sure that these places and caregivers have appropriate evacuation plans for all pets on their sites.
• Keep a photograph of your pet with your personal identification, in case the pet gets lost. You'll be able to show rescue workers what to look for.
• Give your pet a collar with proper identification: pet's name and your telephone number.
• Keep a leash to control your pet.
• Keep proof of all vaccinations to show to any pet caregivers and shelters.
• Stock up on pet food [en] an extra two-week supply per pet.

During a disaster:
• Bring pets inside your residence. Try to keep them calm.
• If you leave your pet at a shelter, make sure you can provide the shelter with your pet's identification collar and rabies tag, a carrier, a leash, a food supply, bowls for water and food, any required medications and special care instructions, and plastic garbage bags for sanitation purposes.
• Do not allow pets to go outside if smoke and fumes are heavy.
• Do not allow pets to drink or swim in floodwater.

After a disaster:
• Allow pets to get used to altered surroundings after a disaster. Walk dogs on a leash. Fires and floods often eradicate the landmarks that pets can recognize (e.g. scents), and they can get lost without reorientation to their environment.
• Beware of downed power lines while walking your pet.
• Beware of snakes while walking your pet. Reptiles are often brought to an area by floodwaters.
• Do not allow your pet to eat food from flood debris.
• Control your pet's water intake. Provide fresh water at regular intervals.
• Beware of contaminants such as fuel oil, sewage, solvents and paint.
• Beware of other dogs and cats that are running wild after a disaster. They can be aggressive, especially if they are injured or hungry.

For other pets:
• Fish can be difficult to transport to a shelter. Try to deliver your fish in an appropriate tank with enough food for two weeks at least 24 hours before a disaster strikes.
• Birds and reptiles require special care. Note that many shelters do not accept them during and after a disaster.
• Discuss pet care concerns with family members, and make sure that they're aware of the proper precautions.
• Let your manager know if you have questions about the care of pets in a disaster.

Figure 10.1 Example of home circular memo: employees' pets.

Memo to: All library employees
From: Head librarian
Date: July 2015

Re: Personal records and archives

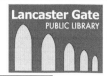

Fires, floods and other disasters often result in the loss of our personal records, many of which are unique and irreplaceable. Consider the following kinds of records, which you might keep in your residence:

- Documents of personal identification: passports, identity cards, work permits, citizenship records.
- Diaries, journals, and business calendars.
- Personal correspondence.
- Educational records, including report cards, transcripts, diplomas and degrees.
- Professional certification, including licences, professional association documentation, certificates of continuing education, and awards.
- Professional career archives, including prized drawings, blueprints, photographs, notebooks and miscellaneous items.
- Resumes, CVs and records of past employment.
- Personal accounting records, including documents pertaining to credit, investments, property ownership, leases, pensions, insurance and taxation.
- Vehicle documentation, including maintenance records.
- Personal health records, including immunization certificates and health insurance documents.
- Pet records pertaining to licences, breed, immunization and health.
- Family archives, including any significant documents from past generations.
- Family photographic records, including still photography, 8mm, video and digital formats. Pay special attention to unique images of special events: graduation ceremonies, weddings, the earliest images of children, surviving images of ancestors, special images of pets, images of family residences.

These records are vulnerable to moisture and extremes of heat and light. Ideally you will store them in a safe place, away from rising floodwaters and bright sunlight. The worst place to store anything fragile is in either the basement or the top floor of a house. Both of these locations are at risk from moisture ingress.

One effective measure to protect documents and photographic materials is duplication. We can scan items, and store the scanned data in remote locations. If the original item is destroyed, its duplicate can preserve the image. Firefighters note that people are especially disturbed when they lose wedding photos and videos of their children. To prevent such losses, you can duplicate the photos and distribute them to other family members in different regions. (Back-up copies of family photos can be welcome gifts.)

How valuable is a particular personal record to you? Imagine losing it. Imagine the inconvenience of reconstructing it, of reapplying for a license or asking an issuing body for a copy. If you are unwilling to lose your records and archives, consider ways to protect them:

- Safe storage, away from heat, light, moisture and insects.
- Good containers: metal document boxes, acid-free folders.
- Duplication and distribution outside the region. (Documents can also be scanned.)

Let your supervisor know if you have any questions about your records, archives or other special materials. Our records manager can advise you about the best ways to protect various items.

Figure 10.2 Example of home circular memo: employees' personal records stored at home.

10.7   Newsletter/Intranet materials

Brief, informative articles regarding aspects of your library's plans can be included
in the library newsletter and on the intranet. Concise and specific, these articles can
cover topics such as:

- the location of emergency equipment and first aid kits
- what to do if you see moisture ingress in the main library or branches: faulty plumbing,
  sprinkler malfunctions, leaky roofing
- what to do in a power outage
- what to do in an earthquake
- after an earthquake: what patrons expect from the library
- dealing with flooding in our community
- if you have security concerns in your department or branch
- working together after a disaster
- holiday safety.

Newsletter and intranet resources can include announcements of orientation and
training sessions. You can include answers to questions that have arisen during the
sessions, and remind employees to review their response and resumption plans (see
Figure 10.3).

'If you're using a website to disseminate newsletter items, be as concise as possible', suggests an emergency communications specialist in Los Angeles. 'Use point
form. Keep sentences short. Do not add long paragraphs of information loosely con-
nected to your topic. Specificity is the key to getting the message across to your
audience.'

10.8   Staff orientation sessions

Staff orientation sessions for your library can take various forms of presentation,
including:

- general sessions for larger groups
- management groups, e.g. branch managers, main library department managers
- departmental sessions – managers and their staff members
- lunch-and-learn sessions.

In many organizations, audience size for an orientation session can vary between 10
and 50 attendees. Orientation sessions offer a broad summary of risk-related topics.
For example, in 45 minutes to one hour, a presenter could cover:

- the local risk profile
- special considerations at the specific site, e.g. the main library or a branch
- emergency response activities
- response, resumption and continuity plans
- risk implications for residences and families
- Q & A.

Ten Office Safety and Security Tips for a Happy Festive Season

1. Don't let strangers walk through your work areas unchallenged and unattended. One holiday bandit dressed up as Santa Claus and wandered around an office complex distributing candy. When he left, his sack was full of laptops, wallets, purses and other valuables.
2. Watch for bogus charity appeals that arrive via email. Do not give out credit card information to charities with which you are unfamiliar.
3. Had a few to drink? Don't drive, plan your departmental budget or attempt to operate your computer. Try to maintain your self-control around your colleagues at the holiday party: discussion of sensitive information at social events is unwise.
4. Lock all gifts and other valuable purchases in your trunk, especially when you park your vehicle in a shopping mall or car park.
5. Don't overload your power sources with holiday lights and other illuminated decorations. Perform a capacity check on your uninterruptible power supply (UPS) to ensure that it can handle any power failures or surges.
6. Don't allow office buffets and party foods to get stale. Discard any uneaten and un-refrigerated food after three hours.
7. If the library shuts down for several days during the holidays, be sure to store all confidential materials in a safe place. Don't leave sensitive files and magnetic media in open areas.
8. Back up all vital data before leaving for your holiday. Store back-up media in a secure place, preferably off-site.
9. Be sure to turn off your work area lights before shutting down for the holidays.
10. Be careful when giving out personal schedules and office timetables to strangers over the telephone. Burglars want to know the best times to break into your office, and the holiday shutdown provides numerous opportunities. Don't give out schedule information unless you are familiar with the caller. Warn your colleagues about strangers who enquire about shutdown dates, and make sure your alarm system is working before you shut down.

Figure 10.3 Example of a newsletter item on holiday safety.

Special equipment (for example, microphone, projector) might not be necessary for orientation sessions, but handouts regarding emergency procedures are often appropriate. Handouts could include:

* the library's emergency response brochure and similar materials
* copies of the disaster plan(s) and related documents
* reprints of articles that have previously appeared in the library newsletter
* lists of emergency supplies for offices and vehicles.

'We achieved the best results in our library system by keeping orientation sessions simple', says a Midwestern US college librarian.

When I ran the sessions, I'd focus on personal safety during and after fires, floods and tornadoes. I avoided getting into details about how our technical services department should assess damage, and similar matters. I emphasized life safety over everything else, and asked my colleagues to think about themselves and their families first and foremost. In the end, that's what people care about. Most library disaster plans don't mention this, but people will worry about their children a lot sooner than they'll consider activating back-up cataloguing data. The point is that you have to plan for what people will do, not for what they should do. I covered that in the orientation session, and I believe that my colleagues were a lot more comfortable about what I had to say after that.

10.9 Management orientation sessions

Management orientation sessions are geared to meet the needs of managers who must provide leadership during emergencies and other contingencies in order to:

- safeguard themselves and staff members
- recognize different kinds of warning signs
- reduce damage and loss of library assets
- ensure timely return to operations
- minimize unnecessary calls for assistance to external first responders (police, firefighters).

These sessions should allow for slightly longer Q & A periods. Further, attendees might provide insights, observations and recommendations that should be followed up and taken into consideration during the updating of various plans and programmes. For example, during a management orientation session in Toronto, a senior corporate librarian noted that her department's planning did not take into account travel risks – serious delays, the outbreak of a disease such as SARS, and the theft or loss of luggage and IT. Since the supervisors in her department travel frequently across North America, mitigation measures have been added to the department's business resumption and succession plans.

Management orientation sessions should not only provide good advice but also encourage people to enhance current planning. 'Once you start thinking about disaster planning from a manager's perspective, you get a different idea of your library, a different way of looking at operations and routines that you took for granted previously', says the manager of a multinational corporation's library research unit based in Berlin.

Even a very brief orientation session can get you considering alternative approaches to post-disaster problems. Frankly, I found the sessions put on by associates from our New York office to be useful not only for disaster preparedness and planning, but also for fresh ways of dealing with various more common issues. For example, strategic alliances with other libraries can support faster post-disaster resumption of operations, but those alliances can facilitate other initiatives unrelated to disasters. After our management orientation sessions, we decided for the first time to share resources and research data with the other libraries in our corporation. So even if a disaster never happens, we reap the benefits from our orientation sessions.

10.10   Operational resumption and continuity orientation and training

It is generally agreed that the best way to provide orientation and training for resumption and continuity is to carry out tabletop exercises. These can be customized to meet a variety of needs in your library. A full range of sample tabletop exercises is included in the Chapter 11.

10.11   Management security seminars

The tabletop exercise format can be used in your library's management security seminars, which can focus on potential security breaches and crisis management issues. These seminars might be necessary ahead of special events such as international political summits and world sporting championships, with exercises based on your library's requirements for a high level of service to patrons coupled with enhanced physical and electronic security. Topics could include:

- projected risks related to electronic access of collections
- anti-theft measures
- enhanced security measures in public areas
- enhanced employee safety
- staff allocation issues during emergencies and disasters that occur during special events in your city or region.

'As the Cloud becomes more important for information exchange and storage, we need more frequent management security seminars', says an IT specialist in a British university library. 'These days our managers need frequent updates about risks to data. To be honest, many managers live in the past when it comes to data protection. They think it's simply a matter of changing your password every decade or so. They need a broader perspective, and must understand that protecting libraries from security threats is more complicated now than ever.'

A retired public library director in New England believes that library security measures should be reviewed more often:

> I'd say that in some jurisdictions, such as big urban areas, public library managers should be reviewing their security every quarter. A library's security coordinator should update managers on recent security breaches, and then an external expert can address the managers on anti-theft techniques or ways to discourage vandalism. In our area, we relied on the local school board, which employed a security specialist who had a lot of experience in dealing with threats to public facilities such as libraries. She gave us invaluable advice. The local police were helpful, too. We found that the police were skillful seminar leaders.

10.12   Training the trainers

Your library trainers can learn to provide in-house orientation and training in response, resumption and continuity by:

- Attending orientation and training sessions provided by external experts in the field, at conferences and through continuing education programmes.
- Taking in-depth training for certificates, diplomas or degrees in emergency management, disaster response and business resumption/continuity planning, and observing how instructors work with students.
- Learning first aid and fire warden skills, and paying attention to how instructors in these fields manage their training sessions and work with students.
- Consulting and working with local first responders: police, firefighters and paramedics.
- Reviewing your library's disaster and security plans and related programmes, and adapting them for educational purposes.
- Participating in and eventually leading tabletop exercises in your library.

'There are lots of different ways to pick up essential training skills', says an emergency response instructor at the Justice Institute in New Westminster, British Columbia.

Some people are natural teachers, and can quickly adapt information related to disaster planning for a library's in-house orientation and training purposes. Other people need more time to develop the skills they need to stand up in front of an audience and present material clearly. In your library – in any organization – you should look for employees who are good public speakers and who command respect when they deliver the facts. You do not want somebody on the podium who mumbles and cannot stay on topic. That could discourage employees from getting involved in emergency management and disaster response activities.

10.13   Session reporting

Your library should maintain a permanent record of all training sessions. This record will demonstrate to auditors that your library is serious in its pursuit of the highest standards of disaster response, resumption and continuity. The record, which can take the form of a ledger, should include the following fields:

- the date of the session
- the location of the session
- the number of participants, or a list of participating departments
- a description of the session (orientation lecture, tabletop, drill,)
- a summary of a tabletop scenario, if applicable
- Conclusions/noteworthy observations and insights.

Orientation and training sessions often involve practical decision making and the identification of issues that have not been considered before. Useful material can be included in the session reporting ledger for review when plans are being updated.

Often insights gained during orientation and training sessions are more valuable than any provided by external sources. Additionally, the more that your employees can contribute to the planning process, the more they will buy into it.

10.14 References

10.14.1 Interviews

In this chapter I have quoted American librarians in California, Texas, the Midwest, New England and New York City. I have also quoted and received much useful information from an emergency planning consultant in London, a corporate librarian in Berlin, an emergency communications specialist in Los Angeles and an emergency response instructor at the Justice Institute in New Westminster, British Columbia.

Basic tabletop exercises

11

11.1   No plan without practice

Paper plans are useless.

That is, unless you and your colleagues have familiarized yourselves with your library's disaster plan contents, and tested them to see if they work. The three-ring binder on your director's shelf cannot protect you and your library until you learn what the binder contains, and find out if its contents will meet your needs before, during and after a disaster.

'You can't expect a binder to save you if you haven't bothered to review it', says a Jamaican information consultant who specializes in information security and resumption planning.

> *Both in-house and external planners have to push library managers to read plans carefully and to make arrangements for staff members to test different components. In some libraries, it's hard enough to get people to participate in simple fire drills, even when government regulations stipulate them. It can be even more difficult to get employees to test disaster plans, which can be more complicated. That's why many planners recommend tabletop exercises to inform employees about their library's disaster plan, and to test the plan.*

A tabletop exercise is defined as an orientation or training process during which participants consider a particular disaster scenario that could occur in their workplace. Participants can then consult their disaster plan, and consider ways to apply it in order to protect themselves and their patrons, and to resume library operations quickly. Ideally the scenario is realistic, and the exercise does not require much time to complete. As the name indicates, a tabletop exercise often takes place around a table, such as that in your library's activity room. But similar and equally effective exercises can be held in a discussion circle, or in a coffee shop.

'In our library, we have stand-up coffee exercises', says a corporate library director in New York City.

> *They're no more than 15 minutes. Sometimes only a few library staff members are able to attend, and that's fine. I present the scenario, which could involve anything from a terrorist attack to a burst pipe in the washroom. Everyone in our library knows our disaster plan, and when they participate in coffee exercises they describe the best courses of action during and after the event. I'm always impressed by the intensity of our exercises, and the ways in which our people use the library's disaster plan. It's not perfect, and we discover weaknesses quite often – almost always through coffee exercises and the perspectives that they offer us.*

This chapter includes a series of generic tabletop exercises that have been developed for the following purposes:

- To test levels of emergency preparedness and business resumption capability in different departments, work units and branches of your library.
- To reveal strengths and weaknesses in your library's disaster response and resumption planning.
- To encourage employee participation in your library's disaster planning process.
- To identify new ways to solve response and resumption problems.
- To support employee orientation to the disaster plans; to act as a teaching tool for all levels of your staff.
- To support the updating and revision of disaster plans and any related programmes.

Customized tabletop exercises that you develop for your library can be derived from:

- risk analyses of your library's sites and their surrounding neighbourhoods
- risk analyses produced by local governments for your neighbourhood, area or region
- any recent local disasters in your region, whether or not they have affected your library's operations.

'You can hold tabletop exercises not only after a local disaster, but also after any disaster that merits a global focus', says an emergency services coordinator in Ottawa. For example, Asian earthquakes often capture worldwide public attention, and people are more interested in finding ways to protect themselves, even if they do not live in seismic zones. That can be a good time to offer a tabletop exercise to employees in any library. You can tell them that you want to make sure that your plans are up to date and ready for activation, and chances are that employees will be eager to participate. They might not be as enthusiastic during times when things are relatively calm, and the media cover matters unrelated to disasters. The point is that you should take advantage of unfortunate events when they happen elsewhere, to prepare your library when something bad happens locally. That's not cynical. That's being practical and realistic.

11.2   Risk assessment and analysis example

Assume that in your library's risk assessment and analysis the following risks prevail at the main library and branches:

- fire and associated risks including explosions and smoke damage
- flooding from faulty plumbing and severe weather
- high winds and winter storms
- toxic spills
- power failures
- data loss.

Your library's risk profile is exacerbated by proximity risks, that is risks at neighbouring sites, including:

- shopping malls and retail areas
- high crime areas

- major roadways
- railway tracks
- bodies of water, including a big river.

Risks prevailing near your library could trigger multifaceted events. For example, a train derailment and consequent toxic spill could result in:

- small but spreading fires
- gas leaks and toxic spills
- explosions and smoke damage
- a temporary but nonetheless serious decline in regional air quality
- multiple casualties, some requiring hospitalization
- gridlock on neighbouring roads, with transportation difficulties to and from library sites
- increased absenteeism and the disruption of library operations.

Your library's tabletop exercises should be developed in light of all of these prevailing risks.

'You see lots of orientation and training exercises that cover only one specific risk', says a school librarian in Atlanta, Georgia.

> *Our school and my library had one exercise for hurricanes. It had been put together in the 1960s, and while parts of it were still relevant, it did not address the more important aspects of safety and recovery. And then 9/11 and Hurricane Katrina hit, and libraries in the southern US recognized the need for better planning, which involves a lot more training and practical exercises.*

A public library branch manager in Texas agrees, and reinforces the idea that it is not only the larger regional disasters that you must anticipate. More likely, and potentially just as damaging to library assets, are smaller events affecting a single community or neighbourhood, or even a single floor of a building.

> *We talk a lot about Katrina and 9/11, and the Fukushima Daiichi nuclear disaster. But we need to prepare for things that are much more likely to happen, smaller disasters that strike libraries every day. That's why the people in my library spend even more time talking about ruptured pipes and minor power failures than the really big disasters. I believe that we need to prepare for the broad spectrum of events, and the best way to do that is to conduct regular exercises with a variety of different scenarios.*

11.3 Generic tabletop exercises

Based on the risk assessment and analysis example in the previous section, the following series of exercises can be carried out in many libraries with minimal adaptation needed. The scenarios provided are derived from reports of actual events.

11.3.1 *Fire and associated risks*

At 4.00 a.m. next Thursday, a faulty electrical circuit causes a fire on the ground floor of your building. The fire spreads through a wall cavity. Using large amount of water from hoses and water cannons, firefighters extinguish the blaze in 45 minutes, but close the building until noon the following Monday.

Casualties:

One patron (who was standing near the main entrance and attempting to find out what was happening inside) and one firefighter are treated for smoke inhalation at a local hospital.

Damage:

- Charring of walls, fixtures and furniture on the main floor, but no serious structural damage.
- Smoke damage and lingering odours of burnt materials throughout the building.
- Water damage throughout the building. Carpets, computers and collections have been drenched.
- Cracked glass in front entrance doors.
- Power to the building will be shut off until 7.30 a.m. the next day.

Crisis potential:

- TV camera crews get first-rate footage of your building enveloped in smoke. Reporters on the scene ask disturbing questions about the safety of the library, 'which serves large numbers of patrons every day'.
- Reporters telephone the Library Director and Board Chair at their homes and ask for comments. 'Is the library really safe? What would you say to somebody whose children visit that building regularly? And could another fire break out?'
- Reporters interview several library employees as they approach the damaged building on their way to work. They ask those employees to comment on the situation.
- A photo of the building enveloped in smoke appears on the front pages of the local newspapers. The Board Chair asks the Library Director to 'clear the air' and 'address the situation'.

Generic tabletop exercise

1. Refer to your current disaster plan and related emergency measures. Make a list of the first steps that you would take to resume business at your site? Write a schedule with realistic time estimates for the steps that you have listed.
2. Assume that 90 per cent of the collections in the building have been soaked with water. Write a list of the kinds of items that:
   a. can be discarded and not replaced
   b. can be discarded and replaced
   c. can be conserved (freeze-dried, etc.) if valuable and still usable
   d. deserve advanced conservation, even in poor condition, owing to historical or monetary value
3. Your staff members are told to resume operations at an alternative site, such as a neighbouring branch or office. Make lists of:
   a. the basic operations that you will be able to conduct within 48 hours from the alternative site (e.g., communicating with key managers, issuing bulletins, dealing with vendors involved in repairs and the resupply of lost assets)

b. the equipment that you will need to offer the basic operations listed above

c. people and organizations that you must contact as soon as possible regarding operational issues.

This exercise will be limited to one hour.

11.3.2   Flooding/water ingress

Note that anecdotal evidence suggests that water damages information assets more frequently than any other risk, owing to riparian flooding, faulty plumbing, leaky roofing, and related problems.

At 11.30 p.m. next Tuesday, a pipe bursts on the main floor of your building, and approximately 1400 gallons pour onto the floor and throughout your offices. Carpets, work area and wiring are soaked. The flood is not discovered until 6.45 a.m. on Wednesday.

Casualties:

Arriving early, one employee slips and falls in a hallway. She suffers a concussion and sprains her ankle. She lies unconscious near the front entrance for an hour before she is discovered.

Damage:

*   Drenched carpets and underlays, which emit an unpleasant odour within three hours.
*   Soaked wiring, which increases the risk of fire and computer hardware malfunction.
*   Soaked ceilings and wall cavities, which emit an unpleasant odour within 12 hours.
*   Soaked hardcopy collections, especially those arranged on shelving less than three feet above floor level.
*   Moisture damage to paper records, especially those in filing cabinets arranged against walls.
*   Moisture damage to artwork, posters and ornaments mounted on walls.

Crisis potential:

*   A roving reporter hears about the flood while having coffee at a nearby cafe. She arrives in the library's information desk and looks for an interview. She calls for a camera crew. The resulting story: 'Office floods are always a risk. Here's what happened to a local library, and all because of a burst pipe. What are they going to do with those wet computers, and all those soggy books?'

Generic tabletop exercise

1. Refer to your current disaster plan and related emergency measures. Make a list of the first steps that you would take to resume business in your water-damaged building. Write a schedule with realistic time estimates for the steps that you have listed.
2. Discuss the availability of moisture control vendors in your area. Determine which vendors have the necessary equipment (dehumidifiers, fans, etc.) and are prepared to respond quickly to your library's call for emergency service.

3. Staff members at your site are told to resume business at an alternative site, such as another branch or neighbouring office. Make lists of:

   a. the basic operations that you will be able to conduct within 48 hours from the alternative site (e.g., communicating with key managers, issuing bulletins, dealing with vendors involved in repairs and the resupply of lost assets). Note: assume that the alternative site lacks a serviceable telephone. You must use your cellular telephones to perform basic operations. Will cellular telephones function as required in these circumstances?
   b. the equipment that you will need to offer the basic operations listed above
   c. people and organizations that you must contact as soon as possible regarding immediate library issues.

   This exercise will be limited to one hour.

11.3.3   Severe weather/power failure

On April 19 next year, a windstorm hits your community. High winds and heavy rainfall cause serious transportation problems across the region. Telephone service – including cellular networks – becomes unreliable owing to overloading and equipment failures. Temperatures drop to just above freezing level during the daytime.

On April 20, the winds become even stronger – up to 110 km/hr. A regional power failure occurs at 2.45 p.m. The immediate effects include:

- A blackout in most parts of your community, with brownouts in other areas of the region.
- Flooding on local roads and sections of a major highway. Power lines are down across the region.
- The closure of numerous offices and retail outlets. Because of the failure of electric-powered gates in parking lots, many people cannot use their vehicles to drive home. Public transport is seriously delayed and overextended.
- Emergency lighting failures at a number of local offices. Ambulance crews are forced to respond to numerous injuries caused by flying debris, downed tree branches and slip-and-fall injuries. Downed power lines lead to road closures.

On April 21, the winds start to abate across the region, but the power failure continues. Work crews are unable to repair many downed wires because of inaccessibility, storm debris and a high demand for equipment. Other effects include:

- Food distributors complain that the power failure has shut down their freezers, and thousands of tonnes of frozen food has started to thaw. Regulations insist that this food be discarded. There could be food shortages for several days.
- Hundreds of organizations lose vital data from their servers, and much of this data has not been properly backed up.
- A seniors' home in the area reports the deaths of four residents owing to hypothermia. The home's emergency generator breaks down during the night and there is no heat in the building. A number of other residents are suffering from chills that could lead to pneumonia. Because the alarm and monitoring systems lacked power, two elderly Alzheimer's patients wandered away from the home and are missing.
- Rumours circulate concerning fuel and prescription drug shortages, break-ins and other criminal activities in neighbourhoods without police patrols, and a general breakdown in government services.

On April 22, the regional government declares a disaster in your community and neighbouring areas. While the storm has abated, temperatures remain lower than the seasonal average. Power remains off throughout much of the region. It could remain off for up to five days in some neighbourhoods.

Your tasks:

1. Determine what each of the participants in your exercise group needs to survive the above scenario in their homes. Take into account the needs of young children, the elderly and yourselves. Assume that you might be isolated in your residence for several days.
2. Determine the potential effects of the storm and failure on your library, its branches, and its stakeholders, e.g. employees and patrons. How can you continue to communicate with stakeholders? What are the essential messages that you should give them?
3. Assume that your library workspace has been cold and dark for several days. Determine the effects of these conditions on office fixtures, IT and other electrical equipment, and your specific work areas. Note: a plumbing leak has caused water damage to offices and carpets in your building. What will you need to resume operations?

This exercise will be limited to one hour.

11.3.4 High winds and winter storms

On a Tuesday during the first week of December, a snowstorm sweeps across your region and buries it under between 25 and 30 inches of snow in 36 hours. Winds cause the snow to drift in various locations, and driving becomes very difficult. Public transport is overloaded, as drivers abandon their vehicles and attempt to get home by bus. Temperatures fall to -35 degrees with wind chill. The cold snap will last for a week.

Casualties:

One senior library manager is injured in a car accident. He is hospitalized for a week. An IT librarian is injured by ice falling from a neighbouring roof. She will be off the job for a fortnight. Several slip-and-fall injuries occur around the outside of your branch, mostly to people entering or leaving the building. A courier is hurt by a car skidding out of control as it leaves the parking lot.

Damage:

- Downed power lines across your region. Falling tree branches and the closure of local parks get people talking about 'a mini-ice storm'.
- Brownouts become frequent. On Wednesday morning at 5.00 a.m., the power at your library site fails altogether for no less than 24 hours. The interior of the building starts to cool down immediately. Your back-up generator – if your building has one – will supply power for one hour only before it runs out of fuel.
- Absenteeism at your library site reaches 40 per cent by Wednesday afternoon.
- Much of the region shuts down for several days.

Crisis potential:

- A local TV station broadcasts a report about a rumoured long-term closure of library facilities, with staff lay-offs. Several regular patrons hang around outside library branches, hoping for information regarding the status of library services.

Generic tabletop exercise

1. Refer to your current disaster plan and related emergency measures. Make a list of the first steps that you would take to continue business in your department. Write a schedule with realistic time estimates for the steps that you have listed.
2. Civic authorities demand that your library building remain open to provide shelter for homeless people and anyone stranded by the weather. Determine the implications of this demand. Will the library be prepared to accommodate homeless and stranded people? If so, for how long?
3. Your department is told to resume operations at an alternative site, such as a neighbouring branch or office. Make lists of:

   a. the basic operations that you will be able to conduct within 48 hours from the alternative site (e.g., communicating with key managers, issuing bulletins, dealing with vendors involved in repairs and the resupply of lost assets)
   b. the equipment that you will need to offer the basic services listed above
   c. the people and organizations that you must contact as soon as possible regarding library operational issues.

   This exercise will be limited to one hour.

11.3.5   Toxic spill

During the Friday morning rush hour, a train carriage containing ammonia overturns on the nearby tracks. The wind sends fumes away from your branch, but there is a risk that the wind will shift, and that fumes will affect your employees and operations. Senior library management decides to evacuate the building as a precautionary measure. Municipal authorities order local roads closed immediately. Employees in neighbouring offices begin to leave the area in droves, causing gridlock and long queues of traffic.

Casualties:

- The driver of the train dies of fume inhalation and other injuries.
- A police officer at the scene must be taken to hospital owing to burns and fume inhalation.
- At your site, three employees complain of headaches and sinus problems, possibly owing to ammonia fumes.

Damage:

- There is no damage at your library site, and fortunately the wind does not shift. The fumes dissipate within 12 hours, but the situation is very tense for several more days. Over the next three days, absenteeism reaches 30 per cent.

Crisis potential:

- A local TV station broadcasts footage of the spill, with your library building and its sign in the background. Various managers from other local institutions call contacts at your library to make sure that it is safe and secure. A brief 'reassurance programme' is called for.

Generic tabletop exercise

1. Refer to current disaster plan and related emergency measures. Make a list of the first steps that you would take to continue operations in your department or library building. Write a schedule with realistic time estimates for the steps that you have listed.
2. Consider your library's current emergency kit. Determine what you should add to it – such as protective masks, goggles – to protect employees during a toxic spill.
3. Your staff members and co-workers are told to resume business at an alternative site, such as another branch or neighbouring office. Make lists of:
   a. the basic operations that you will be able to conduct within 24 hours from the alternative site (e.g., communicating with key managers, issuing bulletins, dealing with vendors involved in repairs and the resupply of lost assets)
   b. the equipment that you will need to carry out the basic tasks listed above
   c. the people and organizations that you must contact as soon as possible regarding library operational issues.

   This exercise will be limited to one hour.

11.3.6   Power failure

Next Thursday morning, damage to the local electrical grid causes a power failure in your library's general area. Power might not be restored for 36 hours. Your emergency generator fails within one hour of activation. The building starts getting cold almost immediately.

Casualties:

- None

Damage:

- Potential computer systems problems and data loss. IT staff members will spend part of the next day attempting to find possible glitches caused by the power failure. Your building becomes uncomfortably cool in approximately one hour. Food in the refrigerators begins to spoil in eight hours.

Crisis potential:

- None

Generic tabletop exercise

1. Refer to your current disaster plan and related emergency measures. Determine whether it is necessary to activate emergency measures. If so, make a list of the first steps that you would take to resume your library's operations. Write a schedule with realistic time estimates for the steps that you have listed.
2. Determine the number and location of functional flashlights and other sources of emergency illumination in your building.

3. Determine the effects of the power failure on your security systems – alarms, CCTV, locks, etc. If the power failure shuts down these systems, how will you protect library assets?
4. Your department is told to resume operations off-site, at a branch in another neighbourhood or at an empty office in a nearby shopping mall. Make lists of:
   a. the basic operations that you will be able to conduct within 24 hours from the alternative site (e.g., communicating with key managers, issuing bulletins, dealing with vendors involved in repairs and the resupply of lost assets)
   b. the equipment that you will need to offer the basic services listed above
   c. the people and organizations that you must contact as soon as possible regarding library operational issues.

   This exercise can be limited to one hour.

11.3.7   Data loss/possible theft and misuse

At a library management group meeting, it is noted that a substantial amount of electronic data and confidential paper files have gone missing from different departments. It remains to be determined whether the data has been stolen or unintentionally erased. The amount of missing data is uncertain at present. There are fears that some of the data regarding borrowers is highly confidential, and that it might be used to embarrass the library. It might also be sold as 'corporate intelligence'.

Casualties:

• None

Damage:

• To be determined. There are *rumours* regarding a disgruntled employee, sabotage and the introduction of a virus into the system. In any event, the missing electronic data might pertain not only to borrowers, but also to the Human Resources department, your library's purchasing plans and the potential sale of library assets. It is difficult to determine exactly how many paper files have gone missing. There is also the suspicion that some paper files might have been surreptitiously photocopied for use outside the library.

Crisis potential:

• There could be a number of crises if the data falls into the wrong hands. If the media report the loss there could be a general decline in confidence in the library. At the very least, there is a reasonable likelihood that the library will be publicly embarrassed.

Generic tabletop exercise
1. Refer to your current disaster and crisis management plans. What parts would be useful to you and your colleagues under the circumstances? Make a list of the first steps that you would take to determine if you have suffered any loss of data (either electronic or paper) in your department. Do you have your essential data backed up for resumption purposes? Are your back-ups current? How long would you need to access this essential data under the circumstances?

11.4 Tabletops for managers

11.4.1 Director/Head Librarian/Board of Directors

- Following a regional emergency such as a severe winter storm and consequent power failure, communication between your library's senior managers and supervisors becomes especially challenging, and transportation will be difficult. For yourself or -selves, outline:
  a. emergency supplies needed in your residence(s)
  b. special concerns regarding family members (small children, elderly relatives, disabled relatives)
  c. at least two different routes to get from your residence to your library office, by car or other means of transport
  d. at least two different routes to get to the library's alternative site, by car or other means of transport
  e. any special risks to your residence(s) in the event of a toxic spill, high winds. or winter storms.
- Following a fire at a library branch, you are ambushed by media representatives looking for interviews. What are the three main points that you will strive to get across to the media? What wording will you avoid at all costs?
- Consult your library's current disaster and crisis management plans. Identify three points that you believe require clarification or updating. Remember that in many cases those plans will be your guide after an emergency.

11.4.2 Assistant Head Librarians

- Following a regional emergency such as a severe winter storm, communication between your library's senior managers and supervisors becomes especially challenging, and transportation will be difficult. For yourself and your key supervisors and other staff members, outline:
  - emergency supplies needed in your residence(s)
  - special concerns regarding family members (small children, elderly relatives, disabled relatives)
  - at least two different routes to get to your library site, by car or other means of transport
  - at least two different routes to get to your library's alternative site, by car or other means of transport
  - any special risks to your residence(s) in the event of a toxic spill, high winds or winter storms.
- Following a serious fire at your library site, external investigators call your office looking for information regarding the situation, any damage to the library's facilities and the security at the damaged site. These are informal enquiries that you can handle without the assistance of other managers. Nevertheless, it is essential to send the right message. What three points will you attempt to get across in telephone calls of no more than ten minutes in duration? What kinds of PR problems could arise under the circumstances?
- Following a fire at one of your library branches, you are ambushed by media representatives looking for interviews and quotes. What are the three main points that you will strive to get across to the media? What wording will you avoid at all costs?
- Consult your disaster plans and related emergency documentation. Identify three points that you believe require clarification or updating. Remember that your plans and documentation will be your guide during and after a disaster.

11.4.3   Departmental Manager/Branch Manager

- Develop a basic plan for an off-site operations centre for the use of the employees in your department or at your branch in the event of a fire that causes serious damage. Assume that you must be away from the building for ten days. Indicate:
  - at least two possible alternative sites for your staff, aside from another branch or library site
  - the number of telephones and computer workstations you will need
  - the vital records (paper and electronic) and portable technology (e.g., laptops) that you will need access to during your time away from the building
  - an approximate cost for the set-up and management of the centre.
- Consulting maps of your region, determine three safe gathering sites for your library's employees following a regional emergency such as a toxic spill. Take into account:
  - locations of the residences of your branch employees
  - potential risks between safe gathering sites and employees' residences
  - advantages and disadvantages of different sites.
- Devise and apply a grading scale (e.g. 'A', 'B + ', 'B', 'C', 'F', etc.) for the different sites.

11.4.4   Any library manager or supervisor

- Design for yourself/yourselves 'a department in a portable/handheld device' in the event of an emergency that seriously damages and limits your access to your site. Develop a list of electronic files that you will need while you are away from the building. These files might include:
  - human resources data
  - facilities management data
  - essential files that must be backed up and available at all times
  - emergency PR bulletins
  - staff telephone numbers and addresses.
- You may also specify what kind(s) of hardware, software and security features you would prefer.

11.5   Pandemic influenza exercise

High levels of access to library sites and resources give rise to concerns about the safety and security of library employees during a pandemic. In recent years, pandemic influenza outbreaks have occurred with disturbing results. The following tabletop exercise can be carried out in libraries of all kinds. Consult Appendix 2 for more information and examples of guidelines.

Background
Recent forms of pandemic influenza are similar in a number of ways to the Spanish Flu that caused millions of deaths worldwide during 1918–19. Victims of these diseases could suffer severe respiratory problems and eventually the failure of multiple organs. In such cases, death can

follow in a short time. At present, public health experts are warning people in their jurisdictions that an outbreak of pandemic influenza is likely at some point in the future; in your region, some scientists and public health officials have suggested that an outbreak is 'inevitable'. Despite efforts to develop mass immunization campaigns and to prepare the local populace for the worst, there are still fears that the results of a pandemic could lead to a global catastrophe. Possible results include:

- millions of deaths
- a long economic downturn: a recession or depression
- the destabilization of various political regimes, mostly in the Third World
- the displacement of populations
- famine
- declines in sectors such as transportation and tourism.

In your region, results could include:

- a general slowdown of local business activity for several months; permanent closure of many small and medium-sized businesses
- the failure of local tourist and hospitality industries
- increasing unemployment.
- the closure of public institutions such as schools, colleges, universities, theatres, government offices, malls and stadiums
- the quarantining of healthcare facilities such as hospitals and seniors' residences.

Your library and its employees could experience:

- increasing absenteeism, owing not only to sickness but also to employees' fear of contracting the disease in the workplace
- work process slowdown and backlogs throughout the organization
- the postponement of projects and other activities
- slowdowns at the offices of organizations with close ties to the library
- morale and productivity problems
- difficulties in arranging travel anywhere outside your region
- concerns regarding the safety of employees who have recently returned from areas where pandemic influenza has hit hard.

Scenario
One weekend this September, eight people die of pandemic influenza in local hospitals. Over 1500 cases are reported in your region among all age groups. The prognosis for many is poor.

The disease has spread quickly across the continent, and city cores are virtually empty. News broadcasts note that people prefer to stay at home. There is a sense of panic across your region.

Local governments are preparing to declare a disaster. Authorities are considering the closure of the local airports. There are grave concerns regarding the failure of transportation and distribution systems for essentials such as foodstuffs, medicines and fuel.

Your tasks

1. Determine the best uses of your library's alternative site(s) under the circumstances of the pandemic scenario. Consider the library's need for ongoing communications with employees, patrons and affiliated organizations. Also take into account the possibility that your library management might choose to continue business on an 'essential services only' basis, and that the alternative site(s) might be the only fully functional work area(s) in your library system.

2. Determine methods to decrease the chances of contracting pandemic influenza while working in the alternative site. These methods might include advanced sanitation procedures, strictly controlled access, restricted ventilation, reduced travel, and wireless communications.
3. Develop procedures to shut down the alternative site(s) when the risk of pandemic influenza infection subsides.

You have 60 minutes. Appoint a recordkeeper to take note of comments and recommendations. Good luck.

11.6   Tabletop exercise management tips

At the beginning of any tabletop exercise, it is wise to appoint an exercise leader, whose responsibilities include:

- Ensuring that participants understand the scenario and tasks under consideration.
- Keeping track of the time, and respecting the time limit. (Note that it is inadvisable to allow an exercise group to exceed a time limit. Awareness of it can sharpen participants' focus and contribute to more useful outcomes.)
- Keeping participants on topic; helping them to avoid distractions and irrelevant discussions.
- Encouraging participation from all members from the group.

Each exercise group should have a recordkeeper to note comments, observations and relevant concerns. Senior library management should review the records of each exercise before releasing them to other library employees and stakeholders. Frequently, tabletop exercises lead to more questions than answers; planners might find these questions useful for the enhancement or revision of plans.

Finally, coffee, tea and snacks are appropriate during exercises, and senior library management should be sure to thank library employees for participating in exercises.

11.7   Conclusion

There are other ways to test plans and train employees: evacuation (or fire) drills, an IT shutdown and reboot from back-ups, or a series of lectures, seminars, films and multimedia presentations. All of these have their uses and benefits. In many libraries, however, tabletop exercises are easier to arrange and carry out. Also, in the experience of many planners, tabletop exercises produce the best results in the shortest time, and can support other forms of testing and training.

11.8   References

11.8.1   Interviews

In this chapter I have quoted a Jamaican information consultant, a corporate library director in New York City, an emergency services coordinator in Ottawa, Canada, a school librarian in Atlanta, Georgia, and a public library branch manager in Texas.

Process and results

12.1 The overwhelming question

Will it work?

Your disaster plan is complete. That is, you have finished a satisfactory draft of the plan, while advising your colleagues that it is 'a living document' that will never be perfect. It should be revised annually, and updated whenever major changes occur at your library.

'There's always something that needs enhancement', says a corporate librarian in Sydney, Australia.

> We decided to conduct tabletop exercises twice a year, and the IT librarian performs quarterly tests in which he shuts down our systems and makes us work with back-ups for a few hours. We have also arranged more strategic alliances, since we discovered that many vendors don't have disaster plans, and if something bad occurred, they would not be able to help us. So we've made alliances with vendors who are better prepared.

As for her planning documents, they are evolving as well:

> Our first draft was 250 pages. Over two years, I managed to delete more than half of it. We had included a lot of material that was out of date or simply unnecessary. The second draft was 100 pages. The IT librarian stripped out 20 pages that he adopted as standard operating procedure for his department. He did not want his IT plan to be included in our full corporate plan because IT had different routines and post-disaster requirements.

Her current draft has 75 pages, with one 'detachable section' that is similar in many ways to the Disaster Manager's Kit in Appendix 4. 'We've uploaded the plan to our library website, and invited staff members to comment on it. I think we're ready for whatever might hit us. We're certainly better prepared than we were years ago, when we didn't have a plan. But the ultimate test will be an actual disaster.'

This librarian has been effective in her role as her library's disaster planner owing to a number of factors. Her personal attributes, essential for anyone charged with planning responsibilities, include:

- skill and experience in her library's management and day-to-day routines
- an interest in risk mitigation and disaster planning
- an awareness of the risks that prevail at her library
- a willingness to set a good example in preparing herself, her family and her workspace for disasters
- persistence and patience in developing the plan, establishing strategic alliances, arranging orientation and training sessions, and answering questions about the entire process

• a determination to get her colleagues involved in the planning process, usually through their participation in tabletop exercises.

Ironically, she hopes that the effectiveness of her efforts and the success of her library's disaster plan are never proven by a disaster. But if one strikes, she believes that her library will be prepared.

Perhaps your situation is similar to hers, in that you have a disaster plan that you have tested and kept up to date. All appears to be in order. You believe that you are prepared for all of the risks indicated in your initial risk assessment and analysis. The question, however, remains: Will your plan work in actual disaster circumstances?

12.2   A case history: in the beginning

Consider the case of a public library in the American Midwest. Located in a medium-sized town, the library comprises a main branch and two smaller branches in outlying neighbourhoods. The main branch was constructed in the 1940s; the other branches are newer. The staff includes eight full-time librarians and approximately 30 full-time and part-time technicians, clericals and other support personnel.

You are familiar with many of this library's activities and challenges. Its collections are heavily used. It offers children's programmes such as storytime and reading clubs. There is a seniors' reading group and a knitting circle. There is also a backlog in the Technical Services department and a need to upgrade much of the IT hardware. The library's website needs to be redesigned and updated. The carpeting in the main branch needs to be replaced; the worn spots of the recent past have become unsightly holes.

As for the employees, their morale is high and their local reputation is good. Staff turnover is low. Everyone appears to get along with each other, and the Head Librarian, a woman in her mid-40s, is popular and well respected. She hopes to expand library services over the next decade, although she recognizes that shrinking budgets could force her to modify her plans.

After events such as 9/11 and Hurricane Katrina, the town's municipal council decided to upgrade its security and disaster plans. At first, council members concentrated on managing the risks at the Municipal Hall. Then they turned their attention to local schools, the reservoir, the municipal works yard, the fire hall and police department, roads, bridges, overpasses, and finally the library.

'The Mayor dropped in one day and told me to do something about disaster planning', says the Head Librarian.

> *He was pretty vague about what I should do, although he mentioned the importance of preparing for bad winter weather. And then he told me that the library could not rely on extra funding from the municipal council because the disaster plan for the Municipal Hall had cost so much that there was no money to spare. So I had to get things done on my own.*

But she was not really on her own. The reference librarians offered her information on security management and disaster planning. The librarian in charge of IT said that he would 'look after the systems side'. Other employees expressed their willingness to participate in orientation and training. Finally, the elderly facilities manager who worked at the three library sites told her that he was ready to concentrate on preventative maintenance, and to 'make the necessary adjustments to the physical plant'.

Meanwhile, the Library Board – six enthusiastic volunteers from the business community – told her that there were ways to raise funds for emergency supplies and anything else that the library might need. 'The Board Chairman – a retired lawyer – showed up at my office', says the Head Librarian. 'He was wearing his [US] Marine Veteran's cap. When he does that, I know he means business. He told me that he and other Board members would come through for the library, and that I was to start work on the disaster plan immediately. And so I did.'

12.3   The process: preparedness

The Head Librarian began with a risk assessment and analysis. She investigated the history of the library, and noted that over the years it had been threatened by natural risks such as tornadoes and winter storms. She also discovered that all three of its buildings had flooded owing to faulty plumbing.

'In the closet where we keep old records, I found a photo album that contained pictures of flood damage over the years', she said.

> There had been one large flood in each of buildings, and a number of smaller floods. These were from burst pipes. In addition, one of the newer branches had problems with its roof, which cracked one winter. When the spring thaw set in, water seeped into the library and caused a lot of damage. But while I had a series of photos of this event, nobody remembered it. The memory of these things can fade with time. But I had to take that leaky roof into account in my planning.

She and the Board Chairman inspected the interiors and exteriors of the library buildings. They noted wear and tear, mostly from winter weather. And they paid particular attention to proximity risks such as the railway tracks that ran near one of the smaller branches and a highway close to the main library: 'Big tanker trucks travel down that highway all the time. Some of them contain chemicals or oil. So I noted the possibility of a toxic spill near that library site.'

She asked her staff for their comments and observations. Did they remember anything related to the library's risk profile? They did. The Head Librarian heard from several employees about matters of interest to anyone developing a disaster plan:

- old, exposed wiring in basements
- potential mould growth in wall cavities and basements
- 'questionable' plumbing, such as old pipes with pinhole leaks
- a database in the Technical Services department that had not been properly backed up
- inadequate storage and security for a collection of antique maps of the region

- clogged drains in two of the library's parking lots
- infrequent fire drills and unfilled fire warden positions
- inadequate fire extinguishers.

The Head Librarian pointed out these items to the Board Chairman. While he asked her to attend to the backing-up of the Technical Services database, he promised to recommend to the Board and municipal council the necessary repairs and upgrades to library facilities. The Head Librarian described the problems and their solutions in the library's risk mitigation plan, along with suggestions for enhanced security at all sites and regular orientation and training for the entire library staff.

12.4   The process: response

The next step was the development of a disaster response plan. The Head Librarian wrote a brochure that resembled the example reproduced in Chapter 3. There were a number of differences. Since the library was not located in a seismic zone, the Head Librarian saw no need to include material on earthquakes. She did not consider bio-chemical mail threats to be a risk to her library. And since none of the library buildings contained sprinkler systems she did not mention them in the brochure. She had a local printer produce a supply of brochures on glossy stock, and handed a copy to each employee, and, to demonstrate her initiative, she sent copies to the Library Board and the municipal council. Everyone was impressed. The Board Chairman told her that she had gumption, which was the highest compliment that he could pay to anyone. 'The brochure was a big hit', says the Head Librarian. 'People in neighbouring towns plagiarized it for their organizations, but I didn't mind. I was flattered, and as far as I was concerned, disseminating useful information has always been my job as a librarian.'

A branch manager asked her about 'in-house disaster education'. Could the library use the brochures for staff orientation and training? The Head Librarian agreed that this was a good idea, but did not want to proceed with an education programme until the other plan components had been developed:

> At that point I started to panic. Planning is not a linear process. Every observation, procedure and piece of advice can have many implications. A library disaster plan can seem comprehensive, with every contingency covered, but the person or people who developed that plan will worry about the inevitable imperfections and gaps. Disasters are chaotic events that can challenge the most sophisticated planning. That's why we must keep working on our plans, and adapt them to new risks that become evident over time. No risk profile is static. I had to ask myself whether my planning was adequate. I had my doubts, but I decided to continue until I had reached the end of the final phase, which covered our operational resumption measures. I would finish the first draft, test it and then try to fill the gaps.

Here she has summarized typical concerns of librarians who accept the responsibility for developing plans. There can be misgivings and a feeling that one has missed essential points; there are concerns about misinterpreting observations from staff members and risk assessment data. Unfortunately, some people give up at this point and leave the plan for somebody else to finish. In many cases, the plan remains forever half-finished. As events unfolded at the library under discussion, the Head Librarian was wise to continue her work on the plan.

12.5 The process: resumption

The Head Librarian discussed different approaches to post-disaster planning with the Library Board, the facilities manager and her staff. She attended a library association conference that featured a workshop on planning, and learned the differences between recovery, continuity and resumption. For her library's purposes, she opted for a resumption plan. The workshop gave her ideas for its contents, and when she arrived back at her office she started working on it.

'I didn't think that we needed anything too elaborate', she says.

> *I didn't want to form teams to handle various post-disaster tasks since I thought that it would be best if the entire library staff worked together as a team, which could deploy members to deal with disaster circumstances as they arose. Besides, we didn't have enough money in the budget to cover the organization and training of separate teams, and I was concerned about the sustainability of individual teams over time. On a [US armed forces] base, there can be dozens of teams to deal with different situations, and team members can go through regular training and retraining to keep up to date. But our library is not a military unit. Naturally our mindset is different. I can understand the appeal of team development in other libraries, but I did not think that it was appropriate for ours.*

She developed a post-disaster plan that is similar in many ways to the Disaster Manager's Kit in Appendix 4. It begins with a list of the safety equipment that she or her deputy would need if a disaster struck. It continues with a reminder to follow the instructions in the library's response brochure. Thereafter, the following contents appear:

- disaster recognition guidelines
- disaster declaration guidelines
- damage assessment checklists
- potential local/proximity effects: roads, supply of essentials including food, gas and pharmaceutical products
- strategic alliances
- emergency communications and transportation
- 'returning to normal' guidelines.

She decided that the library would make no public declaration of a disaster before the municipal council and Library Board had been informed. She let the facilities manager write the damage assessment checklists. The foreman at the municipal works yard contributed a checklist of the potential effects of disasters on local infrastructure, and then added the checklist to the plan for the works yard. He also helped the Head

Librarian to write a strategic alliance plan, and introduced her to people outside the library who could contribute to its resumption efforts. These included a moisture control vendor in a neighbouring town, a moving company and a security firm.

The Head Librarian decided to give the library's strategic alliance partners an orientation session that covered the disaster plan. She invited representatives to a 45-minute meeting where library clericals served coffee and doughnuts, and the Head Librarian delivered an informal lecture on the disaster plan. She told the attendees that their contributions would be essential after a disaster. She ended the session with a tour of the main library. The attendees took notes and discussed the best ways to deal with the library's post-disaster problems. The only complaint came in the form of a question: Why had nobody arranged strategic alliances for the town's institutions before? Such alliances were commonsensical. All organizations should have them. The Head Librarian was pleased to see that she was pursuing the right course.

The provision of post-disaster communications and transportation services was difficult to arrange for the town. The Head Librarian planned for a lack of telephone and bus services for periods of up to one week. Consulting branch managers and their staff, she determined that, despite high levels of absenteeism, the main library and its branches could remain open, although any scheduled programmes might have to be postponed. Her concerns about a power outage were dispelled when a Board member donated a natural gas emergency generator to the main library, and promised to donate smaller generators to the branches in future.

The 'returning to normal' guidelines were made easier to formulate through the library's reliance on post-disaster employee meetings during which people could talk about any disaster that had occurred and how they felt about it. 'I knew that we could depend on employees' high morale to get us past the most of the negative emotional effects', says the Head Librarian.

> Our town does not have a professional mental health team or a resident clinical psychologist. The high school has a counselor, but she told me that she didn't feel competent enough to deal with post-disaster psychological stress. So in the library, we'll talk through our problems with each other. If somebody suffers from PTSD or other serious issues, they can go to their doctor.

The normalization plans of libraries in many small towns are equally simple, but nonetheless effective for many post-disaster situations.

12.6   The process: backtracking

Throughout the resumption planning phase, the Head Librarian became aware of matters that she should have dealt with earlier. Such realizations are common during the planning process, and backtracking is necessary if a plan is to be comprehensive. As she finished the 'returning to normal' guidelines, the Head Librarian recognized the need for a fully-documented IT response plan. She was relieved when the librarian in charge of IT showed her a plan that he had developed, one that resembles that which appears in Appendix 6. 'Our IT librarian had also made strategic alliances with several vendors, who were prepared to replace IT components as required', says the Head Librarian. 'He had also updated our IT security protocols, and made sure that vital data was backed up in different locations. He told me that we could lose all three of our buildings, but we would still have our data. I tried to look happy about this, but it was difficult.'

The Head Librarian increased the library's emergency supplies, adding larger flashlights and extra batteries to the emergency kits on each site. She also included battery-operated radios to each kit so that employees could listen to emergency radio broadcasts if there was a power failure. She advised all employees to carry a supply of any prescription drugs they needed, for illnesses such as diabetes, asthma, depression and hypertension. 'I recommended that everybody have a two-week supply of any prescriptions they needed', she says. 'The local pharmacies could run out of certain drugs if post-disaster transportation were a problem.'

She also realized that the recommendations for risk mitigation had not been acted upon, and reminded the Board Chairman of his promise. She saw that while promises are easy to make, having them carried out can be challenging. In a jovial way, she told the Board Chairman that she would repeat her reminders regularly, and that if he wanted to silence her, he would have to make sure that the library's old fire extinguishers were replaced. The Board Chairman delivered the new extinguishers shortly thereafter. The Head Librarian thanked him, and mentioned the old wiring in the basements. The Board Chairman complimented her on her persistence.

12.7   The process: orientation, training and testing

After she had finished compiling her documents, the Head Librarian worked on a number of tabletop exercise scenarios that described a variety of disasters to her library: fire, flood, a power failure, data losses due to viruses, a pandemic and severe winter weather. She attached a series of tasks to each scenario, and set a time limit of one hour on each exercise. Then she distributed response brochures and copies of the resumption plan to all library work units, and scheduled exercises at each library site. Employees participated with enthusiasm, and the exercises generated a plethora of comments and observations that the Head Librarian would use to enhance the library's disaster plan. In fact, she realized that the enhancement would involve serious revisions, most of which would cover matters that she had not considered.

Employees signed up at a local school to take first-aid training. They chatted over coffee and lunch about home safety preparations. They volunteered to become fire wardens, and to attend warden orientation sessions at the fire hall. The library handed out pamphlets on cold weather safety to patrons. Eventually, the municipal council invited the Head Librarian to address it on regional disaster preparedness. The Head Librarian was delighted to have reaffirmed the usefulness of the library to the community.

But early one morning a fire broke out in the basement of one of the library branches.

12.8   A real scenario

Old and damaged wiring can exist harmlessly for many years, but in seconds it can cause fires and lead to the destruction of substantial assets. In the basement of the branch, behind a pile of empty book cartons, an electrical short in old wiring started a fire that spread through the basement, up a staircase, and into the main floor of the branch. Firefighters arrived quickly and doused the flames; their fast action limited the damage and saved the branch structure.

The Head Librarian arrived on the scene as the firefighters opened their hoses on the blaze:

> *I'll never forget the smoke and steam that poured out of the branch windows. The smell of burned material – carpeting and plastic furniture – was acrid. The Fire Chief told me to stand farther away from the action so that I didn't succumb to the fumes. And then I realized that – my God! – the library had experienced a disaster, the real thing that we had been talking about for months.*

The Mayor and Board Chairman arrived shortly afterwards, along with a number of media representatives. Library employees showed up and asked the Head Librarian if there was anything that they could do.

> *I told them that we were activating the resumption plan as soon as we could. And when the Fire Chief had declared the building safe to enter, we would get to work. I reassured branch employees that their jobs were safe. Frankly I was worried about their having too many resumption activities to carry out in a short time. And that's when the moisture control people arrived – thanks to our strategic alliance plan – and we began the process of getting back in business.*

The moisture control vendor sent a team of six technicians, who worked alongside a team of four movers. In ten hours, they had:

*   inspected the building structure to ensure that it was sound
*   inspected heavy furniture – including all shelving units – to ensure that it was stable
*   inspected all electrical circuitry, plumbing, and heating, ventilation and air conditioning machinery to ensure that it was safe
*   scheduled repairs or replacements to damaged but salvageable items
*   scheduled repairs to damaged wall and ceiling components
*   removed IT hardware beyond repair, and sent it to a recycler
*   removed charred or otherwise irreparable carpets and furniture, and taken them to the local dump
*   recorded all observations and photographed damage for future reference
*   set aside damaged books, periodicals and other items from collections for assessment by library staff
*   commenced mould control and dehumidification measures.

It turned out that while the fire had inflicted serious losses, the water from firefighters' hoses had caused even more damage. As is the case in many libraries in which fires have broken out, the water used to save them can contribute to the further deterioration of assets. This is not an argument for preventing firefighters from doing their job, since they have rescued countless people from burning buildings, and with their hoses and related fire control measures they can prevent the destruction of entire cities. But their success can come at a cost, as librarians have discovered numerous times. In the case of the branch under discussion, more than two-thirds of the branch's hardcover collection was drenched, as were approximately one-half of the paperbacks, periodicals, CDs and DVDs.

'I had to make a difficult decision', says the Head Librarian:

> I could either agree to the moisture control vendor's attempts to save a lot of the water-damaged items, or I could simply discard them and order replacements. I base my decision to save any damaged item on characteristics including uniqueness or scarcity, monetary value, popularity, reference usefulness and the extent of the damage. If the damage is substantial, the item circulates infrequently and the monetary value is negligible, I discard the item. I do not believe in heroic and probably expensive measures to save a book that can be inexpensively replaced, or hasn't circulated in years, or was on the verge of being discarded anyway.

The Head Librarian understands why academic libraries will go to extreme lengths to save collections of incunabula, rare manuscripts, artworks and special editions and printings, and she encourages librarians in charge of such collections to develop highly sophisticated post-disaster conservation programmes:

> Libraries that hold truly valuable collections should consider hiring conservators. At least, those libraries should have conservators on call – experts not just in general conservation but also in the kinds of conservation necessary for specific items. The conservation of a fifteenth-century herbal will differ from that of a modern first edition of an important novel, or a medieval map, or a collection of early photographs. But our branch did not hold such items, and while it was painful to discard so much of the branch's holdings, I knew that we wouldn't have difficulty in replacing works by popular authors such as J.K. Rowling and John Grisham. Within days, we received cash donations from the community to restore the collection. In fact, the firefighters' hoses performed a lot of unintentional weeding for us. I'm sure that would not be the case for libraries with large and valuable collections, but it is for many public libraries such as ours.

12.9   Use of the disaster plan

The Head Librarian is thankful that she had developed a disaster plan. Despite its imperfections, it served its purpose well:

> I don't think that we could have resumed operations at the branch as quickly as we did. It reopened two weeks after the fire. There were big empty spaces on the shelves, and there was no carpeting. The new furniture had arrived from the warehouse of a local vendor, and our IT vendor had delivered new hardware. Most of our services were unavailable, but I thought that it would be best to reopen as soon

as possible and show our patrons that we were still in business. It was good for
branch employees as well. They felt uncomfortable waiting for things to happen, and
were relieved when patrons started walking through the branch's front doors again.
Everybody breathed a sigh of relief.

While some of the instructions and checklists in the plan appeared to be obvious, or
'no-brainers', the Head Librarian and her staff appreciated their inclusion. They admit
that there is much confusion, and at times chaos, after a disaster, and they found the
plan's clear and straightforward procedures to be as reassuring as they were helpful.
This is not to say that the plan forced them into a narrow course of action. Rather, it
allowed them leeway to make a number of decisions on the spot, and to be flexible
regarding the discarding of damaged items.

'I think that you can add too many details to disaster plans', says the Head Librarian.

You have to allow library managers and staff members to react to post-disaster cir-
cumstances as they occur. You can't set strict time limits on activities such as inform-
ing stakeholders and reopening damaged facilities. By their very nature, disasters
can disrupt the best-laid plans. So you have to expect surprises, and figure out quick
ways to deal with them.

12.10   Post-resumption

The branch fire gave the Head Librarian an opportunity to review the plan and
audit its contents. She found a number of gaps that she filled promptly, and she
clarified a number of points regarding reopening procedures and post-disaster site
security. One issue that she noticed was that despite the branch's fast reopening
and resumption of operations, it took months for some employees to accept what
had happened. At a post-disaster debriefing session at the branch, a couple of older
employees said that they felt an overwhelming sense of loss when they saw damaged books and carpeting being discarded. 'They apologized for raising this issue,
but I and other people assured them that their comments were important. In the end,
most of us felt a sense of loss. But later that year, morale returned to normal, and
that's probably because we resumed business and repaired the damage as soon as
we could.'

For the Head Librarian, the final lessons of the disaster were clear:

- It is often the little things that lead to disasters. We are wise to prepare for big natural catastrophes such as hurricanes and earthquakes, but we should not ignore smaller threats such as
old wiring and plugged drains. We should take all risks into account.
- Planning is a process, not a product. For planners, this has become a cliché, but all stakeholders should understand it.
- The planning process does not end with a document in a binder. It continues for as long as a
library exists. It is imperfect but essential for the survival of libraries in dire circumstances.
- A smaller disaster – such as that described above – can be a good teacher, one that shows us
how to prepare for much worse events.

Since ancient times, libraries have been at risk. In the minds of many librarians, our history begins with the Library of Alexandria, which was a wonder of the world. Historians are vague on the details of the Library's destruction, but all agree that it disappeared, most likely owing to a disaster or series of disasters. Its loss teaches us that libraries, like everything else, will one day vanish. Our goal must be their survival, for as long as possible. Hence the need for disaster plans.

12.11   References

12.11.1   Interviews

In this chapter I have quoted a corporate librarian in Sydney, Australia, and the Head Librarian of a public library in a Midwestern US town.

Further reading

The works cited here are practical and readable resources for those who wish to learn more about disasters and disaster planning in general, and the planning process for libraries in particular. Together, these works can serve as a 'planner's shelf' for reference purposes. While there are numerous other titles on the topic, these below are highly recommended.

Alire, C. A. (Ed.). (2000). *Library Disaster Planning and Recovery Handbook*. New York: Neal-Schuman.

Bolt, B. A. (2003). *Earthquakes* (Fifth edition). San Francisco, CA: W.H. Freeman & Company.

Fink, S. (1986). *Crisis Management: Planning for the Inevitable*. New York: American Management Association.

Kahn, M. B. (2012). *Disaster Response and Planning for Libraries* (Third edition). Chicago, IL: American Library Association.

Kovacich, & Dr, G. L. (2003). *The Information Systems Security Officer's Guide: Establishing and Managing an Information Protection Program* (Second edition). Burlington, MA: Butterworth-Heinemann.

Morris, J. (1986). *The Library Disaster Preparedness Handbook*. Chicago, IL: American Library Association.

Raphael, B. (1986). *When Disaster Strikes: How Individuals and Communities Cope with Catastrophe*. New York: Basic Books Inc.

Raven, J. (Ed.). (2004). *Lost Libraries: The Destruction of Great Book Collections Since Antiquity. Basingstoke, Hampshire*. UK and New York: Palgrave Macmillan.

Smil, V. (2008). *Global Catastrophes and Trends: The Next 50 Years*. Cambridge, MA and London, England: The MIT Press.

Wellheiser, J., & Scott, J. (2002). *An Ounce of Prevention: Integrated Disaster Planning for Archives, Libraries, and Record Centres* (Second edition). Lanham, MD and London: UK The Scarecrow Press and Canadian Archives Foundation.

Whittow, J. (1980). *Disasters: The Anatomy of Environmental Hazards*. London: Penguin Books Ltd.

Wilkinson, F. C., Lewis, L. K., & Dennis, N. K. (2009). *Comprehensive Guide to Emergency Preparedness and Disaster Recovery*. Chicago, IL: Association of College and Research Libraries.

Appendix One

Lancaster Gate Public Library Crisis Management Plan

Table of Contents
    I. Purpose and definitions
   II. The Crisis Management Team (CMT)
  III. Recognizing a crisis
  IV. On-the-spot agenda for the head librarian/spokesperson or delegate
   V. Mistakes media representatives make
  VI. Crisis Management Command Centre (CMCC)
 VII. Crisis management tabletop exercises
VIII. Distribution, auditing and revisions
  IX. Sample media releases

I. Purpose and definitions

This Crisis Management Plan is intended to brief members of LGPL's Crisis Management Team on the basics of crisis response. Key terms are defined as follows:

Crisis

A crisis is defined as an instance of bad PR that has negative implications for LGPL's business operations and corporate reputation. Crises can arise from events such as natural disasters and security breaches, as well as from issues of censorship and patrons' complaints.

Disaster/Emergency

A disaster is an event that transcends the control of civil and other authorities, that causes injuries and serious damage, and that impairs the library's ability to conduct business. An emergency is an event that disrupts operations, but which LGPL management and civil authorities can control, settle, or defuse.

Crisis Management Team (CMT)

LGPL's Crisis Management Team comprises senior managers who have been trained to respond to a crisis. Team members can include representatives from all LGPL departments.

Spokesperson

The spokesperson is a senior manager who speaks for LGPL during a crisis. The message of the spokesperson is the official word of LGPL, suitable for quotation in all media. To date, the head librarian has served as LGPL's spokesperson.

Delegate

In the absence of the spokesperson, a delegate will stand in his or her place and accept all of his or her responsibilities for delivering the appropriate message to LGPL members and the general public.

Crisis Response

A crisis response is the total effort made by the LGPL to address a crisis. Crisis responses can last for many months and involve every employee.

II. The Crisis Management Team (CMT)

If a crisis occurs or appears about to occur, the CMT should assemble as quickly as possible. Assembly locations include:

- The head librarian's office
- Another space at the main library location
- A space at a LGPL branch

During a crisis, one of these locations will be considered the Crisis Management Command Centre (CMCC). See Section VI.

CMT members can also discuss the situation during conference calls. (In future, they might be able to deal with a crisis through wireless communications.)

CMT members should include:

- Head librarian
- Assistant librarian
- Department managers
- Human resources manager
- Facilities manager
- IT librarian
- Delegates as required for all of the above positions

If any team member is unavailable, a delegate can assume his or her duties. Other managers and supervisors could be asked to become pro tem CMT members as the situation warrants.

III.   Recognizing a crisis

The equivalent of a risk analysis in crisis management is a determination of the "crisis families" that pertain to a particular organization. LGPL crisis families can be organized as follows:

Disasters and emergencies

- Natural (e.g. flooding)
- Human-caused (e.g. data loss)
- Technological (e.g. toxic spill)
- Proximity (e.g. fire in the building next door)
- Cascading (e.g. winter storm that causes power outages, roof leaks, and data loss)
- Disasters are further broken down by categorizing those that:
- Involve casualties, including fatalities
- Do not involve casualties
- Involve serious damage to facilities
- Involve light or moderate damage to facilities
- Involve loss of electronic data or other sources of corporate information

Death/injury

- Death/injury of a senior librarian
- Death/injury of several employees in a single instance or during a brief time period
- Death/injury of a single employee

Note: Causes of death/injury include aircraft crashes and motor vehicle accidents, disasters, substance abuse, suicide and homicide.

Internal criminal activity

- Workplace violence
- Harassment (sexual, verbal, etc.)
- Vandalism and sabotage
- Information theft
- Data tampering
- Illicit sharing of confidential or sensitive information
- Extortion
- Blackmail
- False accusations / misrepresentation
- Theft

External criminal activity

- Employee indictment for criminal behavior outside the workplace
- Civil disobedience / protests and demonstrations
- Robberies, particularly with violence

- Kidnapping
- Hostage-taking incident
- White powder incident
- Arson
- Bomb threats
- Hacking and cracking
- Information theft and illicit distribution
- Blackmail
- Threat of violent crime on or near a LGPL site
- Violent crime on or near a LGPL site
- Police investigations regarding any of the above
- Court cases involving any of the above

Adverse government action

- Hostile legislation
- Hostile intervention
- Police investigation

Labour issues

[This branch of LGPL's crisis families includes job actions at neighbouring sites, e.g. any unionized organizations with offices or plants near LGPL sites.]

- Strikes
- Lockouts
- Picket lines
- Cases of alleged wrongful dismissal

Adverse journalistic activity/faulty public relations

- Ambush interviews
- Declining reputation
- False accusations
- Image distortion
- Leaks and violations of Privacy legislation and policies
- Premature disclosure
- Public testimony
- Hostile quote out of or in context
- Hostile rumours
- Special interest group activity

Corporate/organizational shift

- Merger with other libraries
- Shut down/permanent closure

Economic problems

- Recession
- Council cutbacks
- Local plant closure(s)
- Disruptions in the agricultural sector
- High local unemployment

IV. On-the-spot agenda for the head libarian/ spokesperson or delegate

You are LGPL's spokesperson, or the spokesperson's delegate. A reporter from a local media outlet approaches you on the street, OR contacts you by telephone. The reporter wants to interview you regarding a potential crisis at LGPL.

Follow these guidelines during the interview:

IDENTIFY (if possible):
- The reporter's name and employer.
- The source of the story. Does it spring from a rumour? Misinformation? Another news outlet?
- An anonymous internal source?
- The names of other LGPL employees whom the reporter has interviewed regarding the story.
- The kinds of documents that might have come into the reporter's possession, e.g. stolen correspondence, anonymous notes, etc.
- The reporter's deadline.

BE HONEST ABOUT:

Your own ignorance. If you know nothing about the story, say so. Promise to investigate it, and tell the reporter that you will contact him or her as soon as you have reliable information.

Your personal knowledge of the story. DO NOT SAY "NO COMMENT". If you know about it, you may say: "That's under investigation at present, and I don't want to give you incorrect information. Please call me back tomorrow." OR: " We will issue a press release tomorrow morning. I'll ask my assistant to e-mail you a copy."

AT ALL TIMES, BE:
- Polite, no matter how aggressive the reporter becomes.
- Accommodating. Let the reporter know that you want to help him/her.
- Dignified. Remember whom you represent, and avoid inappropriate language. Under crisis conditions, even experienced managers can say the wrong thing.
- Sensitive: If the crisis has involved injuries or fatalities, express condolences. Respect corporate confidentiality. Do not reveal details regarding injured or deceased LGPL personnel. Respect employee privacy.

REMEMBER:
- None of your comments to any media representative are off the record.
- Those accused of criminal acts are innocent until proven guilty. Until a court arrives at a verdict, all crimes are alleged.

- You will not have all of the facts concerning a particular incident for a substantial period of time.
- LGPL is proud of its contingency plans. It is prepared to survive a broad range of disasters and crises.
- LGPL's standards for ethical conduct are explicit and strictly enforced.

FOLLOW UP WITH:
- Press releases (See Section IX: Sample press releases)
- Media kits: folders with general information regarding LGPL, including annual reports and product brochures
- References to the corporate web site
- Return calls and e-mails, as required
- Further interviews, as required

V.   Mistakes media representatives make

Media representatives can be misinformed concerning the Lancaster Gate Public Library. Unfortunately, reporters will file stories on crisis-related topics without checking their information on library policies and practices. Among the most common mistakes that media representatives make:

- Confusing LGPL with other libraries in the region
- Working with out-of-date information: old annual reports, clippings, kits, brochures, etc.
- Trusting the wrong internal source for a particular story: a personal assistant does not necessarily know as much about an upper-level management problem as the head librarian.
- Failing to check the accuracy of sources; treating a rumour without confirming its accuracy. (This mistake is particularly common after a natural disaster.)
- Assuming that representatives from one library know the internal workings of another library

VI.   Crisis Management Command Centre (CMCC)

There might be no need to establish an off-site CMCC during or after a crisis. Ideally the main library locatin will suffice for most crisis management activities, including interviews and meetings with media representatives.

Following a disaster that involves damage to the main library location, however, a crisis management command centre can be established at any branch selected by the spokesperson. This branch should have the following features:

- Adequate parking for media vans and other vehicles
- A meeting space with chairs and a table
- Additional security

VII.   Crisis management tabletop exercises

The following tabletop exercises demand responses to different kinds of crises that involve a number of "grey areas". There are adequate responses, but no response is absolutely correct or satisfactory. Nor will any particular response or responses immediately obviate a crisis. Exercise participants should take into account the fact that crises often take months—and occasionally years—to resolve.

Tabletop Exercise No. 1: Body in the Parking Lot

Tomorrow morning at 5:15 A.M. police discover a man's body in the driver's seat of a late-model SUV in the parking lot of the main libary building. The man appears to have been shot in the head at least twice with a small-calibre handgun. The SUV is intact: no bullet holes in the vehicle's body or windows. Police suggest that the assailant might have known the victim. The vehicle had been locked after the shooting, with the engine turned off.

The victim is approximately 35 years old, Caucasian, dressed in dark slacks and a white cotton shirt. He wore eyeglasses and an earring. There were no signs of theft from the victim's body or the vehicle.

Reporters at the scene pick up a rumour that the man is an employee of LGPL who worked in the IT department. This turns out to be false. As the police investigation proceeds, it transpires that the man was associated with a gang involved in narcotics distribution, and that he was murdered by a member or members of a rival gang. The parking lot was a temporary meeting place for the victim and his associates.

Over the next week, local newspapers and broadcasts carry the story. The results:

- Some patrons tell reporters that they no longer feel comfortable visiting LGPL. One patron tells a BBC reporter that she's not sure that she wants to use the library in future.
- Six LGPL branches receive enquiries from patrons regarding the security of those branches.
- Several employees demand enhanced security measures in the parking lot. One requests a transfer to another LGPL site.
- Morale at LGPL declines. The atmosphere is subdued.

Your tasks

1. Review the corporate security policy and procedures. Does it cover situations such as that described in the scenario?
2. Compose a brief press release that informs the media that the victim was not an employee of LGPL. Include an appropriate expression of regret, and condolences for the victim's family.
3. Develop a normalization strategy to reassure all LGPL employees that their workplace is safe. You may recommend group meetings and verbal therapy, trauma counseling, and any other measures appropriate to your corporate culture.

Elect a record keeper to make notes during your discussion. You have 50 minutes. Good luck.

Tabletop Exercise No. 2: IT Fraud and Possible Data Theft

Paul Forbes-Thompson claimed that he had graduated with top honors in computer science from Cambridge. When he applied for a job in the IT Department at LGPL, everyone was impressed with him. His letters of reference praised his technical skills, leadership and team spirit. He worked well with his associates. At the end of his first year at the head office, his job evaluation was excellent. He was offered a substantial raise.

But Paul was not what he appeared to be. His diploma and academic transcripts were phony; his letters of reference were forged. While he was extremely clever, he had an anti-social personality disorder and a substance abuse problem. As his use of cocaine and ecstasy increased during his second year at LGPL, his demeanor became erratic. He was frequently late for work and rude to everyone around him. There were complaints about his tasteless and suggestive remarks to women in the office.

One morning, a senior manager noticed that his wallet and laptop were missing from his office. His executive assistant complained that her purse was missing from a drawer in her desk. An iPad had disappeared from the accounting department. Later that day, a woman in the IT department told her manager that she had seen Paul putting a purse in his briefcase. When questioned, he denied that he had the purse but refused to open his briefcase.

The next morning, Paul did not show up for work. Calls to his apartment went unanswered. Several days later, he was still absent and unaccounted for. The HR manager called the police to make a report. A CID senior officer took down the facts.

"First, his name's not Paul Forbes-Thompson," said the officer. "He's a fraud operating under several aliases. He's good at what he does, which is mostly data theft. But every now and then his drug problem gets out of hand and he loses control of himself. He's wanted in Ireland for forgery, possession of narcotics, possession of an illegal weapon and assault. There are a number of charges against him in America as well. If you see him again—and I doubt that you will—let us know immediately."

The officer also recommended a full systems audit and IT security check.

"Any of your organization's confidential data is saleable, and your former employee has lots of customers for it. He can be nasty, too. I'd check to make sure that he hasn't planted bugs in your network. He defrauded an outfit in Birmingham years ago, and made off with a lot of money. But he also caused the outfit's IT group a lot of grief by erasing data and screwing up electronic ledgers and other files. And he put a truly scurrilous message on the outfit's web site that upset a lot of people. Eventually the media got a hold of the story, and everything got messy. The police never found him. He's a very smart crook, even though he never went to Cambridge."

The next day, the officer called back to say that Paul's apartment was empty. Apparently he had skipped town. But in the dumpster of his building, police discovered boxes of LGPL files and confidential materials, plus a number of receipts from a micrographics firm for scanning of documents.

"Have you started that systems audit yet?" asked the officer.

Your tasks

1. Review LGPL's IT Security Policy. Could it be enhanced to thwart frauds like Paul in future?
2. Review LGPL's IT Security Audit process. How long would it take to perform a full audit?

3. Identify your most sensitive and confidential files and documents in hard copy. Are they protected against theft?
4. Review your Crisis Management procedures. What are the first steps to take if a story about Paul's illicit activities at LGPL appears in the local newspapers?
5. Assume that you will never recover any of the data that Paul has stolen. What are the implications? What are the risks to LGPL's reputation?
6. Review your HR department's background check procedures. How carefully does LGPL look into academic and professional qualifications? Could a fraud get somebody to pretend to be an academic reference?

Elect a record keeper to make notes during your discussion. You have 60 minutes. Good luck.

VIII.   Distribution, auditing and revisions

Distribution

Distribution of this Crisis Management Plan is limited to members of LGPL's Crisis Management Committee and their delegates.

Copies of all versions of this Plan shall be submitted to the manager in charge of corporate records for confidential storage in the corporate archives.

Note: All materials pertaining to the compilation, updating, and use of this Plan should be submitted to the Records Manager as well. These include consultant's reports, correspondence, and Committee minutes.

Auditing

The Crisis Management Team will audit this plan annually. Auditing will comprise:

- A reading of the current Crisis Management Plan in full by at least two members of the Crisis Management Team
- Revisions to any section(s) of the Plan that are inaccurate or out-of-date
- Additions to the Plan as required
- Presentation of the audited Plan with a concise summary of any revisions and additions
- The Crisis Management Team's approval of the audited Plan

Revisions

Revisions to the Crisis Management Plan will usually consist of:

- Correction of any inaccuracies
- Updating of specific information regarding procedures, timelines, the database, the contact list, etc.
- Rewriting of different sections to reflect any recent experience of a crisis at LGPL.

IX.   Sample media releases

A. Kidnap/Hostage incidents

FOR IMMEDIATE RELEASE   DATE

LANCASTER GATE PUBLIC LIBRARY IN GOOD SHAPE AFTER HOSTAGE INCIDENT

London—Officials of Lancaster Gate Public Library (LGPL) met today with local police authorities to assist in the investigation of yesterday's ___(event)___ .

(Brief description of event, such as: "Close to closing time yesterday, a man dressed in army fatigues... ")

LGPL has had a contingency plan in place for some time to deal with an event such as this, and branch employees credit the staff with keeping people calm and protected.

At no time were patrons or the integrity of their personal records in jeopardy.

LGPL is working with local police to track down those responsible.

Lancaster Gate Public Library was founded in____ and will continue to serve the general public.

CONTACT:

Name:

Title:

Work phone:

Home phone:

B. Physical damage to premises/equipment by vandalism

FOR IMMEDIATE RELEASE   DATE

LANCASTER GATE PUBLIC LIBRARY IN GOOD SHAPE AFTER VANDALS TARGET BRANCH (EQUIPMENT)

London—Vandals overnight targeted Lancaster Gate Public Library (LGPL), leaving equipment overturned and damaged.

Although some of the damage is substantial, an official with the library said none of the machines stored any personal member account information.

___(name)___ , ___(title)___ , added he/she is confident that patrons will not be affected by the damage. The library maintains an off-site backup set of patron information, plus continual backups of all vital information.

As well, current regulations protect patron privacy.

All branches, including____ , will be open today.

LGPL is working with local police to track down those responsible for the damage and is offering a $_____ reward for information leading to their conviction.

CONTACT:

Name: Title:

Work phone:

Home phone:

C. Physical damage to premises/equipment by act of God

FOR IMMEDIATE RELEASE   DATE

LANCASTER GATE PUBLIC LIBRARY IN GOOD SHAPE AFTER FLOOD/ FIRE/ETC. DAMAGES EQUIPMENT

London—Lancaster Gate Public Library (LGPL) was damaged by a_____ overnight, leaving some equipment out of operation.

Although some of the equipment is affected, an official with the library said none of the machines stored any personal member account information.

The_____ branch, as with all other branches, will be open today.

___(name)___, ___(title)___, added s/he is confident that patrons will not be affected by the damage. LGPL maintains an off-site backup set of patron information, plus continual backups of all vital information.

As well, current regulations protect patron privacy.

CONTACT:

Name:

Title:

Work phone:

Home phone:

Appendix Two

Pandemic Management Program

Table of Contents

Overview

System-wide Issues

Section One: System-wide responsibilities
Section Two: Workplace sanitation
Section Three: Pandemic development and monitoring process
Section Four: Travel planning and safety
Section Five: Stand down procedures

Senior Management

Section One: Preparedness and mitigation
Section Two: Pandemic watch and warning
Section Three: Critical functions and essential services
Section Four: Personnel and skill sets for critical functions and essential services
Section Five: Additional coping techniques for critical functions and essential services

Departments, Branches and Work Units

Section One: Preparedness and mitigation
Section Two: Critical functions and essential services
Section Three: Personnel and skill sets for critical functions and essential services
Section Four: Additional coping techniques for critical functions and essential services
Section Five: Alternative organization chart
Section Six: Supplier confirmation

Appendices

Appendix One: Critical Function Offsite Operation Form
Appendix Two: Pandemic Impact Report

Overview

In light of the ongoing risk of a global influenza pandemic, LGPL has developed this Pandemic Management Program with the following intentions:

- To enhance the safety of employees and visitors to the Central Library and branches
- To increase the security of all LGPL operations during a pandemic
- To ensure the continuance of all critical functions during a pandemic
- To ensure that LGPL meets the expectations of patrons, sponsoring bodies and the general public; and that LGPL meets its community and financial obligations
- To provide individual LGPL departments, branches and work units with the most effective methods of dealing with challenges that arise during and after a pandemic
- To serve as an orientation and training tool. This Pandemic Management Program is intended to cover all LGPL employees and operations for the foreseeable future. Since an outbreak of pandemic influenza could occur at any time, this program will be updated regularly. This program will form a part of LGPL's disaster plans.

System-wide Issues

Section One: System-wide responsibilities

During a pandemic, LGPL will continue to acknowledge its responsibilities to patrons, sponsors and the general public. LGPL's system-wide responsibilities will include:

- Continued communications with the Board; continuing work on current projects and administrative matters
- Continued communications with sponsoring agencies
- Continued communications with the general public via media releases regarding LGPL business operations and services, as needed

Responsibilities to LGPL employees will include:

- Ongoing measures for employee security and safety, e.g. high levels of sanitation at the main library and branches
- Sensitivity to employees' needs in the event of illness
- Adjustment of work processes and schedules as required
- Adjustment of workspace as required to restrict disease transmission. During the pandemic, LGPL senior management will continue to provide leadership and, as much as possible, to direct day-to-day operations. In the event of absences among the management team, their responsibilities can be carried out temporarily by their immediate subordinates, or by prearranged deputies.

Section Two: Workplace sanitation

To protect yourself and your colleagues, make sure that your workspace has a high standard of sanitation. Follow these precautions:

- Frequent hand washing: after washroom use, before meals, after using public facilities such as buses, theatres and malls. Use soap and warm water.
- Cough and sneeze etiquette: cover nose and mouth when sneezing or coughing. Use Kleenex. Avoid unnecessary contact with sick persons.

- Disposal of paper towels and tissues: use proper receptacles and make sure that they are emptied regularly.
- Keeping surfaces clean: make sure that handrails, elevator buttons, keyboards, telephone handsets and cellular phones and other frequently touched surfaces are regularly cleaned.
- Recognize sickness in people with symptoms including cough and chest mucous, shortness of breath, runny nose, and fever. Persons with these symptoms should seek medical attention and stay at home if possible.

Section Three: Pandemic development and monitoring process

Local government authorities support the World Health Organization's (WHO's) definitions of various phases of a pandemic (see http://www.phac-aspc.gc.ca/influenza/ pi-pp-eng.php and http://www.ncbi.nlm.nih.gov/books/NBK143061/). Adapted for LGPL's purposes, these phases are:

Interpandemic period

Phase 1: No new forms of influenza have been identified by health authorities. Animals and human beings have not been affected by any but the standard forms of influenza.

Phase 2: A new influenza subtype has affected animals such as chickens. There are reports that these animals have infected human beings.

Pandemic alert period

Phase 3: There are further reports of animals infecting human beings. As yet, however, there are few confirmed instances of human-to-human transmission.

Phase 4: Small, localized groups of human beings develop the disease through human-to-human transmission. The first affected groups will most likely appear outside North America.

Phase 5: Larger localized groups of human beings develop the disease through human-to-human contact. At this point, the virus is adapting to human beings, but is still not fully transmissible. Nevertheless the risk of a pandemic is now substantial. Travel outside the country might be limited. LGPL management may choose to commence the implementation of the Pandemic Management Program.

Pandemic

Phase 6: Full pandemic, with potential for global morbidity. There could be closures of public facilities and other high-traffic sites. LGPL may experience higher absenteeism and surging demands from patrons and other stakeholders for pandemic-related information.

Section Four: Travel planning and safety

During Phases 5 and 6 of a pandemic, the following measures would be advisable:

- Avoid / discourage travel if possible. Do not travel to areas where influenza morbidity is especially high. Do not travel while sick.
- Enhance electronic communications to avoid travel. Rely on telephones and conference calling, e-mail and wireless resources.
- Take slower, less-traveled routes to avoid infection; depend on low-traffic routes and sites to obtain supplies, information, etc.

•   Postpone non-essential out-of-town events, conferences and training sessions

Section Five: Stand down procedures

Pandemics come to an end. To resume normal operations, carry out the following stand down procedures:

•   Listen for announcements from WHO, government authorities and local health authorities regarding the decreasing morbidity and pandemic risk.
•   Watch for decreasing absenteeism, but advise any employees who are still sick to stay home until they are fully recovered.
•   Resume normal operations in phases, particularly in response to patrons' demands for service and requests from regulators.
•   Reorder supplies and equipment as required.
•   Resume any projects that had been postponed owing to the pandemic.
•   Inform the Board and other stakeholders that LGPL is normalizing operations.

Senior Management

Section One: Preparedness and mitigation

Before the outbreak of a pandemic, make the following preparations to manage operations at the main library. Keep these preparations up-to-date:

Communications

❏   Ensure that managers have the necessary cellular phones and computer equipment that they need—laptops, tablets and other handheld devices, etc.
❏   Review and update a list of questions that patrons will ask regarding pandemic-related issues, e.g. province-wide emergency measures. Ensure that this list is distributed electronically as required.
❏   Update contact lists and directories with new telephone numbers, e-mail addresses, and other information as required. Note any changes in LGPL contact persons.

Managers and their executive assistants

❏   Encourage employees to stay at home if they fall ill.
❏   Encourage employees to wash their hands upon entering LGPL buildings, before eating, and after washroom use.
❏   Organize annual pandemic updating and orientation sessions (30 minutes) for LGPL employees. Sessions will include an update on the current pandemic risk, safety measures in the workplace and employees' residences, and the acquisition of any new equipment and supplies to be used for the purposes of pandemic management.
❏   Ensure that senior managers have deputies / backups, and that the corporate succession plan is up-to-date.

Sanitation

❑ Ensure that there is a small hand washing station at the reception desks, i.e. the desks nearest the main door to the LGPL work spaces.
❑ Remind employees to maintain the highest levels of sanitation in their residences and vehicles.

Section Two: Pandemic watch and warning

According to epidemiologists and public health authorities, a pandemic will most likely originate in Asia, and spread via air travel and commerce. In the beginning, the media will note the following circumstances:

• Increasing casualties and global morbidity
• Increasing numbers of refugees in areas where the pandemic has struck during its early stages
• Calls for assistance from governments in afflicted regions
• Flight cancellations
• Closure of harbours and airports
• Cancellation of public events, e.g concerts and sporting events
• Economic fallout in afflicted areas: disruption of food and fuel supplies

The first cases to occur locally will lead politicians at all levels to consult their pandemic management plans and strategies. Activation of LGPL Pandemic Management procedures should take place under the following circumstances:

• On the advice of government agencies, including BC government organizations concerned with health and safety
• At the demand of the Library Board
• In the event that the pandemic spreads locally, with a growing number of cases reported in local hospitals
• In the event that a LGPL employee falls ill and is diagnosed with pandemic influenza
• In the event that tenants in LGPL buildings fall ill and are diagnosed with pandemic influenza

Note: The actual timing of the activation is the responsibility of the manager or his/her deputy. It is prudent to activate Pandemic Management procedures promptly when advised to do so by senior government officials.

The activation process should include:

❑ A meeting of LGPL managers to announce the activation of the Program and its procedures
❑ A request to all LGPL managers to ensure that the Program is activated without delay in all departments
❑ A message to all Library Board members and sponsoring agencies regarding the Program's activation
❑ A message to the public regarding the Programs's activation

Section Three: Critical functions and essential services

Procedures

1. As soon as possible after the activation of the Pandemic Management Program, **all available managers will meet** in the main library boardroom. The purpose of the meeting is to confirm that:
   - ❏ LGPL is in pandemic management mode
   - ❏ Up-to-date information is available regarding key contacts and suppliers
   - ❏ The managers are ready to continue their operations either on of off site, as circumstances necessitate.
2. As the pandemic progresses, work locations may change at the discretion of the senior management. Initial work locations are indicated in the following table:

Critical function number	Critical Function	Surge potential (high, medium, low)	On site or off site
1	Announce and monitor activation of the Pandemic Management Program and procedures	High	On site
2	Communicate with LGPL employees as required	High	On or off site
3	Communicate with patrons and the general public	High	On or off site
4	Communicate with the Library Board and government authorities as required	High	On or off site
5	Delegate responsibilities in the event of increasing absenteeism	High	On site
6	Advise sponsoring agencies re: the status of ongoing operations, as required	High	On site
7	Activate system-wide succession plan as required	High	On site
8	Manage standard operations at normal levels, if possible	Medium	On or offsite

3. At any time during a pandemic, and particularly during new waves of pandemic cases, management may elect to hold meetings off site, or through conference calls. In the event that a manager and the patrons of his / her staff are forced to work offsite during the pandemic, they should confirm their offsite locations with the each other, the Director and the receptionists. Offsite activities can be recorded on the form in Appendix One of this program. Managers should also confirm that they have the necessary up-to-date applications and equipment offsite for continuing operations. Information regarding applications and equipment will be included in Appendix One of this program.

Ongoing measures

4. The Director or his / her deputy should be available to receive reports from managers regarding their **progress on carrying out critical functions** and essential services. These reports will arrive either electronically or in hard copy. See Appendix Two of this program for a sample of the report form.
5. The Director or his / her deputy should **review progress and new developments** regarding LGPL's major critical functions **every workday** if possible, preferably by telephone or e-mail. While some branches and departments might suffer serious absenteeism and disruptions, others will not. The latter should be able to work at almost full capacity, depending on the availability of in-house resources, services and materials from outside suppliers, and the reliability of transportation and communications systems.
6. In the event of increased absenteeism, management and staff will carry out their critical functions **at levels as close to normal as possible,** in order to avoid backlogs, and to support corporate morale.

Section Four: Personnel and skill sets for critical functions and essential services

LGPL's Succession Plan should contain the necessary advice concerning the skill sets required by the managers and key employees in departments such as IT, as well as the steps needed for orderly succession.

Section Five: Additional coping techniques for critical functions and essential services

Additional coping techniques include:
1. Change from face-to-face processes (e.g. meetings in the main library) to **conference calls or social media**
2. Change the **mode of delivery,** e.g. from postal service to courier, or from hard copy to electronic formats, as required.
3. In the event of a growing backlog or unexpected demand for service, **change the schedule or delivery date of a service or product.**
4. **Reduce decision-making steps;** making personnel responsible for more steps in a service delivery process
5. Farm out processes to **third parties.** Ask other managers for assistance if necessary.
6. Consider developing **an offsite capability** for certain critical functions. With the appropriate technology and security, which tasks can be completed at employees' residences?

Departments, branches and work units

Section One: Preparedness and mitigation

Before the outbreak of a pandemic, make the following preparations to manage operations in your workspace. Keep these preparations up-to-date.

Communications

❑ Ensure that the staff have the necessary cellular phones and computer equipment that they need—laptops, tablets and other handheld devices, etc.

❑ Update contact lists and directories with new telephone numbers, e-mail addresses, and other information as required. Note any changes in contact persons.

Staff

❑ Encourage employees to stay at home if they fall ill.

❑ Encourage employees to wash their hands upon entering the office or branch, before eating, and after washroom use.

❑ Organize annual pandemic updating and orientation sessions (30 minutes) for the all employees. Sessions will include an update on the current pandemic risk, safety measures in the workplace and employees' residences, and the acquisition of any new equipment and supplies to be used for the purposes of pandemic management.

❑ Ensure that managers have deputies with the appropriate skill sets

Sanitation

❑ Remind employees to maintain the highest levels of sanitation in their residences and vehicles.

Section Two: Critical functions and essential services

Procedures

1. As soon as possible after the activation of the Pandemic Management Program, **all available employees will meet** in their workspace. If the manager is unavailable, staff will meet in the office of his / her delegate. The purpose of the meeting is to confirm that:
   ❑ LGPL is in pandemic management mode
   ❑ Up-to-date information is available regarding patrons, key contacts and suppliers
   ❑ Employees are ready to continue their operations on and offsite
2. As the pandemic progresses, the priority of different critical functions may change at the discretion of the manager or his / her delegate. Critical functions are indicated in the following table:

Critical function ID number	Critical Function	Surge potential (high, medium, low)	On site or off site
1	Communications with the public	High	On or off site
2	Ongoing work on current projects	High	On or off site
3	Departmental management, resupply, etc.	High	On site

Note: At least 25% of the critical functions of LGPL could be carried out offsite. With enhancements to software and hardware, it would be possible to carry out most critical functions offsite.

3. Employees planning to carry out critical functions offsite should confirm their schedule their manager or his / her delegate during the pandemic. They should also confirm that they have the necessary up-to-date applications and equipment on site for continuing operations. Information regarding applications and equipment will be included in Appendix One of this program.

Ongoing measures

4. Employees should advise senior management or his / her of their **progress on carrying out critical functions** and essential services.
5. The department manager or his / her delegate should **review progress and new developments** regarding the critical functions **every day** if possible, preferably by telephone or e-mail. The manager will submit a weekly pandemic impact report to the Director delegate while this Pandemic Management Program is in effect. See Appendix Two of this program for the Pandemic Impact Report form.
6. In the event of increased absenteeism, staff will carry out the critical functions **at levels as close to normal as possible,** in order to avoid backlogs.
7. For more information regarding critical functions and essential services, staff should consult the **system-wide disaster plans.**

Section Three: Personnel and skill sets for critical functions and essential services

Critical function ID number	Minimum number staff to complete function	List position(s)	Certification required	List name of backup or alternative	Signing authority
1					
2					
3					

Section Four: Additional coping techniques for critical functions and essential services

Additional coping techniques include:
1. In the event of a growing backlog or unexpected demand for service, **change the schedule or delivery date of a service or product.**
2. Change the **mode of delivery,** e.g. from postal service to courier, or from hard copy to electronic formats, as required.
3. Change from face-to-face processes (e.g. meetings in the office) to **conference calls or social media.**
4. **Reduce decision-making steps;** making personnel responsible for more steps in a service delivery process
5. Farm out processes to **third parties.** Ask other departments for assistance if necessary.

The following tables contain guidelines for alternative procedures:

Critical function / essential service 1

Description:

Alternative procedure:

Critical function / essential service 2

Description:

Alternative procedures:

Critical function / essential service 3

Description:

Alternative procedures:

Section Five: Alternative organization chart

Alternative organization and management provisions and procedures include the following:

- ❏ In the event that a department manager is absent owing to pandemic-related circumstances, his / her deputy will assume the department's management duties on a temporary basis, and vice versa.
- ❏ In the event that the manager and his / her deputy are both absent owing to pandemic-related circumstances, the Assistant Director or his / her delegate will take over the management of the department on a temporary basis.
- ❏ In the event that the Assistant Director is unavailable owing to pandemic- related circumstances, the Director will delegate the critical functions of the department, or suspend them until such time that the appropriate staff are available to carry them out. In the event of a suspension of a department's critical functions, various LGPL departments, branches and work units might have to slow down or suspend operations for an indeterminate period. This provision is for a worst-case scenario, and LGPL's senior management will do everything possible to prevent it.

Section Six: Supplier confirmation

The most important suppliers during a pandemic will be:

Supplier	Contact information	Pandemic plan in place?
[Telecommunications]		
[IT hardware]		
[IT software]		
[Payroll and accounting]		
[Courier]		
[Stationery]		
[Facilities and sanitation management]		
[Security]		

CRITICAL FUNCTION OFFSITE OPERATION FORM

Lancaster Gate
PUBLIC LIBRARY

PANDEMIC MANAGEMENT

CRITICAL FUNCTION NUMBER

CRITICAL FUNCTION DESCRIPTION

EMPLOYEE NAME

OFFSITE ADDRESS

OFFSITE TELEPHONE NUMBER 1

OFFSITE TELEPHONE NUMBER 2

FAX NUMBER

ALTERNATIVE E-MAIL ADDRESS

COMPANY-SUPPLIED EQUIPMENT LIST

1   2

3   4

5   6

7   8

PRELOADED SOFTWARE CHECKLIST

Applications	Tested	Applications	Tested
❑	Yes ○ No ○		Yes ○ No ○
❑	Yes ○ No ○		Yes ○ No ○
❑	Yes ○ No ○		Yes ○ No ○
❑	Yes ○ No ○		Yes ○ No ○

BACKUP STAFF CONTACT INFORMATION

NAME	DEPARTMENT	TELEPHONE NO.	E-MAIL

PANDEMIC IMPACT REPORT

Lancaster Gate
PUBLIC LIBRARY

WEEK OF

DEPARTMENT

PANDEMIC MANAGEMENT

MANAGER/DELEGATE IN CHARGE

NUMBER OF EMPLOYEE ABSENCES THIS WEEK

(Number of person/days)

IMPACT ON THE DEPARTMENT'S OPERATIONS

ADDITIONAL   COMMENTS

Appendix Three

Main Library and Branch Post-Disaster Security Plan

Strictly Confidential

Lancaster Gate Public Library Main Library and Branch Post Disaster Security Plan

Table of Contents

    I.   Statement of responsibility
   II.   Identification badges
  III.   Visitor sign-in
   IV.   Controlled access to building
    V.   After-hours access to building
   VI.   Alarm systems
  VII.   Lock-up procedures
VIII.   Key management system
   IX.   Access card management system
    X.   Security of personal belongings
   XI.   Vandalism/light damage repair procedures
  XII.   Post-disaster additional security
 XIII.   Parking security
  XIV.   Audit schedule

Additional Information

A. Post-Disaster Security Risk Analysis
B. Security Manager's Immediate Post-Disaster Tasks
C. Information Security and Confidentiality

I. Statement of responsibility

The Security Manager will be responsible for the post-disaster security of LGPL sites. He or she should choose an appropriate delegate from the Facilities Management Department, and be prepared to assist in the auditing and updating of post-disaster security plans for LGPL branches.

II. Identification badges

Unless a visitor is a first responder, he or she must wear an identification badge. Visitors are required to return badges upon departure from LGPL sites. Badges should be numbered, and the visitors' names and badge number should correspond in the sign-in book. Note: All strategic alliance vendor representatives must wear LGPL identification badges.

III. Visitor sign-in

After a disaster, all visitors will be required to sign in at the Information Desks (or alternative reception areas) on arrival, and to sign out on departure. This policy applies to journalists and other media representatives.

IV. Controlled access to building

In the event of a post-disaster malfunction in the controlled access system, the Security Manager may restrict access to all except those involved in response and resumption activities.

V. After-hours access to building

After a disaster all after-hours access to the head office will be restricted to those involved in business resumption activities. The Security Manager should exercise caution in dealing with after-hours loiterers near LGPL sites.

VI. Alarm systems

If alarm systems are damaged during or after a disaster, the Security Manager will advise the Facilities Manager and assist in activating the appropriate strategic alliance(s). Repair or replacement of alarm systems is a top priority.

VII.   Lock-up procedures

After a disaster, the Security Manager should review LGPL's lock-up procedures and ensure that they meet current security needs.

VIII.   Key management system

The Security Manager will assist the Facilities Manager as required with the post-disaster administration of the LGPL's key management system. This will include:

*   Secure storage of all spare keys
*   Logging of all key distribution
*   Retrieval of all keys no longer needed by departing employees
*   Disposal of all obsolete keys
*   Ordering of new keys as required

IX.   Access card management system

The Security Manager will assist the Facilities Manager as required with the post-disaster administration of the access card management system. This will include:

*   Secure storage of all spare and temporary cards
*   Logging of all card distribution
*   Retrieval of cards no longer needed by departing employees
*   Disposal of all obsolete cards
*   Ordering of new cards as required

X.   Security of personal belongings

Primary responsibility for personal belongings rests with the individual owners. As in normal circumstances, thefts and mysterious disappearances should be reported to the Security Manager without delay. Note: Investigations of missing property may be postponed until the business resumption process (i.e. the first 72 hours after a disaster) is complete.

Personal belongings should be locked away in desks or lockers. Those belongings necessarily held in workspaces should be kept out of sight if possible.

XI.   Vandalism/light damage repair procedures

Post-disaster remediation of vandalism and light damage is the responsibility of the Facilities Manager, but the Security Manager should investigate all cases of vandalism and report extreme cases to the police.

XII.   Post-disaster additional security

The Facilities Manager will administer a strategic alliance with a security firm, which will provide temporary security personnel to guard perimeter areas of any LGPL sites that are insecure owing to damage. The Security Manager should work with the Facilities Manager to ensure that the appropriate number of guards is available for LGPL's purposes after a disaster.

XIII.   Parking security

Parking area security measures include:

* Lighting
* Cautionary signage: "This area is regularly patrolled and monitored ..."
* Nighttime escorts to vehicles
* Regular patrols

In conjunction with the Facilities Manager, the Securrity Manager should allocate space for the vehicles of emergency and clean-up crews, strategic alliance vendors, and visitors. This space should be at reduced risk from any debris, and permit easy exit from LGPL parking areas.

XIV.   Audit schedule

The Security Manager should audit and revise this Post-Disaster Security Plan annually. Audits should include a review of all new security technology, maintenance contracts for all security hardware, and the post-disaster working relationship between the Facilities Manager and the Security Manager. Division of tasks in extreme circumstances will remain an ongoing issue for everyone involved in the head office's security.

Additional Information

A. **Post-Disaster Security Risk Analysis**
   Taking into account LGPL's risk assessment and analysis, the Security Manager should be aware of the following post-disaster risks at LGPL:
   ❑   Water ingress, leaks and flooding from burst plumbing and water mains
   ❑   Smouldering fires, smoke and fumes from fires
   ❑   Downed wires and cables
   ❑   Broken glass and debris
   ❑   Power outages and brownouts
   ❑   Malfunctioning technology

❑ Intruders (mostly curious onlookers)
❑ Thieves and looters, particularly around the perimeter.

B. Security Manager's Immediate Post-Disaster Tasks

The Security Manager's tasks immediately after a disaster will be:

*   To cordon off damaged and hazardous areas.
*   To advise staff of risks from structural and non-structural damage, and to warn them away from hazardous areas. (This duty could be shared with the Facilities Manager.)
*   To advise the Library Management Group of any post-disaster security risks.
*   To call for additional security as required, as per the appropriate strategic alliance.
*   To monitor entrances and exits as required.
*   To ensure that post-disaster visitors to the LGPL sites have appropriate identification.
*   To give directions to first responders, repair crews, and the media as they arrive at the LGPL sites.

C. Information Security and Confidentiality

The Security Manager should play a role in LGPL's information security and confidentiality. The main issues covered in the policy and procedures are as follows:

*   Levels of confidentiality:
    *   Classified information: Library Management Group members only
    *   Confidential information: Library Management Group and employees only
    *   Private information: Relating to one individual only, usually personal data
    *   Public information: Can be released to the general public
*   Security implications of different kinds of media:
    *   Paper
    *   Digital
    *   Microfilm
    *   Multimedia
    *   Miscellaneous
*   Secure On-Site Storage of LGPL Information
    *   Cabinets, locked and unlocked
    *   Loose records (on desktops, etc.)
    *   Computer password controls
    *   Audits of data back-ups
    *   Storage area security
    *   Secure destruction of obsolete records held on-site
*   Secure Off-Site Storage of LGPL Information
    *   LGPL standards for off-site storage vendors
    *   Archival security
    *   Indexing of information stored off-site
    *   Post-disaster retrieval of vital records held off-site
    *   Secure destruction of obsolete records held off-site
*   LGPL Information in Transit
    *   Secure lock-up of LGPL information in staff-owned vehicles
    *   Secure transport of laptop computers and other portable IT devices
    *   E-mail security
*   Information Technology Security
    *   Anti-theft: securing hardware to supporting surfaces
    *   The importance of up-to-date firewalls and encryption

- The importance of regular, fully-tested data backups
- Preserving vital documentation: manuals, contracts, reports, and ledgers

All of the above items are matters of concern during the resumption process. The Security Manager should be available to provide ongoing support for information security at LGPL sites after a disaster

Appendix Four

Lancaster Gate Public Library

Disaster Manager's Kit: Ten Steps to Response, Resumption, and Continuity

Lancaster Gate Public Library Disaster Manager's Kit: Ten Steps to Operational Resumption and Continuity

Following an emergency or disaster at the LGPL Main Library or branches, take the following steps:

Step One: Are you fit and prepared to act as LGPL's Disaster Manager (DM)? If so, carry out the procedures in this kit. If not, allow your delegate to assume DM responsibilities.

Step Two: Ensure that you have the following items in your DM Kit:
- ❑ Cell phone or BlackBerry with LGPL contact directory
- ❑ Flashlight
- ❑ Spare shoes
- ❑ Work gloves
- ❑ Spare eyeglasses
- ❑ Camera
- ❑ Binoculars

Step Three: Open this manual and follow the instructions as required. For your personal safety, pay particular attention to the SECTION A: the Disaster Manager's Situational Safety Procedures.

Step Four: Complete SECTION B: Disaster Recognition and Declaration Procedures / Record of Events. Note: You may allow another member of senior management to complete this section.

Step Five: Complete SECTION C: the Damage Assessment checklists.

Step Six: Complete SECTION D: Review LGPL's Strategic Alliance List and activate the alliances required under the circumstances.

Step Seven: Review SECTION E: LGPL's Emergency Communications Plan

Step Eight: Review SECTION F: LGPL's Emergency Transportation Plan

Step Nine: Review SECTION G: LGPL's Normalization Program

Step Ten: Disaster Manager's Residential Emergency Procedures

Note: This generic kit contains material from previous chapters.
This kit is intended to serve as an example of a brief disaster plan.

Section A: DM Situational Safety Procedures

First, determine what kind of event has occurred, and follow the appropriate safety guidelines:

Fire

After evacuation:

- Avoid flames, smoke and fumes. Allow firefighters to enter the LGPL facilities.
- Once outside, go to your safe gathering site: [Space for location]
- Upon arriving at the safe gathering site, assemble available LGPL managers. If possible, contact absent members with your cell phone. Report any missing person(s) to your Fire Warden.
- Do not attempt to re-enter the building without the consent of the firefighters.
- Depending on the time of day and the severity of the threat, determine whether to allow employees to return to the site, to send them home, or to activate an alternative site.

Explosion

After evacuation:

- Go to your safe gathering site and wait for instructions from the Fire Warden or the police. Report any missing person(s) to the Fire Warden.
- Upon arriving at the safe gathering site, assemble the available managers. Contact absent members with your cell phone. Report any missing person(s) to your Fire Warden.
- Do not attempt to re-enter the building without the consent of the firefighters or police.
- Depending on the time of day and the severity of the threat, determine whether to allow employees to return to the site, to send them home, or to activate an alternative site.

Leaks/floods

Following the detection of water ingress:

- Avoid wet wires, electrical equipment and power outlets. Do not attempt to use a moisture-damaged computer, printer, fax machine or photocopier.
- Do not walk through water.
- Do not begin cleanup until after a safety inspection of wiring, outlets and equipment.
- If a LGPL building must be closed for more than two hours, assemble the available supervisors. Contact absent members with your cell phone.
- Depending on the time of day and the severity of the water damage, determine whether to allow employees to remain in the building, to send them home, or to activate an alternative site.

Bomb threat

After evacuation:

- Do not attempt to re-enter the building without the permission of the police.
- Consult police regarding the inspection of the involved site(s).

- Attempt to determine when LGPL employees will be allowed to return to their workplace(s).
- Depending on the time of day and the severity of the threat, determine whether to allow employees to return to the building, to send them home, or to activate an alternative site.

White powder incident / biochemical threat

After evacuation:

- Avoid touching any suspicious materials. If you come into contact with any potentially poisonous material, inform police immediately. Do not allow anyone but a HAZMAT specialist assist you in washing, removing clothes, etc.
- Do not attempt to re-enter the building without the permission of the police.
- Consult police regarding the inspection of the involved site.
- Attempt to determine when LGPL employees will be allowed to return to their workplace(s).
- Depending on the time of day and the severity of the threat, determine whether to allow employees to return to the building, to send them home, or to activate the Emergency Operations Centre.

Intruder/protester/threatening behaviour

Following departure/apprehension of the intruder or protester(s):

- Call 911 and request police response.
- If an intruder leaves any parcel, envelope, or suspicious item near your work area, do not touch it. Inform the police. Treat this scenario as a white powder incident.

High winds/snowstorm

- Expect power outages and telephone line disruptions.
- Avoid overhead hazards: tree branches, power lines
- Avoid glass and debris on sidewalks and streets.
- Travel only when necessary. Drive slowly.
- Make sure that your car has an emergency kit and a full tank of gas.
- Listen to your radio for emergency bulletins and traffic advice.
- Depending on the time of day and the severity of the damage, determine whether to allow employees to remain in the building, to send them home, or to activate an alternative site.

Toxic spill/gas leak

- Avoid the spill as much as possible. Do not loiter in the area. Call 911.
- Do not use matches or other open flames in the vicinity of the spill. Do not smoke.
- If you notice heavy fumes or toxic material seeping into the building, evacuate. Avoid fumes, vapour and smoke. Follow the firefighters' instructions.
- Depending on the time of day and the severity of the threat, determine whether to allow employees to remain in their work space, to send them home, or to activate an alternative site.

Power outage / brownout

- Keep flashlight in a handy place.
- Do not attempt to use computers, photocopiers and other electrical equipment.

- Avoid moving around in dark areas unless you have a flashlight. Do not attempt to examine, repair or open electrical equipment.
- Await instructions from maintenance personnel before restarting electrical equipment.
- Depending on the time of day and the severity of the threat, determine whether to allow employees to remain in the building, to send them home, or to activate an alternative site.

General precautions

- Know your limitations. Do not attempt physical tasks that are beyond your capability.
- Provide first aid as required.
- Be prepared to pass on DM responsibilities to your delegate if necessary.
- Do not move into or around spaces or areas that appear unsafe. Do not allow other LGPL employees to do so.
- To spot risks / threats: Look up, down, all around.
- In general, make sure that you know which LGPL supervisors are available at any given time, and which are on holiday, on leave, or travelling on business. Work with available supervisors to keep LGPL operations going.

Section B: Disaster Recognition and Declaration Procedures / Record of Events

To complete this section, complete the following steps in order:

Step One: Recognition of Events
Step Two: Information Gathering
Step Three: Decision to Declare a Disaster
Step Four: Disaster Declaration

Step One: Recognition of Events

When LGPL is threatened, the Disaster Manager will investigate the circumstances as quickly as possible and determine whether the event is:

a. An incident, e.g. a minor breach of security, a small loss of data, or a minor injury at the LGPL site.
b. An emergency, e.g. a number of minor casualties, a small fire or flood, or the loss of valuable equipment or documents.
c. A major emergency, e.g. a serious casualty or casualties, damage to work or public areas, or loss of physical assets that will involve substantial inconvenience, or a power outage that disrupts library operations *for up to 48 hours.*
d. A disaster, e.g. any damage to the building or physical assets that will disrupt library operations *for more than 48 hours,* any natural event (e.g. severe weather) that disrupts transportation or communications for more than 48 hours, or any serious loss of vital data (e.g. technical services files that have not been backed up).
e. A catastrophe, e.g. a large regional disaster that disrupts conditions for an extended period of time, and that involves multiple casualties, the loss of facilities, and damage to critical information assets.

f. A proximity event, e.g. an incident, emergency or disaster near the LGPL site or site(s) that could affect library operations. For example, a fire in a neighbouring building could force firefighters to seal off the area for several hours and cause serious inconvenience.

g. A crisis, e.g. an event involving negative media coverage of LGPL operations before, during or after any of the events described above.

Remember:

- Incidents, emergencies and major emergencies can be controlled and rectified by civil authorities and LGPL management. Civil authorities cannot control disasters, catastrophes, and crises.
- Following a toxic spill or any other disaster that affects the region, communications and transportation systems will slow down and possibly stop altogether for up to several days.
- The region's risk profile is unique. What occurs in parts of North America will not necessarily occur in Europe.
- It is not necessary to declare an incident, an emergency, or a major emergency. As serious as these events can be, they need not affect LGPL's operations for an extended period or cause large financial losses.
- In the event of a disaster or a catastrophe, a declaration is essential to begin library-wide resumption and continuity activities. In itself, the declaration indicates that LGPL acknowledges the gravity of the situation and is working to resolve the problems that the disaster has caused.

Step Two: Information Gathering

Having confirmed the occurrence of an event and determined its effects on LGPL, the Disaster Manager or delegate should collect the following data as soon as possible.

a. The general effects of the event on LGPL and equipment, including work space, shelving, cabinets, IT hardware, paper records and other information media, and communications.

b. The general effects of the event on the operations of senior management, employees, and suppliers.

c. The effects of the event on the library in general, particularly areas where members are served.

d. The effects of the event on major lifelines including highways, local bridges and overpasses, and key local roads.

e. The effects of the event on telephone lines.

f. The effects of the event on power sources, including local electricity providers and any other UPS resources.

g. The effects of the event on transportation and delivery systems including airports, bus service, courier services, and the postal system.

To determine the effects in a–g above, consult the following sources of information:

- Local radio stations
- Television, including local cable networks
- Internet sources
- Word of mouth
- Direct observation from a safe vantage point
- Out-of-town sources such as those neighbouring counties, states, or provinces and national news outlets

Note: To record the data collected during this step, the Disaster Manager should fill out Damage Assessment Form in Section C.

Step Three: Decision to Declare a Disaster

Based on the data collected, the Disaster Manager or delegate will perform the following tasks:

- Immediate notification (through 911) of first responders such as police, firefighters, and paramedics
- Notification of all LGPL supervisors and employees
- Notification of the City Hall
- Activation of strategic alliances (e.g. with moisture control vendors, computer systems suppliers, and couriers) as required

To declare a disaster is to recognize that the above measures will not be enough to contain the event as it unfolds. A disaster will have far-reaching effects, and will require the activation of most or all of LGPL's disaster plan components.

The Disaster Manager or delegate will also carry out the following tasks:

- Brief available managers
- Ask LGPL managers to inform employees *that a disaster has occurred.*
- Ensure that all necessary strategic alliances have been activated
- If necessary, approve the move to an alternative site
- Make oneself available for on-the-spot decisions regarding operational resumption of business processes in LGPL work units
- Make oneself available to consult with LGPL departments regarding damage to the LGPL sites.

Having declared a disaster, the Disaster Manager or delegate will record the following information in the space provided:

a. Date of disaster:

_____

b. Time of event:

_____

c. Basic description of event (e.g. toxic spill, flood etc.):

_____

d. Available supervisory staff informed of the declaration:

_____
_____
_____
_____

e. Time at which LGPL senior management was notified, and by what means (telephone, email, etc.):

_____

f. Time at which strategic alliances were activated:

_____

g. Additional comments:

_____

_____

_____

_____

_____

_____

Section C: Damage Assessment Checklists

LGPL has experienced:
- ☐ Fire/Smoke/Fumes
- ☐ Bomb threat
- ☐ Explosion
- ☐ Powder Incident
- ☐ Flood/Leak/Moisture Damage
- ☐ Power Failure
- ☐ High Winds/Severe Weather
- ☐ Winter Storm
- ☐ Toxic Spill
- ☐ Hostile Intruder
- ☐ Major Theft/Vandalism

LGPL areas inspected:
Fourth Floor (if applicable)
Damage [Severe, Moderate, or Light] to:
- ☐ Ceilings _____
- ☐ Floors _____
- ☐ Walls _____
- ☐ Air quality _____
- ☐ Collections _____
- ☐ Information Desk _____
- ☐ Shelving units _____
- ☐ Cabinets _____
- ☐ Carpets _____
- ☐ Computer hardware _____
- ☐ Telephones/fax machines _____
- ☐ Photocopiers _____
- ☐ Wiring/cables _____
- ☐ Paper records _____
- ☐ Microfilm/fiche/scanners _____
- ☐ Other information media _____

❑ AV equipment   _____
❑ Stationery supplies/forms   _____
❑ Art and ornaments   _____
❑ Kitchen equipment/supplies   _____
❑ Emergency supplies   _____
❑ Adjacent washrooms   _____
❑ Loss of work space: Partial_____ Total_____
❑ Loss of vital records: Partial_____ Total_____
❑ Loss of computer hardware: Partial_____ Total_____
❑ Casualties:_____ Estimated no.:_____
❑ Additional comments:

_____

_____

_____

_____

_____

Third Floor (if applicable)
Damage [Severe, Moderate, or Light] to:
❑ Ceilings   _____
❑ Floors   _____
❑ Walls   _____
❑ Air quality   _____
❑ Collections   _____
❑ Information Desk   _____
❑ Shelving units   _____
❑ Cabinets   _____
❑ Carpets   _____
❑ Computer hardware   _____
❑ Telephones/fax machines   _____
❑ Photocopiers   _____
❑ Wiring/cables   _____
❑ Paper records   _____
❑ Microfilm/fiche/scanners   _____
❑ Other information media   _____
❑ Stationery supplies/forms   _____
❑ Art and ornaments   _____
❑ Kitchen equipment/supplies   _____
❑ Emergency supplies   _____
❑ Adjacent washrooms   _____
❑ Loss of work space: Partial_____ Total_____

❑ Loss of vital records: Partial_____ Total_____
❑ Loss of computer hardware: Partial_____ Total_____
❑ Casualties:_____ Estimated no.: _____
❑ Additional comments: _____

_____

_____

_____

_____

Second Floor (if applicable)
Damage [Severe, Moderate, or Light] to:
❑ Ceilings   _____
❑ Floors   _____
❑ Walls   _____
❑ Air quality   _____
❑ Collections   _____
❑ AV equipment   _____
❑ Information Desk   _____
❑ Shelving units   _____
❑ Cabinets   _____
❑ Carpets   _____
❑ Computer hardware   _____
❑ Telephones/fax machines   _____
❑ Photocopiers   _____
❑ Wiring/cables   _____
❑ Paper records   _____
❑ Other information media   _____
❑ Stationery supplies/forms   _____
❑ Art and ornaments   _____
❑ Kitchen equipment/supplies   _____
❑ Emergency supplies   _____
❑ Adjacent washrooms   _____
❑ Loss of work space: Partial_____ Total_____
❑ Loss of vital records: Partial_____ Total_____
❑ Loss of computer hardware: Partial_____ Total_____
❑ Casualties:_____ Estimated no.:_____
❑ Additional comments:

_____

_____

_____

_____

Ground Floor
Damage [Severe, Moderate, or Light] to:

❑ Ceilings   _____

❑ Floors   _____

❑ Walls   _____

❑ Air quality   _____

❑ Server room   _____

❑ Collections   _____

❑ Information Desk   _____

❑ Shelving units   _____

❑ Cabinets   _____

❑ Carpets   _____

❑ Computer hardware   _____

❑ Telephones/fax machines   _____

❑ Photocopiers   _____

❑ Wiring/cables   _____

❑ Paper records   _____

❑ Other information media   _____

❑ Stationery supplies/forms   _____

❑ Art and ornaments   _____

❑ Kitchen equipment/supplies   _____

❑ Emergency supplies   _____

❑ Adjacent washrooms   _____

❑ Loss of work space: Partial_____ Total_____

❑ Loss of vital records: Partial_____ Total_____

❑ Loss of computer hardware: Partial_____ Total_____

❑ Casualties:_____ Estimated no.:_____

❑ Additional comments:

_____

_____

_____

_____

_____

_____

Basement Areas / Parking Lot (if applicable)
Damage [Severe, Moderate, or Light] to:

❑ Ceilings   _____

❑ Floors   _____

❑ Walls   _____

❑ Air quality   _____

- ❑ Collections   _____
- ❑ Information Desk   _____
- ❑ Shelving units   _____
- ❑ Cabinets   _____
- ❑ Carpets   _____
- ❑ Computer hardware   _____
- ❑ Telephones/fax machines   _____
- ❑ Photocopiers   _____
- ❑ Wiring/cables   _____
- ❑ Paper records   _____
- ❑ Other information media   _____
- ❑ Stationery supplies/forms   _____
- ❑ Art and ornaments   _____
- ❑ Kitchen equipment/supplies   _____
- ❑ Emergency supplies   _____
- ❑ Adjacent washrooms   _____
- ❑ Loss of work space: Partial_____ Total_____
- ❑ Loss of vital records: Partial_____ Total_____
- ❑ Loss of computer hardware: Partial_____ Total_____
- ❑ Casualties:_____ Estimated no.:_____
- ❑ Additional comments:

_____

_____

_____

_____

Information Technology Department Assets (if applicable)

Damage [Severe, Moderate, or Light] to:

- ❑ Walls   _____
- ❑ Electrical outlets   _____
- ❑ Other power sources   _____
- ❑ Wiring/cables   _____
- ❑ Heating, ventilation and air conditioning
     (HVAC)   _____
- ❑ UPS   _____
- ❑ Fire controls   _____
- ❑ Fire Suppression System   _____
- ❑ Locking hardware   _____
- ❑ Servers   _____
- ❑ Desktops: keyboards and mice   _____
- ❑ Notebook computers and portable devices   _____
- ❑ Modems   _____
- ❑ Routers   _____
- ❑ Telephones   _____

- ❑ Fax machines _____
- ❑ Printers _____
- ❑ Monitors _____
- ❑ Projectors _____
- ❑ Wireless access points _____
- ❑ Scanners _____
- ❑ Power bars _____
- ❑ Camera equipment _____
- ❑ Specialty devices including microphones,
  webcams and overdrive station _____
- ❑ Security cameras/DVRs _____
- ❑ Raised floor _____
- ❑ CDs _____
- ❑ Disaster recovery documentation
  and media _____
- ❑ Furniture/fixtures _____
- ❑ Carpeting _____
- ❑ Stationery supplies/forms _____
- ❑ Additional comments:

_____

_____

_____

_____

Library Stakeholders Affected By the Event:
- ❑ LGPL Senior Management
- ❑ LGPL Main Library
- ❑ LGPL branch employees
- ❑ LGPL customers
- ❑ LGPL suppliers
- ❑ Gift Shop

  Additional comments:

_____

_____

_____

_____

Effects of the Event on the Local community:
- ❑ Casualties
- ❑ Missing persons
- ❑ Communication breakdowns
- ❑ Transportation problems (e.g. gridlock, lifeline failure)

- ❏ Power failure
- ❏ Damage to numerous buildings
- ❏ Resource shutdown (e.g. schools, offices)
- ❏ Neighbourhood shutdown
- ❏ Evacuation(s)
- ❏ Increased absenteeism
- ❏ Government declaration of emergency or disaster
- ❏ Supply shortages (e.g. water, food, medical supplies, fuel)

Additional comments:

_____

_____

_____

_____

The Effects of the Event on Major Lifelines
- ❏ Gridlock
- ❏ Flooding
- ❏ Power lines down
- ❏ Roadway damage (e.g. fissures, sinkholes)
- ❏ Debris blocks (from buildings, power poles, flooding)
- ❏ Detours

Closures:
- ❏ Highway(s)
- ❏ Arterial route(s)
- ❏ Side street(s)
- ❏ Bridge(s)
- ❏ Overpass(es)
- ❏ Airports
- ❏ Other:_____

Additional comments:

_____

_____

_____

_____

Effects of the Event on Telephone Lines:
- ❏ N/A
- ❏ All lines down:
  2 hours 4 hours 8 hours 24 hours 48 hours 72 hours or more

- ❏ Some lines functional: Local Long distance
- ❏ Cellular networks down:
  2 hours 4 hours 8 hours 24 hours 48 hours 72 hours or more

- ❏ Estimated time to full recovery of telephone system:
  2 hours 4 hours 8 hours 24 hours 48 hours 72 hours or more

The Effects of the Event on Power Sources:

❑ N/A

❑ Total regional blackout:
  2 hours 4 hours 8 hours 24 hours 48 hours 72 hours or more

❑ Blackout in some neighbourhoods:
  2 hours 4 hours 8 hours 24 hours 48 hours 72 hours or more

❑ Blackout at the Main Library:
  2 hours 4 hours 8 hours 24 hours 48 hours 72 hours or more

❑ Blackout at LGPL branch(es):
  2 hours 4 hours 8 hours 24 hours 48 hours 72 hours or more

❑ Brownout:
  2 hours 4 hours 8 hours 24 hours 48 hours 72 hours or more

❑ Intermittent power failures throughout region:
  2 hours 4 hours 8 hours 24 hours 48 hours 72 hours or more

Source(s) of Regional Data:

❑ Local radio stations

❑ Television and local cable networks

❑ Internet sources

❑ City Ha;;

❑ Word of mouth

❑ Direct observation (from the windows and roof of the building. Note: Emergency supplies should include a pair of binoculars)

❑ Out-of-town and out-of-province sources such as major news outlets

Section D: Strategic Alliances

For immediate activation:

_____

_____

_____

_____

For activation in 72 hours:

_____

_____

_____

_____

Confirmation of notification:

- ❑ Mayor's Office
- ❑ City Hall Chief Clerk
- ❑ City Hall Communications Department
- ❑ Required strategic alliance partners

Other:_____

Section E: Emergency Communications Procedures

Table of Contents
a. Disruptions in organizational communications
b. Communications Monitor
c. Emergency communications fallback procedures
d. Departmental self-reliance

a. Disruptions in library communications

LGPL relies on a variety of technologies for the communications purposes, the foundation of which is the telephone, email and voiceover systems. Most disruptions in telephone service are due to either overloading or line breakage.

Overloading occurs in the following circumstances:
- ❑ A regional disaster such as a toxic spill, winter storm or flood
- ❑ Commencement of a snowfall or other severe weather in the general area
- ❑ A major disaster with national or international implications, e.g. 9/11
- ❑ A major political event, e.g. an election or resignation of an important government figure
- ❑ A major sporting event held locally
- ❑ Major holidays

In most regions, overloading has rarely lasted more than twelve hours during or following any of the above circumstances.

Line breakage occurs in the following circumstances:
- ❑ Line cut during construction
- ❑ A regional disaster, especially involving high winds, winter storms or heavy snowfalls
- ❑ A systems malfunction at the telephone company
- ❑ Shutdowns for emergency repairs or upgrades
- ❑ Sabotage or tampering

After any disruption, LGPL must wait for telephone service to be restored before resuming normal operations.

Other communications disruptions

Damage to roadways could disrupt postal delivery schedules and LGPL's couriers. Note that these organizations will not deliver to sites that appear to be damaged or otherwise unsafe.

b. Communications Monitor

In the event of a telephone system failure, the Main Library receptionist (and in some cases, the branch receptionists) will assume the role of Communications Monitor and perform the following tasks:

- Check with IT staff to determine whether the failure is internal or external
- Inform all available managers and supervisors, and ask them to inform their staff members.
- Tune in to local radio stations for reports of areas affected and estimated time of service resumption
- Accept messages delivered to the Information Desk and distribute to the appropriate staff members
- Accept couriered (or taxied) envelopes and parcels and distribute them to the appropriate staff members

In the event of a disaster, the Communications Monitor will keep the Disaster Manager and other LGPL managers informed of all new developments regarding telephone service. As soon as service resumes, the Monitor should inform the Disaster Manager.

Following telephone system downtime, the Communications Monitor should be prepared to answer questions regarding the following:

- Resumption of normal service and business hours at LGPL sites
- Possible loss of voice mail messages and e-mail left for employees shortly before the telephone system failure
- Possible loss of electronic transactions shortly before the telephone system failure
- Whereabouts of various managers and staff members
- Arrival of envelopes and parcels
- General inquiries regarding the security of LGPL, its employees and operations

The Communications Monitor should attempt to reassure members and other callers that operations are returning to normal, and apologize for any inconvenience. It is essential, however, to use caution in answering any questions regarding:

- The operation of LGPL's security systems
- Staffing levels at any LGPL department
- Residential addresses and telephone numbers of employees
- Any damage to LGPL facilities or other losses incurred during the telephone system failure

c. Emergency communications fallback procedures

In the absence of normal communications channels, LGPL must temporarily rely on:

- Delivery of messages through the use of employee vehicles
- Delivery of messages via taxis
- Delivery of messages via walking and cycling

Above all, personal safety must be considered before an employee attempts to deliver messages between sites, either on foot or in a vehicle. See the Damage Assessment Form for a checklist regarding post-disaster risks on roadways.

d. Departmental self-reliance

LGPL need not cease all operations owing to a disaster or disruption in communications. To continue operations in different departments, the following measures should be available:

❑ Communications monitoring on each floor

❑ Operational resumption/continuity planning for each floor

❑ Manual procedures for use in the event of an IT systems failure

❑ Appropriate post-disaster reporting of operations during a communications blackout

Section F: Emergency Transportation Plan

Table of contents

   I. Recommended strategic alliances
  II. Emergency use of employee-owned vehicles
 III. Post-disaster assessment of lifelines
  IV. Post-disaster routing
   V. Maps
 VI. Additional supplies in vehicles

I. Recommended strategic alliances

For LGPL's post-disaster transportation needs, the following strategic alliances should be organized as soon as possible, with all details agreed on in writing:

a. With courier companies: A strategic alliance that guarantees that the companies will make their best efforts to provide service after a disaster. The alliance will make LGPL a favoured client under emergency circumstances, at a pre-arranged price.

b. With a taxi company: A strategic alliance that guarantees that the company will make its best effort to provide service to specific sites after a disaster. Note: With their radio network, taxis are often well informed regarding the condition of lifelines following a disaster. LGPL could also use this strategic alliance for information-gathering after a disaster.

II. Emergency Use of Staff-Owned Vehicles

At their discretion, LGPL employees may use their own vehicles for business purposes in an emergency.

Emergency management orientation and training for LGPL employees should contain information on post-disaster road safety, particularly in light of problems arising from inclement weather, bottlenecks, and poor road conditions.

III. Post-Disaster Assessment of Lifelines

Following any region-wide emergency or disaster, post-disaster assessment of lifelines such as streets, highways, bridges, tunnels, and overpasses becomes essential. It is prudent for LGPL employees to be able to assess both the potential and real effects of winter storms, toxic spills, and floods on local lifelines.

LGPL employees must be prepared for the following post-disaster problems related to lifelines:

- Gridlock, particularly on major highways
- Road closures, either partial (i.e. single-lane traffic only) or full
- Roadway damage: potholes, sinkholes, washouts, and fissures
- Bridge damage and closure
- Overpass damage and closure
- Flooding from broken mains, reservoirs and bodies of water
- Risks from toxic spills
- Risks from fires and explosions
- Accidents, including multi-vehicle pile-ups and casualties
- Risks from broken power lines
- Risks from debris from damaged buildings and trees
- Abandoned vehicles
- Displaced persons on foot

IV. Post-disaster routing

Rather than insist on the use of specific means of transportation after a disaster, LGPL should implement flexible responses to circumstances beyond the control of civil agencies. This is especially true when lifelines have been damaged or closed, and rerouting is necessary. Ideally there will be three different routes to locations of any LGPL site. If one route is closed, there will be two others on which LGPL vehicles (or the vehicles of couriers) can travel to reach their destination.

In an area that depends on bridges for essential lifelines, the three-route plan can be difficult to devise. Nevertheless there should always be more than one route by which LGPL employees can reach a particular destination. Otherwise the chances increase sharply that the LGPL facilities will not be able to receive documents, information, etc.

V. Maps

LGPL should maintain a small collection of maps for the safety and convenience of all employees involved in post-disaster transportation. This collection will comprise maps of all municipalities and routes along which employees must travel to reach them. Much of the collection can be stored at the Information Desks for fast access.

In light of changing routes, new road construction, and urban growth, the map library should be updated every two years.

Note that an up-to-date collection of maps will be an invaluable resource after any disaster that damages lifelines and necessitates rerouting of traffic.

VI. Additional supplies in vehicles

Ideally all LGPL employees will carry the following items in their personal vehicles:

- Up-to-date map(s) of the region and its communities
- Flashlight and flares
- AM/FM Radio

❑ First aid kit with a small supply of any required prescriptions, e.g. heart medication, asthma puffer

❑ Tire-change kit and spare, fully-inflated tire

❑ Spare footwear, e.g. running shoes, work boots

❑ Sunglasses and spare pair of regular eyeglasses

❑ Emergency blanket, e.g. tarp or foil sheet

❑ Package of green or orange garbage bags

❑ Heavy-duty gloves

❑ Package of basic dust masks

Employee vehicles should be regularly serviced. Fuel tanks should never be less than one-third full.

Post-disaster travellers in and around the region should comply with the directions in the Emergency Response Plan.

Section G: Normalization Program

Table of Contents
  I. Definition
 II. Problems arising from incomplete normalization
III. Checklists
 IV. Testing and revisions

I. Definition
Normalization is the general consensus among LGPL employees and members that the library and its operations have returned to normal, and that the changes to the library following a disaster are acceptable.

Among those post-disaster circumstances that require substantial time for acceptance are:

❑ Casualties at LGPL sites

❑ Serious damage to LGPL buildings or their immediate vicinities

❑ Substantial changes of personnel

❑ Substantial changes in senior management

❑ Substantial replacement of fixtures

❑ A move to new facilities owing to loss of a LGPL site

❑ An ongoing crisis arising from LGPL operations, or activities perceived to be related to LGPL

❑ Substantial changes to LGPL's IT system, especially when downtime has affected work flow

Normalization is a subjective quality that is closely linked to morale levels and productivity. The purpose of this Normalization Program is to support a return to general normalcy after any emergency or disaster at any LGPL site or sites.

II. Problems arising from incomplete normalization

It is essential to acknowledge the insidious and less obvious effects of an emergency or disaster on LGPL employees. At any LGPL site, the following problems could arise if normalization is incomplete:

❏ Absenteeism

❏ Post-traumatic Stress Disorder (PTSD)

❏ Prolonged sick leave

❏ Requests for transfer

❏ Staff attrition

❏ Loss of expertise

❏ Prolonged crisis / bad press

❏ Loss of market share

❏ Loss of reputation

❏ Decreased productivity

❏ Poor quality work, including unfinished and poorly executed tasks

❏ Disinclination to contribute to new projects and initiatives

❏ Labour Union issues

❏ Tension and increasing stress

❏ Rumours

❏ General decrease in morale and poor working environment

Any or all of these problems are possible following a disaster and a delay in normalization. Adding to the problem are:

❏ Disinclination of managers to recognize patterns in absenteeism and quitting

❏ Disinclination to discuss post-disaster problems, either formally or informally
❏ Failure to acknowledge change officially through the appropriate "organizational ritual"

❏ Ineffective in-house communications, especially from senior management

❏ Ineffective orientation and training on new systems and equipment

❏ Disinclination of managers to discuss specific problems with individual employees

III. Normalization Checklists

For all LGPL employees:

To ensure that normalization takes place and employee morale is restored in a reasonable time, the following processes and procedures should be carried out:

❏ Debriefing with employees in each department as soon as possible after the business resumption phase, approximately 72 hours after a disaster

❏ Recognition of employees' efforts during the resumption/continuity phase, especially during follow-up meetings

❏ Announcement of recovery accomplishments in the library newsletter or bulletin

❏ Discussions between managers and individual employees regarding specific problems in the workplace, and under certain circumstances, in the home

❑ Recognition of the need for a recovery period, during which employees might not be as productive as before

❑ Approval of time off for all medical appointments, for the individual employee or a member of that employee's family

❑ Availability of ongoing professional counselling for emotional/psychological problems, especially those arising from PTSD

❑ Press releases and media packages for local journalists and broadcasters covering LGPL's success in getting back in business

❑ Availability of senior managers for interviews regarding the wind-up of business recovery activities

❑ "Rap and Wrap" sessions for final debriefing and celebration of effective resumption and continuity

Professional counselling should be available through LGPL's employee assistance program (EAP). The Human Resources Department should make sure that EAP providers have counsellors experienced in dealing with PTSD cases.

IV. Testing and revisions

LGPL's Human Resources Department should test this Normalization Program through tabletop exercises and enhance it to meet specific needs. The main questions relate to:

❑ The ability of LGPL's EAP provider(s) to offer post-disaster counselling, particularly for PTSD sufferers

❑ The ability of LGPL's library communications vehicles to reach all employees and to keep them informed regarding recovery accomplishments

❑ The willingness of individual managers to make sure that their staff members are accepting necessary post-disaster changes to LGPL's facilities, processes, and procedures.

❑ The Human Resource Department's roles in LGPL's operational resumption and continuity

Disaster Manager's Residential Emergency Procedures

- **FIRE/EXPLOSION**
- **LEAK/FLOOD**
- **INTRUDER / THREATENING BEHAVIOUR / PROWLER**
- **HIGH WINDS**
- **SNOWSTORMS**
- **TOXIC SPILL/GAS LEAK**
- **POWER OUTAGE / BROWNOUT**
- **GENERAL PRECAUTIONS**

Fire/explosion

- Call 911
- For a spreading blaze, evacuate the residence. Tell all residents / family members to leave the building

- Walk, don't run. Use the nearest exit. Do not try to pack belongings or take extra items with you.
- Avoid flames, smoke and fumes. REMEMBER: the closer to the floor, the lighter the smoke and fumes.
- Once outside, go to an area away from smoke and fumes.
- Make sure that everyone in your residence has evacuated safely. Report any missing person to the firefighters.

Leak/flood

Most leaks/floods are not life-threatening, but in a serious case of water ingress:

- Avoid wet wires, electrical equipment and power outlets. Do not attempt to use a moisture-damaged computer, printer, TV or sound system.
- Do not walk through water.
- Let plumbers and other tradespersons know the source of the water: window, pipe, bathroom, etc.
- Do not begin cleanup until after a safety inspection of wiring, outlets and equipment.
- Be alert for mould growth in wall and ceiling cavities, particularly in basement areas.

Intruder / threatening behaviour / prowler

- ❑ Call 911 as soon as possible. Avoid remaining alone with any intruder.
- ❑ If you surprise a burglar, do not threaten him or attempt to restrain him.
- If any burglar or intruder appears angry or threatening, keep a safe distance away. Listen to what he/she says. Do not argue or raise your voice. Try to calm him down.
- Avoid heroics. Do not make abrupt or unnecessary movements. Try to leave the scene.
- When the police arrive, assist them by offering the following information:
  - ❑ Description of the intruder: height, weight, age, sex, hair, eyes, distinguishing marks
  - ❑ Accent?
  - ❑ Intoxicated?
  - ❑ Armed or unarmed?
  - ❑ Leave on foot or by vehicle?
  - ❑ Items missing from your residence?

High winds/snowstorms

- Expect power outages and telephone line disruptions.
- Avoid overhead hazards: tree branches, power lines
- Avoid glass and debris on sidewalks and streets.
- Travel only when necessary. Drive slowly.
- Make sure that your car has an emergency kit and a full tank of gas.
- Listen to your radio for emergency bulletins and traffic advice.
- Keep children and pets indoors if possible.

Toxic spill/gas leak (petroleum, chlorine, etc.)

A toxic spill could occur on any street. If so:

- Avoid the spill as much as possible. Do not loiter in the area. Call 911.
- Do not use matches or other open flames in the vicinity of the spill. Do not smoke.
- If you notice heavy fumes or toxic material seeping into the building, evacuate. Avoid fumes, vapour and smoke.

Power outage/brownout

- Keep flashlights and other emergency supplies such as additional food and water stored in handy places: kitchen, bedside tables, basement work areas
- Do not attempt to use computers and other electrical equipment.
- Avoid moving around in dark areas unless you have a flashlight. Do not attempt to examine, repair or open electrical equipment.
- Await instructions from municipal and Hydro crews before restarting electrical equipment.
- If a power outage has been longer than two hours, check food in fridges for spoilage.

General precautions

- Take first aid and CPR training. Keep your certification up-to-date.
- Be sure that you know the locations of the nearest first aid kit, flashlight, ladder and fire extinguisher.
- All family members should be familiar with exit routes.
- Make sure that everyone in your family and residence knows safety measures against fire.
- Make sure that your vehicle's gas tank is always at least one-half full.
- Your personal, out-of-region contact number is: (   )

Appendix Five

Main Library and Branch Post-Disaster Staff Allocation Plan

Lancaster Gate Public Library Post-Disaster Staff Allocation Plan

Table of Contents

I. Introduction: Business Resumption Priorities
II. Library Management Group (LMG)
III. Disaster Manager
IV. Resumption Tasks

I. Introduction: Business Resumption Priorities

Following an emergency or disaster, the following priorities will prevail:

a. The safety and security of all LGPL employees and patrons, as well as visitors to LGPL sites
b. The safety and security of all LGPL facilities, buildings and physical assets
c. The security, integrity and availability of LGPL's information technology (IT), including hardware, software, and telecommunications links at all LGPL sites. Within the IT Department, administrative and patron services systems will take precedence over all others for resumption purposes.
d. The security, integrity and availability of LGPL's paper records and documentation, particularly its vital records.
e. The ongoing provision of service to patrons, at LGPL sites and electronically
f. The restoration of services and facilities damaged or lost during or after an emergency or disaster

II. Library Management Group (LMG)

The Library Management Group comprises:

- Head Librarian
- Assistant Head Librarian

- Area Coordinators
- Manager, IT
- Manager, Human Resources
- Manager, Facilities
- Branch Heads (or delegates, usually senior supervisors)

Note: The above people should be notified of the meeting by mobile. In the event of a disaster, emergency or crisis, some people might not be available. The LMG meeting will proceed without them.

Tasks

- Ensures that LGPL resumption plans are tested and updated regularly
- Recognizes and declares a disaster as required
- Assumes responsibility for managing the overall business resumption process
- Reports directly to the LGPL Board and other stakeholders during the business resumption period
- Approves all media releases and interviews, and elects a single spokesperson to provide information to external bodies including news agencies and government departments
- Approves all substantial library expenditures
- Allocates all resources as required at LGPL sites
- Makes the final decisions regarding the priority of library functions / operations to resume
- With the assistance of civil and government authorities, makes decisions regarding the opening and closure of LGPL sites following a disaster
- Ensures that LGPL branch managers and staff members receive interim reports and a final debriefing about the disaster, its effects on LGPL, and the progress of LGPL's operational resumption.

III.   Disaster Manager

The Disaster Manager assumes his or her roles and responsibilities at the beginning of the resumption phase, and carries out response and resumption tasks until LGPL has resumed a basic level of business, acceptable to the LMG.

Note: He or she should have at least one delegate on site as backup during business hours.

Disaster Manager Tasks

- Works with and reports directly to the LMG
- Coordinates the corporate business resumption process
- Assists in determining the extent of the damage to LGPL assets and facilities
- Assists in the collection and assessment of information for the LMG
- Based on the assessment of information collected, recommends necessary actions to the LMG
- Assists in the recognition and declaration of a disaster
- Assists with the activation of an alternative site or sites

- Provides direction and ad hoc assistance to those employees carrying out business resumption tasks
- Assists with the arrangements for the transportation of employees, equipment and supplies to the alternative site(s)

IV. Resumption Tasks

The LMG will ensure that the following business resumption tasks are carried out in the appropriate departments during the operational resumption phase:

Administration (3 persons required)

Tasks

- Sends and receives messages and information from branches, staff and patrons;
- Records damage assessment data as required, with a digital camera if necessary
- Confirms the ability of branches to open for business, or to remain closed owing to damage and continuing risk
- Assists in the activation of strategic alliances as required
- Deals with miscellaneous administrative problems as they arise during the resumption phase

Requirements

- ❏ 3 cellular telephones
- ❏ 1 fax line
- ❏ 3 workstations with printers
- ❏ 200 no. 10 envelopes
- ❏ 15 pads of lined paper, 8½ × 11
- ❏ 10 ballpoint pens

Financial Services (3 persons required)

Tasks

- Ensures confidentiality, integrity and availability of accounting data and systems
- Reports all lost or unavailable accounting data to the LMG
- Works with IT if required. (Note: IT systems will need substantial testing before they can be fully reactivated, either at their normal site or at an alternative site. Accounting personnel will play a crucial role in post-disaster testing of these systems.)
- Ensures that the LGPL payroll is met

Requirements

- ❏ 2 cellular telephones
- ❏ 1 fax line
- ❏ 3 workstations with printers
- ❏ 1,500 cheques
- ❏ 2,000 no. 10 envelopes
- ❏ 25 pads of lined paper, 8½ × 11
- ❏ 50 ballpoint pens
- ❏ Blank ledgers

Human Resources (2 persons required)

Tasks

*   Sends and receives messages and information regarding post-disaster staff allocation at different sites and in different departments
*   Assists in the activation of the 1-800 line, if available: development of a voice message announcing office closures, relocations, staff requirements, and safety advice.
*   Allocates staff to various departments and work areas following a disaster
*   Receives and allocates volunteer assistance
*   Maintains ad hoc records regarding business resumption staff activities, shifts, absenteeism, and casualties
*   Provides psychological support and arrange counseling for staff as required

Requirements

❑ 1 cellular telephone
❑ 1 fax line
❑ 1 workstation
❑ 10 pads of lined paper, 8½ × 11
❑ 10 ballpoint pens

Facilities Management (3 persons required)

Tasks

*   Inspects the Main Library and branches to determine physical damage, particularly to the structure, electrical and HVAC systems, and plumbing
*   Works with civil authorities to ensure the safety and accessibility of LGPL sites
*   Advises the LMG concerning workplace safety and security matters after a disaster
*   Activates strategic alliances for the repair or replacement of building components as required
*   Advises LMG concerning the safety and security of LGPL branches, in light of reports from different areas
*   Works with branch staff to maintain the security and safety of LGPL branches.

Note: The Facilities Manager's first priority is the Main Library building and site.

Requirements

❑ 3 hard hats
❑ 3 cellular telephones
❑ 3 heavy duty flashlights
❑ 3 pairs of work boots
❑ 3 pairs of heavy-duty gloves
❑ 12 dust masks
❑ 3 pairs of goggles
❑ 1 pair of binoculars   ❑   1 fax line

- ❏ 1 workstation
- ❏ 10 pads of lined paper, 8½ × 11
- ❏ 10 ballpoint pens
- ❏ Digital camera (Note: Cellular phones containing digital cameras will suffice for LGPL's emergency purposes)
- ❏ Access to all first aid kits and emergency cabinets
- ❏ Access to all LGPL facilities and their technology storage areas, including electrical rooms and IT areas

Information Technology (IT) (3 persons required)

Tasks

- Sends and receives messages and information to and from vendors, particularly those supplying hardware and telecommunications support. (Note: The first operational priority for IT are the administrative and patron services systems and their ongoing security, integrity and availability)
- Provides support to cellular phone users
- Preserves and has available all vital systems inventories and documentation
- Assesses damage to hardware, software and telecommunications links
- Assesses data losses
- Provides and activates workstations as required for business resumption
- Trouble-shoots for operators of workstations
- Activates IT in alternative sites as required
- Provides access to backup data as required
- Activates the 1-800 line (if available) with the assistance of the Human Resources Department

Requirements

- ❏ A fully functional alternative site, with emergency supplies and communications options. (Note: This alternative site should be capable of full activation—power, systems set-up—within two hours.)
- ❏ Transportation between the Main Library and the alternative site(s). If travel is necessary, a strategic alliance should be arranged to transport IT personnel. Note: In the event of a regional emergency, air travel might be restricted or unavailable for several days. Alternative travel arrangements will have to be made: with bus companies, etc.
- ❏ An up-to-date set of LGPL's IT systems documentation, including configurations, network diagrams, and inventories
- ❏ 3 workstations
- ❏ 4 cellular telephones
- ❏ 10 pads of lined paper, 8½ × 11
- ❏ 10 ballpoint pens

Main Library services (3 persons required)

Tasks

- Sends and receives messages and information from LMG
- Safeguards collections as much as possible
- Notes any significant losses to collections and other assets

- Communicates with branches as required
- Updates the LMG regularly regarding matters affecting Main Library services to patrons
- Assists in reassuring patrons regarding any closure of library facilities

Requirements

❏ 3 cellular telephones
❏ 1 fax line
❏ Access to external news sources, preferably through laptops or other portable IT
❏ 5 pads of lined paper, 8½ × 11
❏ 5 ballpoint pens

Branch Operations (at least 2 persons per branch)
Note: All branch employees at a branch site during a disaster may contribute to resumption efforts)

After an emergency or disaster, each branch personnel should perform the following tasks:

- Inspects the branch building and site for damage, and reports damage to the LMG and Disaster Manager. (See Damage Assessment Form.)
- Makes decision to close the branch if damage is serious enough to endanger employees, patrons or visitors to the branch
- Works with civil authorities as required to shut down the branch if necessary
- Posts appropriate signage in the event that the branch must be closed
- If the branch can remain open, ensures that signage indicates that the branch is open for business
- Ensures security of the branch at all times
- Performs basic cleanup as required.

Note: Use caution when working with or around broken glass, faulty wiring, unstable heavy furniture, and leaky plumbing. Refer to LGPL's emergency response brochure.)

Requirements

❏ Access to the branch first aid kit and emergency cabinet
❏ 2 pairs of work gloves
❏ 6 dust masks
❏ 2 cellular telephones
❏ 1 fax line
❏ 1 workstation
❏ 2 pads of lined paper, 8½ × 11
❏ 5 ballpoint pens
❏ 2 flashlights and spare batteries
❏ Battery-operated radio for news updates and situation reports
❏ Emergency signage: "Temporarily Closed," "Open," etc. A supply of poster boards, felt pens and heavy tape is recommended.

Appendix Six

Information Technology Disaster Recovery Plan

[A sample that can serve as a template]

Lancaster Gate Public Library

Information Technology Disaster Recovery Plan

Name	Date
Drafted by:	
Approved by:	
Implemented by:	
Tested by:	
Revised by:	

Information Technology Disaster Recovery Plan

Table of Contents

1.0 Introduction
    1.1 Using This Plan

2.0 Objective
3.0 Scope
    3.1 Class I
    3.2 Class II
    3.3 Class III

4.0   Risk Assessment and Control
5.0   System Description
6.0   Backup and Restore Procedures
         Backup and Restore Strategy (Detail)
         Onsite
         Offsite
         Restore
7.0   Data Protection and Recovery Software
         7.1   Virus Protection

8.0   Alternative Site
         8.1   Restoration Procedure at Alternative Site

9.0   Business Impact Analysis Results
         9.1   Critical Functions

10.0   Assumptions
11.0   Class I Event Action Plan
12.0   Class II Event Action Plan
13.0   Class III Event Action Plan
14.0   Exercising and Maintenance of the Plan
15.0   Plan Distribution

Appendix A — LGPL Contacts
         1.1   Lancaster Gate Public Library
         1.2   Support Specialists
         1.3   Technology Contractors and Vendors

Appendix B — LGPL Applications

1.0   Introduction

This plan contains information and procedures required to recover and resume critical operations at LGPL or a third party site in the event of a disaster that affects the technology area. It also describes the current system configuration, applications, and the controls in place to reduce the damage and ease recovery efforts as much as possible.

1.1   Using This Plan

To Find Information On	See
Types of disasters that this plan addresses	Scope
Assessment of risks	Risk Assessment and Control
Current systems	System Description
Regular backups	Backup and Restore Procedures

To Find Information On	See
Data protection	Data Protection and Recovery Software
Critical functions	Business Impact Analysis Results
Things to do when a disaster occurs	Class I Event Action Plan, Class II Event Action Plan, Class III Event Action Plan
Whom to call	Contacts

2.0   Objective

The plan is intended to provide guidance so that critical systems can be operational as promptly as possible.

All IT personnel should be familiar with its contents in order to:

* notify personnel and stakeholdersaffected by system disruptions
* recover data and systems and resume critical operations in timely fashion
* provide LGPL senior management with status updates

3.0   Scope

The plan provides the necessary information for recovery from three classes of events that could disrupt operations in the technology area. The three classes are described below.

3.1   Class I

A Class I event causes the loss of data or use of equipment but still allows staff access to LGPL sites. Events that could trigger loss of computer system access include:

* general server failure
* server hard disk failure
* power surge
* water damage
* program or operating system failure that destroyed data
* accidental formatting or corruption of databases, programs or data
* a virus that corrupted data and programs
* heating, ventilation or air conditioning failure (HVAC)

3.2   Class II

A Class II event results in loss of access to the LGPL IT areas and systems for an extended period of time. The goal would be to recover at an alternative site in three days if building access were denied for more than three days. Events that could trigger loss of building and technology access include:

- fire or other damage to the whole building or a significant portion of the building
- extended labour dispute
- extended power outage
- localized flooding
- pandemic/quarantine
- hazardous materials incident / toxic spill

3.3   Class III

A Class III event causes the loss of access to LGPL sites and a significant portion of the surrounding area. The goal would be to recover at an alternative site in three days. Events that could trigger loss of building and surrounding area access include:

- earthquake
- serious flooding
- severe damage from fire or explosion

4.0   Risk Assessment and Control

As part of the development of this plan, an assessment was made of:

- possible damage that could result from the three classes of events
- current mitigation controls in place
- potential improvements that could be made to eliminate or reduce damage

As a result of the risk evaluation, improved measures have been undertaken. These include:

- upgrades to the network servers and their physical environment described in the section entitled **System Description**
- documentation of backup and recovery procedures included in the section entitled **Backup and Restore Procedures**
- implementation of data protection and recovery software described in **Data Protection and Recovery Software**
- off-site backup storage arrangements outlined in **Off-site Storage**
- arrangements for alternative sites and systems to be available in case of a disaster outlined in **Alternative Site**

5.0   System Description

This section should include a comprehensive and up-to-date description of LGPL's IT systems, as well as labelled diagrams of key components.

6.0   Backup and Restore Procedures

Backup can be categorized into two sections, Onsite and Offsite.

Onsite backup is accomplished by utilizing a spare hot-swap hard drive available on each computer. These drives are I TB in capacity. A full backup is run each weekend and stored on these drives. Incremental backups are made nightly and also stored on the same drive. The drives have enough capacity to store one month of data. Earliest files are then deleted and the process carries on.

Offsite backups are made initially and whenever a major change has been made. These backup are images of the entire disk and can be replicated to almost any computer if there is any kind of catastrophic failure.

Email archives are maintained by a dedicated server and follow the normal backup procedures.

Backup and Restore Strategy (Detail)

Synopsis — The backup strategy at LGPL is divided into two distinct categories, onsite and offsite. These two categories are again divided into two distinct technologies, image and file/folder. If the offsite backup must be used in the event of total destruction, then up to five business days of data and email could be lost. If the onsite backup is utilized in the event of failure then file/folder data could be restored up to, and including, the previous day. Email could suffer a loss of up to five business days (additional notes below). Since offsite backup data is transmitted over the internet there is very limited bandwidth available at reasonable cost. There is a trade-off in the quantity of data that can be moved for storage offsite.

The Volume Shadow Copy (VSS) service inherent in Microsoft's server technologies is available to all LGPL personnel.

- Volume Shadow Copy Service creates snapshots of files so users can restore deleted files themselves.
- VSS can back up Server or Exchange files that are open or locked.

Onsite

1. An image of each virtual server was made at the time of installation and is stored on the removable backup drive. A server could be restored in a matter of minutes.
2. Each weekend a complete backup is made of the main directory. This directory contains all of LGPL historical data, daily work files, user profiles, and user directories. This backup is about 20 GB in size.
3. Each business day a differential backup is made of the same directory as described above. Each week these differential backups are deleted.
4. Each weekend a complete backup is made of the E-change server. If there is an E-change server failure then the backup would be used and up to five days of data loss might occur. The approximate size of the mailbox store is 15 GB. Some or all of the missing five days in the event of failure, could be made up from the database. Of course the data loss could be less than five days, depending on the day-of-the-week failure occurs.

Offsite

1. An image of each virtual server was made at the time of installation and is stored on the removable backup drive. The drive is held offsite at a secure location managed by the municipality.
2. Each weekend an internet download of both the E-change server mailbox file and the directory is made to the back-up site.

All files and images stored offsite are protected by backup password protection and 256 bit encryption.

Restore

Previous restores and related processes have been tested successfullly. Future restores will be implemented, both for a changing environment and for an environment that is settled and secure for long-term use.

7.0   Data Protection and Recovery Software

7.1 Virus Protection

Virus sweeping is performed on a regular basis.

LGPL has a very thorough antivirus solution. Viruses are checked for on all points of entry. The Electric Security Corporation checks all emails coming in and out of LGPL for viruses. In addition, LGPL uses a comprehensive network antivirus package. The firewall at LGPL backs up that solution and performs the same tasks, the e-mail server checks to make sure that viruses cannot enter public folders, servers have their own antivirus program, and user workstations also have their own antivirus program. A server acts as a distribution point to all antivirus programs on the LGPL LAN. Every night, it updates and distributes, if necessary, program updates across the network.

8.0   Alternative Sites

If a Class II or Class III event occurs, or any other disaster happens that disrupts computer operations at LGPL for an extended period of time, an alternative site can be chosen where internet services are available.

Current alternative sites include:

*   [Site A]
*   [Site B]
*   [Site C]

These sites are located at least 15 miles from LGPL, and include other public libraries, academic libraries, government data centres, and anywhere that might have power and internet access. Several possibilities have been tested. An operational hot site is prohibitively expensive and is no guarantee against certain disasters. Equipment requirements for temporary use are minimal and could be easily obtained and set up.

8.1   Restoration Procedure at Alternative Site

Once the restoration has been done, the recovery process can begin. Because of the complexities in restoring LGPL servers, a key vendor with server recovery expertise should be on hand to assist in the recovery process. Arrangements have been made with this vendor, ith whom LGPL has a strategic alliance.

9.0   Business Impact Analysis Results

In order to develop the recovery plan, it was necessary to identify the critical business functions that must be resumed as quickly as possible in the event of a disaster.

All LGPL opeational activities involving technology applications were identified. Each was examined in terms of the platform and development tools used, developer or support provider, and users. Each activity was assessed as to whether it was critical or non-critical in terms of business resumption and recovery efforts.

9.1   Critical Functions

The following applications were identified as critical:

- Monitoring systems
- Database processes
- Website applications
- All documents

10.0   Assumptions

The action plans for the three classes of disaster are based on the following assumptions:

- backup procedures and off-site storage methods described above have been carried out on schedule
- backup tapes, data and documentation can be retrieved
- alternative site/equipment contracts are in place
- personnel are familiar with the required activities as a result of orientation and training, delivered through regular tabletop exercises
- documentation for system restoration, applications, and procedures for critical functions are available from secure on-site or off-site storage
- immediate actions to save lives and limit damage have been taken if necessary, e.g., evacuate building, emergency shutdown for computer system, damage containment, police, fire 911 called

11.0   Class I Event Action Plan

1. IT Manager or delegate — notify that there is a problem. *See Contacts for a list of senior supervisors.
2. Senior supervisor — assess situation.
3. Senior supervisor — notify support contacts required according to nature of problem.
4. IT Manager and Support Specialist — determine the extent of the damage and estimate potential downtime.
5. IT Manager — decide on course of action.
6. Depending on the situation, some of the following may be necessary:
- restore system from in-house backups if appropriate
- notify users if only some applications are unavailable
- retrieve off-site back-ups for restoration if necessary
- determine data loss from last back-up to system failure
- collect and re-enter lost data
- contact data providers and arrange for re-transmittal of data or alternative method of delivery
- contact supplier for replacement equipment
- notify stakeholders of possible delays
- update management on situation status
- if system not likely to be available within three days, notify alternative site vendor and proceed to alternative site with necessary backups

When system is operational and data recovered, run the necessary batch files to update the databases and distribute information according to instructions from IT Manager.

IT Manager will notify stakeholders that the situation has returned to normal.

12.0   Class II Event Action Plan

1. IT Manager — Notify alternative site supplier that facility is needed.
2. IT Manager — notify Senior Supervisor to proceed to alternative site.
3. IT Manager — arrange for transportation and accommodation for alternative site if necessary.
4. IT Manager or Senior Supervisor — retrieve off-site back-ups, documentation, supplies for delivery to alternative site.
5. Senior Supervisor and Support Specialist — activate system at alternative site.
6. IT Manager— alert required personnel that alternative site has been activated. They should be prepared to report to that site.
7. Senior Supervisor — determine data missing since last off-site back-up.
8. IT Manager — contact data providers and arrange for re-transmittal of data or alternative method of delivery for missing data.
9. Senior Supervisor — re-enter lost data.
10. IT Manager — notify business partners and clients of possible delays.
11. IT Manager — Notify those affected by any changes to normal procedures.
12. IT Manager — Update management on situation status.

When system is operational and data recovered, run the necessary batch files to update the databases and distribute information according to instructions from team leader.

IT Manager will notify stake holders when the situation has returned to normal.

13.0   Class III Event Action Plan

1. IT Manager — notify alternative site supplier that facility is needed.
2. IT Manager — notify Recovery Team Leader to proceed to alternative site.
3. IT Manager — arrange for transportation and accommodation for alternative site if necessary.
4. IT Manager or Senior Supervisor — retrieve off-site back-ups, documentation, and supplies for delivery to alternative site.
5. IT Manager and Support Specialist — activate system at alternative site.
6. IT Manager — notify business partners and clients of possible delays.
7. IT Manager — notify business partners, clients and suppliers of address and how to communicate.
8. IT Manager — arrange to collect and distribute information according to situation.
9. IT Manager — update management on situation status.

When system is operational and data recovered, run the necessary batch files to update the databases nd distribute information according to instructions from the IT Manager.

The IT Manager will notify stakeholders when the situation has returned to normal.

14.0   Exercising and Maintenance of the Plan

In order for this plan to be effective, it must be tested on a regular basis in order to:

• check for errors or missing information
• identify areas that are not addressed by the plan
• provide training to personnel in recovery procedures
• ensure that personnel are familiar with the procedures

The plan should be tested and reviewed at least every six months. This is especially important because of the frequency of changes in software programs, hardware and personnel areas.

As a minimum, the Class I scenario should be tested twice per year. Activation of alternative-site may be limited to once per year testing if cost is a factor.

The plan should be revised where necessary as quickly as possible after each exercise and revisions distributed promptly. Revisions for changes in personnel, contact information or procedures should be distributed as necessary.

15.0 Plan Distribution

Copies of this plan should be distributed as follows:

- one copy in LGPL Administration Library Collection
- one copy in fireproof on-site storage
- one or more copies in off-site storage
- copies to anyone who may have to use it in the event of a disaster
- copies for key personnel to retain at their residences if LGPL building access denied
- copies to LGPL senior management so that they are familiar with procedures to be followed. (This means status updates during disaster situations will be simpler, since management is aware of what should be happening and can just be briefed on the status of plan activation.)

Distribution of copies of the plan should be recorded so that updates can be circulated correctly. Employees that leave LGPL should return all copies in their possession.

Appendix A — LGPL Contacts

1.1 Lancaster Gate Public Library

Name	Title	Work phone	Cellular/Pager	Home phone
	IT Manager			
	Senior Supervisor			
	Assistant Supervisor			

1.2 Support Specialists

Name	Specialist Title	Work phone	Cellular/Pager	Home phone

1.3 Technology Contractors and Vendors

Company	Contact	Phone	Fax	E-Mail

Appendix B — LGPL Applications

Application	Development Tool	Developer	Users	Update	Platform	Status
Core Library Business						
Word Processing						
Spreadsheet						
Presentation						

Index

A

Absenteeism, 81
Adult services coordinator, 1
Advanced communications systems, 68
Alarmist, 2
Alliances identification, 62
  alternative sites, 62
  building and site clean-up, 62
  emergency moving and storage, 62
  employee counselling, 62
  IT systems
    hardware, 62
    software, 62
  post-disaster site security, 62
  secondary priorities, 62
    accounting, 62
    emergency conservation, 62
    general public, communications with, 62
    office supplies and furniture, 62
    patrons, communications with, 62
    sponsoring bodies, communications
      with, 62
  structural damage assessment, 62
  telecommunications, 62
  transportation, 62
Artillery bombardment, 5
Assistance, repeated offers of, 72
Avian influenza, 3

B

BIA. *See* Business impact analysis (BIA)
Biblio triage process, 40
Binder dependence, 87
  syndrome, 87
Building components, stabilization of, 70
Business impact analysis (BIA), 11
Business resumption training, 89

C

CCTVs. *See* Closed-circuit television
  cameras (CCTVs)
Central library strategic alliances, adaptation
  of, 67

Chicken little, 2
Circumstances for substantial time for
  acceptance, 80
Civil unrest, 5, 31
Closed-circuit television cameras (CCTVs),
  16
Cloud based information exchange, 96
CMCC. *See* Crisis management command
  centre (CMCC)
CMT. *See* Crisis management team (CMT)
Collection
  displacements, 76
  security, 21
Committees, 12, 20, 33, 62
  advantages, 12
  disadvantages, 12
    costs, 12
    distractions, 12
    planning process, 12
Conservator, 64, 68
Continuity, 29, 31, 61, 64, 87, 96
  plans, 31
    alternative site plans for business
      operations, 32
    clean team, development of, 32
    employee training, 32
    multi-layered data management and
      recovery, 32
    plans auditing, 32
    plan updation, 32
    site security plans, 32
    specialized teams, training of, 32
    strategic alliances with allied operations,
      32
Convergence, 69
Cookie-cutter solutions, 30
Corporate libraries, 19
Courier service for emergency conditions, 64
Crisis management, 59, 62, 96, 109
  Lancaster gate public library, 127
    crisis management command centre
      (CMCC), 132
    crisis management tabletop exercises,
      132

Crisis management *(cont.)*
    distribution, auditing and revisions, 135
    mistakes media representatives, 132
    purpose and definitions, 127
    recognizing of, 129
    sample media releases, 136
  plan, 29, 59, 127, 135
Crisis management command centre
    (CMCC), 132
Crisis management team (CMT), 128
Currency values, 52
Current planning enhancement, 95

D
Damages
  assessment of, 37, 87
    evaluation, 37
    form, 43, 44
    observation, 37
    prioritization, 37
    recordkeeping, 37
  books, 40
    treatment of, 63
  collections, inspecting of, 40
    full clean-and-mend, 40
    light clean-and-mend, 41
    light damage, 40
    moderate, 40
    moderate clean-and-mend, 41
    normal clean-and mend, 41
    serious, 40
    severe, 40
  site evaluation, 41
  wiring, 120
Data back up
  risk mitigation, 19
    inventory, 20
    off-site storage facility, 20
    storage media reliability, 20
    storage schedule, 20
    testing schedule, 20
    transportation system, 20
Data loss, 53
Data protection, 96, 188, 190, 192
Decision
  making, 53
  trees, 24
Delivery, methods of, 90
  home circulars, 90

  management orientation sessions, 90
  management security seminars, 90
  newsletter/intranet materials, 90
  staff orientation and training sessions, 90
Digital photography, 18, 43
  use of, 18
Disaster. *See also* Emergencies
  and crises, 58
  declaration, 29, 52, 53, 58, 59, 117, 160
    notification
      of all other employees, 58
      of external administrative
        stakeholders, 58
      of patrons, 58
      by word of mouth, 58
  definition of, 52
  manager's kit, 113, 117, 157
    damage assessment checklists, 117, 163
    disaster recognition and declaration
      procedures, 160
    DM situational safety procedures, 158
    emergency communications procedures,
      171
    emergency transportation plan, 173
    normalization program, 175
    residential emergency procedures, 177
    strategic alliances, 170
  planning, 1, 9, 12, 29, 51, 63, 87, 89, 99,
    100, 109, 113
    committee, 12
    process, 15
    response, 21, 22, 116
      brevity, 22
      clarity, 22
      design and layout attractiveness, 22
      handling ease, 22
      media adaptability, 22
      organizational culture
        appropriateness, 22
      readability, 22
      revision, ease of, 22
      site specificity, 22
      staff appropriateness, 22
      staff members, ease of distribution
        to, 22
  post. *See* Post disaster
  recognition of, 52
    procedures form, 53, 54
  related stress, 34

Discussion sessions, 83
Dust jackets, 52

E

EAP. *See* Employee assistance programme
     (EAP)
Earthquakes, 2, 4, 11, 18, 25, 70, 116
Electronic distribution, 24
Emergencies
   conservation techniques, 87
   and disasters, emotional reactions to, 25.
        See also Disaster
      age, 25
      military and paramilitary experience, 25
      personality, 25
      physical conditioning, 25
      prevailing state of mind, 25
      sociocultural background, 25
      training
         medical emergencies, 25
         response, 25
   information programmes, 76
   kit, library, 39
   response procedures, 87
Emotional responses, 51
Employee
   assistance programme (EAP), 65, 83
   questions after damage, 79
   reassuring of, 79
   safety, 69
   training programme, 87
Engineering library, 52
Enterprise risk, 9
   management (ERM), 9
Equipment inventories, 24
ERM. *See* Enterprise risk management (ERM)
Exercise leader responsibilities, 112

F

Facilities, closure of, 70
Facility management personnel, 68
Financial donations promises, 73
Fire struck, 70
Friends of the library, 75

G

Generic tabletop exercises, 101
   data loss/possible theft and misuse, 108

   fire and associated risks, 102
   flooding/water ingress, 103
   power failure, 107
   weather/power failure, 104
   winds and winter storms, 105

H

Hazardous material (HAZMAT), 39
HAZMAT. *See* Hazardous material
     (HAZMAT)
Head librarian, 59, 115, 118
Heating, ventilation and air conditioning
     (HVAC), 14
Hierarchical management, 11
Home circulars, 90
   advantages, 90
   memos, 90–92
Human
   carelessness, 6
   caused risks, 5
      apathy, 6
      carelessness and clumsiness, 6
      detail inattention, 6
      false assumptions, 6
      forgetfulness, 6
      internal policies, ignorance of, 6
      laws and external regulations,
         inattention to, 6
   resources department, 83
HVAC. *See* Heating, ventilation and air
     conditioning (HVAC)

I

Incomplete normalization, problems arising
     from, 81
Incunabula, 121
Information
   gathering, 53
      casualties, 53
      damage to collections, 53
      damage to facilities, 53
      data loss, 53
      local transportation systems, effects on, 53
      neighbouring community, effects on, 53
      power and telephone lines, sewerage
         and water supply, effects on, 53
      roads, bridges, overpasses and tunnels,
         effects on, 53

Information *(cont.)*
  security, 99
  technology disaster recovery plan, 187
    alternative sites, 192
    assumptions, 193
    backup and restore procedures, 191
    business impact analysis results, 193
    class I event action plan, 194
    class II event action plan, 194
    class III event action plan, 195
    data protection and recovery software, 192
    exercising and maintenance of the plan, 195
    introduction, 188
    objective, 189
    plan distribution, 196
    risk assessment and control, 190
    scope, 189
    system description, 190
In-house disaster education, 116
Inspection at the perimeter, 38
Internet, 20, 24, 30, 61, 76, 191, 192
  shutdown, 5
Investment brokerage library, 52
IT managers, 66
IT security protocols, 118

J
Job loss, 79

L
Lancaster gate public library
  and branch
    access card management system, 153
    after-hours access to building, 152
    alarm systems, 152
    audit schedule, 154
    controlled access to building, 152
    identification badges, 152
    information technology disaster
      recovery plan, 187
    key management system, 153
    lock-up procedures, 153
    parking security, 154
    personal belongings, security of, 153
    post disaster security
      additional, 154
      plan, 151

post-disaster staff allocation plan, 181
  business resumption priorities, 181
  disaster manager, 182
  library management group (LMG), 181
  resumption tasks, 183
statement of responsibility, 152
vandalism/light damage repair
  procedures, 153
visitor sign-in, 152
crisis management plan, 127
  crisis management command centre
    (CMCC), 132
  crisis management tabletop
    exercises, 132
  crisis management team (CMT), 128
  distribution, auditing and revisions, 135
  mistakes media representatives, 132
  purpose and definitions, 127
  recognizing of, 129
  sample media releases, 136
disaster manager's kit, 157
  damage assessment checklists, 117, 163
  disaster recognition and declaration
    procedures, 160
  DM situational safety procedures, 158
  emergency communications
    procedures, 171
  emergency transportation plan, 173
  normalization program, 175
  strategic alliances, 170
Letters to local newspaper editors, 73
Librarians, for human safety, 1
  discouraging factors, 21
  encouraging factors, 21
Library
  administrator, 15, 30, 33, 38, 63
  of Alexandria, 123
  assets, 7, 19, 95, 101, 108
    issues of, 24
      back-up data recovery, 24
      essential data, 24
      fire control technology, use of, 24
      insurance policies, 24
      strategic alliances with organizations, 24
      strategic alliances with vendors, 24
    loss of, 19
  board, 1, 11, 21, 58, 115, 117, 143

building, 3, 17, 32, 42, 64, 71, 106, 115
  exteriors, 14, 38
  inspection, 14
business resumption, 61
closure, 71
crisis manager, traits of, 59. *See also* Crisis
    management
  ability to speak publicly, 59
  admit ignorance, willingness to, 59
  good listening skills, 59
  grace under pressure, 59
  information-gathering skills, 59
destruction, 123
director, 11, 66
disaster planners, 7
emergency kit, 39
employees, 1, 31, 70, 79, 110
insurance coverage, 19
interiors, building of, 39
internal and external inspectors, 37
management, 37
managers, roles of, 26, 33, 73
  drills, 34
  encouragement from management, 34
  internal promotion, 34
  orientation and training sessions, 34
  planning decisions, 34
  tabletop exercises, 34
  training sessions, organizing of, 34
records, 97
recovery, 29
resources, 63
sites, 110
stakeholders, 112
unfit members, activities of, 75
  damage assessments, 75
  damaged books moving, 75
  damaged furniture moving, 75
  re-shelving items, 75
Library management group (LMG), 181
Living document, 113
LMG. *See* Library management group (LMG)

M

Management
  orientation sessions, 95
  roles, 33
  security seminars, 96
    topics included, 96

Message
  centres and missing children, 76
  circulated by senior managers, 79
Military-style continuity plans, 32
Moisture control vendor, 64, 120
Morale levels, 81
Moving companies, 65

N

Natural risks, 2
  drought, 3
  earthquakes, 3
  fire, smoke and fumes, 2
  flooding and water ingress, 2
  landslides and avalanches, 3
  pandemics, 3
  pests, 3
  secondary, 2
  tsunamis, 3
  volcanoes, 3
  weather, 2
Nervous employees, 79
Newsletter/Intranet materials, 80, 93, 94
  topics covered, 93
Normalization
  checklists, 82
    employees for, 82
      employee morale restoring, process
        involved, 82
    patrons for, 84
  defined, 80
  delay, 81
  plans, 118
  programmes, 175
    testing of, 85

O

Older facilities, gradual replacement, 18
Online library services, 85
Operational
  recovery activities, 83
  resumption, 29
    and continuity, 96
    and recovery, 74
  teams, 34
Organizational culture, 31
Organization charts, 24
Orientation programme, 96
  assumptions, 89

Orientation programme *(cont.)*
  definition of, 87
  inhouse methods, 97
  issue identification, 97
  practical decision making, 97
  purposes of, 88
    business resumption training, 89

P

Pandemic
  influenza exercise, 110
  management program
    departments, branches and work units,
      145
    overview, 140
    senior management, 142
    system-wide issues, 140
  risk, 85
Paper plans, 99
Patrons, 42, 69
  reassuring of, 72
    signs included, 72
  safety, 21, 70
  unwanted donations, 72, 73
  updating of, 74
Personal attributes, for planning, 113
Personal safety, 21
  concerns, 69
Physical assets, 63
  computer hardware, 63
  electronic data, 63
  facilities, 63
  furniture and fixtures, 63
  hardcopy books and periodicals, 63
  paper records/files, 63
  software, 63
Planning consultant, 11
PMP. *See* Preventative maintenance program
  (PMP)
Post disaster
  circumstances, 68
  patron behaviour, 84
  planning, 117
  priorities, 42
    general safety of entrances, 42
    library facilities, reopening of, 43
    non-structural components, soundness
      of, 42
    normalization operations, 43

    physical safety of employees, 42
    positive public relations, re-
      establishment of, 43
    security of the building, 42
    serviceability of
      elevators and escalators, 42
      furniture, 43
      HVAC, 42
      lighting, 42
      power sources, 42
      shelving, 43
    staff moral, recovery of, 43
    structural integrity of building, 42
  programmes, 76
  public relations, 87
  resumption, 122
  service for branches, 68
    reasons involved, 68
  staff allocation plan, 181
    business resumption priorities, 181
    disaster manager, 182
    library management group (LMG), 181
    resumption tasks, 183
    vendors for resumption and continuity, 64
post-disaster procedures
  post-disaster
    data management, 29
    post-disaster procedures, 29
    post-disaster transportation procedures, 29
    staff allocation plans, 29
    strategic alliances, 29
    testing, auditing and revision schedules, 29
Post-traumatic stress disorder (PTSD), 81
Power outage, 72
Preventative maintenance program (PMP),
  17
Prioritization, 42
Process
  backtracking, 118
  orientation, training and testing, 119
  planning, 2
  preparedness, 115
  response, 116
  resumption, 117
Production mistakes, 24
Proximity risks, 5, 6, 14
  air traffic, 7
  bodies of water, 7
  crime hotspots, 7

examples, 100
gas stations and fuel tanks, 7
neighbouring buildings, 7
parking lots, 7
retail shopping areas, 7
roadways, 7
PTSD. *See* Post-traumatic stress disorder
        (PTSD)
Public library, 11, 51
    beginning, case history, 114

R

RAA. *See* Risk assessment and analysis (RAA)
Rap and wrap sessions, 83
Recordkeeping, 43
Records
    centres, 3
    digitization of, 88
    management, 88
Recovery plan, 32
Regional disaster, 66, 69, 76
    preparedness, 119
Response, 87
    planning, leadership in, 24, 26
        liability issues, considering of, 26
        library board, informing to, 26
        library's response measures, keeping
            of, 26
        staff members, listening to, 26
    teams, 27
Resumption, 29, 87
    clean-up arrangements, 29
    crisis management plans, 29
    damage assessment procedures, 29
    disaster declaration procedures, 29
    normalization programmes, 29
    orientation and training programmes, 29
    planning, 99, 117
    post-disaster procedures
        communications, 29
Risk
    analysis. *See* Risk assessment and analysis
        (RAA)
    assessment. *See* Risk assessment and
        analysis (RAA)
    managers, 9
    mitigation, 1, 17, 20, 88, 113, 116, 119
        data back up, 19
            inventory, 20

off-site storage facility, 20
storage media reliability, 20
storage schedule, 20
testing schedule, 20
transportation system, 20
        insurance, 19
        key, 20
        older facilities, gradual replacement, 17
    prevalence, 1
    profile, 2, 58, 115
Risk assessment and analysis (RAA), 1, 9, 11,
        15, 17, 115, 116, 129, 154, 188, 190
    discussions with external experts, 15
    documentation, 16
    example, 100
    frequency, 17
    history taking, 13
        administrative records, 13
        employees, 13
        library board records, 13
        media coverage, 13
        on-site records, 13
        published history of site, 13
    impact, 17
    inspection, 13
    interviews, 14
        formal or informal, 14
    likelihood, 17
    onset timing, 17
    potential threats listing, 17
    scope of disasters, 17
    sustainability, 17
Rumour
    circulation, 79
    growth of, 73

S

Safety
    entrance and exit, 39
    inspectors, 37
        certified tradespeople, 37
        professional engineers, 37
    seminars, 24
SARS. *See* Severe acute respiratory
        syndrome (SARS)
Security
    breaches, 96
    risks, 2, 7
        arson, 8

Security *(cont.)*
    bomb threats, 8
    fraud, 8
    hostile intruder, 8
    malware, 8
    sabotage, 8
    theft, 7, 8
    vandalism, 9
    workplace violence, 8
Self-reliance, 87
Senior library
  management, 112
  managers, 66, 79
Session reporting, 97
Severe acute respiratory syndrome (SARS), 3
Sick leave, 81
Single-site event, 69
Site
  activation and management, 87
  qualifications, 64
Situation management, 87
Slowness of repairs, complaints to
            authorities, 73
Social engineering, 8
Staff
  attrition, 85
  orientation sessions, 93
      handouts for emergency procedures, 94
      presentation forms, 93
          departmental sessions, 93
          general sessions, 93
          lunch-and-learn sessions, 93
          management groups, 93
      risk-related topics, 93
  and patron safety, 21
Standard management hierarchy, 27
  budget limitations, 27
  library hierarchy, strength of, 27
  orientation and training, limited time for, 27
  response speed, 27
Strategic alliance, 170
  activation, 87
  documentation, 65
      best-efforts clause, 66
      exchange of information, 65
      letter of agreement, 65
      pre-arranged price, 65
  need determination for, 61
  updating of, 66

Succession plan, 30
System-wide strategic alliance vendor
    qualifications of, 67

T

Tabletop
  exercise, 34, 85, 90, 96, 99, 101, 112
      customized, 100
      generic, 100
      management tips, 112
  for managers, 109
      assistant head librarians, 109
      departmental manager/branch manager,
            110
      director/head librarian/board of
            directors, 109
      library manager or supervisor, 110
Technical services
  database, 116
  and reference department, 30
Technological risks, 3
  aircraft accidents, 5
  dam failure, 5
  data loss, 4
  gas leaks, 4
  IT failure, 4
  nuclear power plant failure, 5
  power outages and brownouts, 4
  telecommunications disruptions, 4
  toxic spills, 4
  train derailments, 4
  transportation disruptions, 4
Telecommunications, 62, 185
  disruptions, 4
  for risk assessment and analysis, 62
  vendor, 64
Telephone service
  line breakage, 5
  overloading, 4
Temporary closure signage, closure
            processes, 70, 71
Three-ring binder, 99
Toxic spills, 76
Training programme, 96
  assumptions, 89
  binder dependence, 87
  business resumption, 89
  definitions of, 87
  session reporting, 97
  trainers, 97

Transportation, 3, 20, 27, 29, 53, 62, 101, 117
    disruptions, 4, 69
Twitter, 80

U

Unwelcome provision of assistance, 72
Updates spreading channels, 74
    newsletters, flyers and brochures, 74
    newspaper articles on library managers, 74
    radio and TV interviews with library
        managers, 74

    social media, 74
    website announcements, 74

V

Verbal therapy, 83
Volunteer assistance, 76
    acceptance of, 75

W

Websites, 24, 34, 71, 80
Workplace practices, 88

CPI Antony Rowe
Eastbourne, UK
April 09, 2015